THE NEW CENSORS

Movies and the Culture Wars

In the series

CULTURE AND THE
MOVING IMAGE

edited by Robert Sklar

THE NEW CENSORS

MOVIES AND THE CULTURE WARS

Charles Lyons

TEMPLE UNIVERSITY PRESS

Philadelphia

Temple University Press, Philadelphia 19122
Copyright © 1997 by Charles Lyons
All rights reserved
Published 1997
Printed in the United States of America

♾ The paper used in this publication meets the requirements of the American
National Standard for Information Sciences—Permanence of Paper for Printed
Library Materials, ANSI Z39.48-1984

Text design by Gary Gore

Library of Congress Cataloging-in-Publication Data

Lyons, Charles, 1960–
    The new censors : movies and the culture wars / by Charles Lyons.
        p.   cm.—(Culture and the moving image)
    Includes bibliographical references and index.
    ISBN 1-56639-511-9 (cloth : alk. paper).—ISBN 1-56639-512-7 (pbk.)
    1. Motion pictures—Censorship—United States.   I. Title.   II. Series.
PN1995.62.L96   1997
363.3′1′0973—dc20   96-36587

For Nick, Mari, Jennifer, Paul, and Tony

Contents

Acknowledgments ix

Introduction: Don't Watch That Movie! 1

1 Warning—"Political Propaganda" 26
The Case against *If You Love This Planet* (1982)

2 Murder of Women Is Not Erotic 53
Feminists against *Dressed to Kill* (1980)

3 No More Racist Movies Here 81
Asian Americans against *Year of the Dragon* (1985)

4 We Are Not Invisible 107
Gays and Lesbians against *Basic Instinct* (1991–1992)

5 This Film Is Blasphemy 146
Religious Opposition to *The Last Temptation of Christ* (1988)

Conclusion: Winners and Losers 183

Notes 193

Index 223

Acknowledgments

A host of people have been close to this project from its inception and deserve to be singled out: My parents, Nick and Mari Lyons; my siblings, Jennifer, Anthony, and Paul; Professor Leif Sjöberg (Stony Brook, retired); Professors Annette Insdorf and Charles Musser (who sponsored and advised me through this book's earlier form, a dissertation at Columbia); Professors David Kastan, David Sterritt, and Andrew Sarris, who sat on my defense; Professor Frank Couvares (Amherst) and Professor Robert Sklar (NYU), whose advice was invaluable; and Janet Francendese (Temple University Press), who has patiently guided this book to its present form.

I also thank Everette Dennis, Marion Maneker, Roya Kowsar, Tim Bent, Arlene Donovan, Robert Benton, Lisa Hacken, Glenn Elliot, Chris Hill, Neal Gabler, Steve Brennan, Helena Hjarlmarsson, Trudy Ship, Lyle Mayer, Michael Medved, Lance Hickey, Mimi McGraph, Tina Gianquitto, Rebekah Rudd, Mark Gompertz, George and Dan Hess, Steve and Lori Herek, Miranda Viscoli, and Ibra Morales—each of whom has helped me along the way. For kindly allowing me to interview them, I thank Terri Nash, Mitchell Block, Charles Sims, Dorchen Leidholdt, Janet Sakomoto, and Ellen Carten. Finally, I am especially grateful to Bobbe Needham (a terrific copy editor), David Bartlett, and the entire staff at Temple University Press and P. M. Gordon Associates for conscientiously creating this book.

THE NEW CENSORS

Movies and the Culture Wars

Don't Watch That Movie!

Protesters stand in front of your neighborhood movie theatre. Some chant, some carry banners, some distribute
flyers. All seem frenzied. What's the commotion? you wonder. What's so outrageous about the movie against which
they are protesting? You decide to cross their picket line, to
watch the film yourself, to know, definitively, the reason for
the all fuss and bother. Boldly, you approach the ticket window. Just as boldly a protester blocks your way. "Don't watch
that movie!" he barks. "It's a lie!" Is this censorship or simply
a healthy instance of democratic freedom of expression?

In this book I argue a simple central point: Although
some antimovie actions by groups or institutions may produce censorious results, in a democracy it is far more healthy
to risk such an outcome than in any way to limit groups'
right to "peaceably gather" and protest. I also have found
that between 1980 and 1995 the Right was far more successful in achieving censorship of movies than was the Left.

In making these arguments, I explore how censorship
operates within the movie industry today and reflect on the
separate histories of both pressure group and governmental activity against five selected movies. For only by following the history of censorship controversies over a period of
time can we approach such questions as these: What do the

successes of some groups and the failures of others in effecting censorship tell us about power and about the operation of corporate capitalism in the United States today? What does the relationship between protest and legal censorship tell us about contemporary U.S. democracy? Government involvement in movie censorship invites a separate series of questions, most importantly, when one branch of the government in the early 1980s decides to label an antinuclear film "political propaganda" and attempts to limit public access to it, what does this reveal about that government's ideological agenda?

Between 1980 and 1995, protests over cinematic imagery came to reflect larger cultural debates over a wide variety of art. But the battles over movies deserve separate attention for at least two reasons: because groups on the Left and Right so visibly and aggressively participated in them, and because they demonstrate how direct-action campaigns have come to overshadow the only remaining formal means of movie regulation, the rating system.

Since the Supreme Court held censorship of films unconstitutional in 1952, and especially since the motion picture industry abolished the Hays Production Code in 1968, special-interest pressure groups have emerged as the primary protagonists in an ongoing drama about how movie content should be controlled. For groups on the Right as well as, in one instance, a branch of the U.S. government, the movies were too free in their depiction of environmental viewpoints, sex, and religion; for groups on the Left, the moviemakers' abuse of freedom in the depiction of women, ethnic groups, and gays and lesbians made movies objectionable. Although their methods of protest or censorship often appeared the same, the results achieved by the Right and Left were strikingly different.

Years from now, cultural historians and statisticians may argue over whether the 1980s and early 1990s actually produced more censorship than did, say, the 1930s or 1950s. What is clear is that between 1980 and 1995—a period whose first twelve years were controlled by a Republican White House—movie censorship controversies became inexorably linked to larger political struggles. Protests by historically marginalized groups such as women, Asian Americans, homosexuals, and simultaneously by conservative groups from the New Christian Right, distinguish these years as a time when movies were battlegrounds in the ongoing culture wars.[1] These wars included skirmishes over works ranging from art funded by the National Endowment for the Arts, to library books, to rap albums and music videos.

While some of these skirmishes erupted late in the decade, 1980 signaled a sudden increase in the lengths to which political groups were willing to go to combat images in movies. (Steven Vineberg has labeled the opposing forces "the conservative and politically correct camps.")[2] For groups on the Left, protests tested the extent to which the empowerment they had fought for since 1960 had been realized and could be defended. For conservatives, the 1980 election of President Ronald Reagan seemed the beginning of a new era during which what they saw as baneful cultural change might be halted or reversed, and "traditional" or "family" values reinstated. That year was marked by controversy over a large number of films either released or in production: *Dressed to Kill; Fort Apache, the Bronx; Charlie Chan and the Curse of the Dragon Queen; The Gods Must Be Crazy; Monty Python's Life of Brian; American Gigolo; Windows;* and *Cruising.*

Why so many protests in 1980 alone? How did it happen that traditionally Left groups—responsible for all but the actions against *Life of Brian*—had grown so sensitive to the way Hollywood depicted them? Did defeat in the political arena breed a sense of powerlessness among minority groups and inspire them to combat negative images with renewed energy? I believe that studying each protest campaign against a representative movie during years since 1980 will help explain what was at stake for each group of protesters and for the government—and why they believed the stakes were so high.

The Evolution of Movie Censorship

In the United States today, censorship has become a high-profile social phenomenon. According to posters, buttons, and bumper stickers, "Censorship is un-American." Censorship challenges, whether over library books, rap albums, photographs, or movies, quickly become media circuses, with pouting politicians and insolent artists shouting at each other on national television talk shows, or private free for alls, with relatives and friends caught in heated exchanges. Although the debates seem constant and ubiquitous, they offer little clarity about what precisely censorship is or how it operates.

According to *Oxford English Dictionary* (OED), *censor* can refer to (1) "the title of two magistrates in Ancient Rome, who drew up the register or census of the citizens, etc., and had the responsibility of the supervision of public morals," or to (2) "an official in some countries whose duty is to inspect all books, journals, dramatic pieces, etc., *before publication,* to insure that they shall contain nothing immoral, heretical, or offensive to government."[3] In legal circles, *censorship* tends toward the OED's second definition. Many constitutional lawyers hold that a democracy guarantees a free marketplace of ideas and that the public therefore has the right to see or read any expression in that marketplace. The most feared scenario occurs when, as eminent constitutional lawyer Thomas I. Emerson notes, the communication is banned "and never reaches the marketplace [of ideas] at all."[4] In legal parlance, this is known as "prior restraint." Most legal thought about censorship considers prior restraint and censorship to be practically synonymous.

Outside law, a broader view of censorship predominates with regard to both extralegal (or de facto) censorship and actions that occur *after* an expression has reached the marketplace. Writing generally about the phenomenon of censorship in modern capitalist societies, Sue Curry Jansen questions the whole liberal notion of a marketplace of ideas, which

> discourages inquiry into the most serious forms of censorship operating in Liberal societies today: censorships routinely undertaken by state bureaucracies in the name of "national security" and censorships routinely sanctioned by the "profit principle." By reducing dialogues on censorship to litigations involving publishers' claims to profits, the Anglo-American legal community has removed an emancipatory concept from the vocabulary of the people.[5]

Jansen, objecting to a narrowly legal view of censorship in the United States, points to a wider range of actions, including press censorship during times of national emergency or choices by media executives that have only commercial gain rather than the artists' work in mind. In other words, she locates outside of the law some of the numerous censorships that occur in modern capitalist societies—a goal shared by this project.

Even those who acknowledge the existence of extralegal censorship associate most censorship with repressive acts performed by public officials who preach conservative agendas. In the United States in recent years, censorship has come to mean any repression that results from either official acts or pressure. In the context of film production, distribution, and exhibition, censorship refers to a set of practices by institutions or groups, either prior to or following a film's release, that result in the removal of a word, a scene, or an entire film from the marketplace. The most obvious forms of movie censorship are the actions of federal, state, and municipal governments and the mechanisms of self-regulation established by the motion picture industry itself—today, the Motion Picture Association of America's (MPAA) movie ratings. A third kind of censorship occurs as a result of group protests—the focus of this book. Not all protests lead to censorship; many are primarily a means of publicizing a group's complaint. But when, because of protests, a movie is reedited or pulled from theatres, such protests can be said to result in censorship.

Traditionally, opponents of censorship have objected more to federal, state, and municipal censorship than to industry self-regulation or to group protests. Government censorship threatens the free-speech guarantee expressed in the First Amendment of the U.S. Constitution; it also places the power to control what the public sees in the hands of a select few and thereby appears antidemocractic. While censorship by government agencies was common during the formative years of the motion picture industry, censorship wasn't legally sanctioned until 1915, when the Supreme Court considered *Mutual Film Corporation v. Industrial Commission of Ohio.* Justice Joseph McKenna, who drafted the Court's majority opinion, concluded that movies were "a business pure and simple, originated and conducted for profit . . . not to be regarded . . . as part of the press of the country or as organs of public opinion."[6] As a result of this decision, state and city censorship increased.

To avert federal censorship, the motion picture industry introduced a system, often termed "self-regulation," that codified rules governing motion picture content. The most significant of these were the "Thirteen Points" and twenty-six other subjects established by the National Association of the Motion Picture Industry(NAMPI), in force from 1916 to 1922; the "Don'ts and Be Carefuls" created by the Motion Picture Producers and Distributors of America (MPPDA, 1922–1930); the Hays Production Code created by the MPPDA and administered by the Production Code Administration, which granted or withheld its Seal of Approval (1930–1961); and the rating system instituted by the MPAA (1968–present). In many well-documented instances, such self-regulation, especially during the years of the Hays Code, resulted in censorship.[7] The Hays Office forced the deletion of sexually explicit scenes from *Madame du Barry* (Warner Brothers 1934) and *Klondike Annie* (Paramount 1936), among many others. Since all the studios had supported self-regulation and the Hays Code, there was little anyone could do to resist censorship decisions other than try to release a movie without Hays Office approval and thereby risk financial doom. Only the most powerful producers were successful in challenging the Hays Office, as in the infamous case when David O. Selznick won the right to use the banned word "damn" in the last sentence of his "Gone with the Wind" (MGM 1939), a film censored in many other scenes.

During the 1950s and early 1960s, legal censorship came under attack. In a routine decision, the New York Board of Regents labeled a small Italian "art" film, Roberto Rossellini's *The Miracle* (1951), "sacrilegious" and temporarily restricted its exhibition. Joseph Burstyn, a distinguished liberal lawyer, came to the film's defense, arguing in the 1952 case *Burstyn v. Wilson* that individual states could not claim "sacrilege" as a standard for restricting a film. Though Burstyn lost in the local courts, later that year the decision was reversed by the Supreme Court. Justice Tom C. Clark ruled that "sacrilege" was not a "viable standard" by which to suppress a movie and simultaneously overturned the thirty-seven-year-old opinion that movies could not be protected by the First Amendment and ought to be regarded as a "business pure and simple." Movies from this point on would be considered protected speech, suddenly part of the press of the nation. Clark's ruling also made it increasingly difficult for states and cities to censor films on legal grounds, except in cases involving imagery that the courts considered legally "obscene."[8]

The formal methods of movie censorship were quickly vanishing. A series of U.S. films released in the 1950s and early 1960s challenged the aging MPPDA Hays Code. The release of such films as Otto Preminger's *The Moon Is Blue* (1953) and Sidney Lumet's *The Pawnbroker* (1965) without the Production Code Administration's Seal of Approval paved the way for a streamlined code. The industry was finally responding to social reality. By 1968, with all of the code's provisions abandoned, the U.S. screen appeared freer from censorship than ever before. The question now became, To what extent would tacit controls replace the obsolete formal restrictions? During the civil rights movement, an increasing number of minority groups sought political and social empowerment and came to recognize the role images play in reinforcing power structures. In the 1970s and after, such awareness led to an unprecedented number of protests against movies, which during the same period were also a regular target of groups associated with the New Christian Right. How would such protests affect movies released during the 1980s and 1990s?

At this juncture, something needs to be said about how I use the problematic terms *liberal* and *conservative* in this book. During the 1988 presidential campaign, George Bush labeled the politics of his opponent, Michael Dukakis, with the "L" word, capitalizing on the increasingly negative public perception of liberalism—especially the idea that the Great Society as envisioned in the 1960s had failed.[9] All of the country's greatest problems could be solved, Bush seemed to suggest, if only that dangerous weed called liberalism were plucked from the garden of U.S. politics. Bush's victory confirmed the success of his strategy. In 1988, at least, intellectuals continued to wonder, Where have all the liberals gone?

Why *liberal* and *conservative* today mean most as cultural labels relates to our discussion of censorship. For John Stuart Mill, ideological opposition between liberals and conservatives could be understood in the historical antagonism between individuals and institutions and between freedom and oppression. From the opening paragraph of his essay *On Liberty:* "The subject of this Essay is not the so-called liberty of the will . . . but Civil or Social Liberty; the nature and limits of the power which can be legitimately exercised by society over the individual." To be human, Mill suggests, is to be free from chains and from imprisonment—most of all, to be free to choose. But in nineteenth-century England Mill saw as a denial of freedom the insidious tendency of institutions such as estates, churches, and unions, as well as of the powerful elite, to choose for the individual. "There is in the world at large," he wrote, "an increasing inclination to stretch unduly the powers of society over the individual, both by the force of opinion and even by that of legislation."[10]

Even more to our purposes, Mill introduced the idea that "force of opinion" could easily result in infringements of one's physical freedom as well. Mill's often-quoted statement that "we can never be sure that the opinion we are endeavoring to stifle is a false opinion; and if we were sure, stifling it would be an evil still" is best understood in the context of his larger concern for freedom from a tyrannical government.[11] He did not view free speech, in other words, as a right separable from the need to be free from greater restraints.

In the twentieth century, liberal more often than conservative ideas found easy adaptation in the United States. No longer did they mean Mill's celebration of individual rights, but rather a wide public embrace of Franklin Delano Roosevelt's New Deal politics: Now liberals supported welfare, trade unionism, old age pensions, and other social programs. By the mid-1930s liberalism had, as Alonzo Hamby writes, "become a norm in American politics."[12]

As fashioned in the late 1950s and early 1960s, liberalism became more clearly associated with minorities' claims to equality, called by some "identity politics." Civil rights now jumped to the top of the liberal agenda. The utopian liberal ideal of the Great Society in which all people were finally and totally equal suggested just how high this new breed of liberals' hopes aimed. A decade later, such hopes would face the strongest conservative challenges in the twentieth-century to that date. Deep in the political and military morass of Vietnam, President Richard Nixon and his neoconservative advisors came to question the assumptions and techniques of liberalism. To them, the Great Society, as Hamby writes, "had become too ambitious, too wasteful, too redistributionist, too anti-democratic."[13] Neoconservatives also believed that the liberals comprised a party of an intellectual, mostly eastern elite, and further that "the people," Middle Americans, were being left out of the equation. Nixon campaigned for a politics of stability in direct opposition to the 1960s politics of chaos. By the mid-1970s, the wheels of political change were spinning fast.

Throughout the 1980s and early 1990s, few liberals would deny that there had been failures during the turbulent previous two decades, by loyal liberals rejected the idea, promoted by conservatives, that liberalism had in fact been rooted out of U.S. politics. As neoconservatives joined with groups associated with the New Christian Right to fight against women's right to abortion, against pornography, and in favor of prayer in school, liberals rallied to a cultural liberalism that united theories, definitions, and practices of earlier periods. In fact, issues of culture had become central tenets of both political parties' platforms in the 1980s and early 1990s.

For the purposes of this book, the most significant differences between conservatives and liberals, here termed also *Right* and *Left,* lie in their respective attitudes toward freedom of expression, as described by David Spitz: "Liberalism is committed to individual liberty and the freedoms of inquiry of expression, while conservatism is far more concerned with the applications of an already existing objective *Truth* and the consequent curbing of erroneous and promiscuous doctrines."[14] Today's cultural liberals tend to be more tolerant of a wide latitude of speech, whereas their conservative counterparts tend to be more wary of the excesses of speech that they believe threaten "family values," religion, and patriotism.

It is ironic that the movies, once hailed as the most democratic art, became during the 1980s and 1990s a battleground for contrasting visions of democracy. The ideal focal point of Left and Right attacks on the media, movies offered groups the opportunity to advertise their complaints against not only a single film but also an industry with a long history of presenting demeaning or otherwise offensive imagery.

Why Not Violence?

That violence is not among the subject areas I treat here—sex, environmental issues, ethnicity, religion, and homosexuality—requires some explanation, for its depiction certainly has been and continues to be controversial. Yet between 1980 and 1995, few specific movies triggered protest by groups against violence in the media, and, despite general attacks by politicians, no single movie caused the U.S. government to seriously consider censorship.

Over the years, in fact, opposition to violence in the media has tended to be general rather than pointed at a single

film. (In contrast, each of the other subject areas I have selected has generated a long history of censorship efforts).
Films that depict crime, which usually involves violence,
have worried censors since the 1920s and 1930s, particularly
those depicting public officials as criminals. In 1928, *The
Racket,* produced by Howard Hughes, exposed links between organized crime and politicians, police officers, and
city officials in Chicago. Soon after its release, censorship
boards in Dallas and Portland banned it. As a reviewer for
Motion Picture Classic noted at the time, "This Picture has
been judged as altogether too realistic by the very men it
tells of [that is, public officials]. Their testimonials have
come in what is perhaps the most unique form in screen history. The very types of men it deals with have done their best
to stop its showing." Another reviewer suggested that "the
Portland ban was "apparently a political decision, the chief
reason offered being that the film showed city officials as being crooks. Pure minded Portland must never see an official
on the screen who was not honest. It might begin suspect-
ing the home folks."[15]

In a larger censorship struggle, the Hays Office ordered
Hughes to reduce the amount of violent crime depicted in
the film *Scarface* (1932) and returned the Ben Hecht script
with a warning: "Under no circumstances is this film going
to be made. The American public and all conscientious
State Boards of Censorship find mobsters and hoodlums repugnant. Gangsterism must not be mentioned in the cinema. If you should be foolhardy enough to make *Scarface,*
this office will make certain it is never released."[16] Ignoring
Hays, Hughes produced the film. After New York State
censors chopped many violent scenes, Hughes filed suit and
ultimately defeated the censors in court. The movie was

nevertheless banned in Chicago and in several other cities because it linked public officials to crime.

Between 1934 and 1968, in spite of the provisions of the MPPDA Code, few films were refused PCA Seals solely because they depicted violent crimes and criminals.[17] Moreover, outside of the industry's self-regulation, legal censorship of violence declined. As legal scholar Richard Randall notes, among the four states and three major cities censoring films in 1965, only Chicago had laws on the books that censored extreme brutality and violence. Although municipalities in Wisconsin and Kansas also objected to specific types of violent imagery, the more common censorship challenges addressed the combination of violence and sex. In 1968, Randall concluded that "films of excessive violence and brutality . . . account for a very small percentage of censorship orders today. This is due more to a lack of statutory censorship authority, though, than to a want of such films."[18]

With the 1970s, concern shifted from violent crime and criminals to violence in general when social scientists reported that exposure to violent imagery could cause violent behavior.[19] Among the commentators who see a broad cultural trend, Michael Medved points out, "the reservations raised over the level of brutality in films today seldom center on a single shocker, or even a cluster of cutting-edge releases that test prevailing boundaries of good taste. They focus on an industry-wide epidemic that has infected an appalling percentage of motion pictures."[20] Nevertheless, recent films singled out for opprobrium include *Boulevard Nights* (1979), *The Warriors* (1979), *Colors* (1988), *New Jack City* (1991), *The Program* (1993), *Natural Born Killers* (1994), and *Money Train* (1995). Each became controversial when it was associated with real-life violence. Gangs vandalized several Massachusetts theatres showing *The Warriors*, and after one screening, a sixteen-year-old boy was knifed. The victim's family filed suit against the producing studio, Paramount Pictures, and the film's exhibitor, USA Cinemas. When several theatres declined to schedule *The Warriors*, Paramount decided to tone down its ad campaign for the film, and the producers demanded that the director reedit the movie to eliminate some of its violence.[21] United Artists' *Colors* drew angry protests while it was being filmed in Los Angeles, and after its release, members of the NAACP and the Guardian Angels picketed Los Angeles–area theatres. Such protests, coupled with attempts at legislative censorship, caused a total of fifteen theatres to cancel engagements.[22] *The Program* and *Money Train* received wide media coverage when they apparently inspired real-life, copy-cat violence. More recently, Bob Dole attacked "Hollywood's dream factory" for turning out "nightmares of depravity," singling out *Natural Born Killers* as the epitome of what is wrong with today's Hollywood films.[23]

But none of these movies, nor those preceding them, galvanized a specific group's anger or resulted in an ongoing censorship debate. The general cry against violence in the media rather offered occasions for politicians to bolster their image among members of the Right. Perhaps because violence has become so much a part of today's movie fare, few protestors actually suggested it be eliminated. In the early to mid 1990s, the phrase "sensitivity not censorship" became a politically wise way for those tired of "the new blood culture," as Frank Rich called it, to voice their complaint.[24] And although it appeared to some that by the end of 1995 the movie industry had in fact undergone an immense change marked by less on-screen violence, no specific film since 1980 could claim the credit.[25]

Five Controversies, Five Movies

The five movies I chose for this book each ignited a debate over environmental issues, sex, ethnicity, religion, or homosexuality; each brought to the national spotlight the concerns of a political constituency, not merely of a handful of lobbyists or politicians.

If You Love This Planet

During and after both world wars, in the McCarthy era, and, to a lesser degree, while Ronald Reagan was president, U.S. government agencies censored movies perceived to threaten U.S. interests, often denigrating them as "political propaganda." During these periods, members of the film industry as well as state and local censors were especially sensitive to depictions of members of the armed forces and of communists. As early as World War I, in an effort to sell Americans on the idea of active participation in the hostilities, the government injected pro-U.S. sentiments into movies. Later, such films as *Spain in Flames* (1937), *Blockade* (1938), and *Professor Mamlock* (1939) were banned in several states because of their pro-Left or antifascist positions. While politicians deliberated over whether the United States should enter World War II, U.S. moviegoers were prevented from seeing almost any movies that treated communism in anything but the most unfavorable light. Movie censorship became an integral part of World War II policy when President Roosevelt formed the Office of War Information (OWI) in 1942, which quickly established a Hollywood liaison "to insure," as historians Clayton Koppes and

Gregory Black write, "that the studios implemented their pledge to help the war effort."[26] To this end, the OWI required studios to submit all scripts for review, encouraged movies that promoted U.S. and world unity and that depicted the struggle for democracy abroad, and discouraged exporting U.S. movies that suggested "economic preparations for a long war."[27]

Just after the war, President Harry Truman abolished the OWI and soon afterward instituted a federal program to remove communists from the government. On March 21, 1947, Truman issued Executive Order No. 9835 establishing the elaborate Federal Loyalty and Security Program, primarily aimed at ridding government of communists or communist sympathizers.[28] Truman also encouraged the House Un-American Activities Committee (HUAC) to purge Hollywood of movies containing sympathetic portraits of Russians, while Senator Joseph McCarthy spearheaded his infamous attacks on Hollywood writers and directors. In some instances out of fear, in others as overt acts of support for McCarthy and his practices, studios engaged in more political self-censorship during the late 1940s and 1950s than ever before.

With the 1960s and 1970s came movies critical of the dominant values of society. What became known as countercultural filmmaking reached its peak with such films as *All the President's Men* (1976), *Network* (1976), and *The Deer Hunter* (1978). Their success proved that politics was alive and commercially viable in Hollywood, and perhaps because they caught the spirit of the times, none such films were censored.

Not long after taking office in 1980, President Reagan and his advisors revived the rhetoric of the Cold War, and not far behind came an increase in the censorship of movies containing "political propaganda." With Russia once again the enemy, Reagan's government demonstrated a renewed fear of foreign-produced documentaries distributed in the United States, particularly those critical of U.S. policies. In 1983, the Justice Department forced three Canadian environmental films to carry the disclaimer "political propaganda" and attempted to restrict their U.S. distribution. One of them, *If You Love This Planet*, was a twenty-minute documentary detailing the environmental and medical effects of a nuclear war and subtly criticizing U.S. policy on weapons testing. The Justice Department's restrictive label warning viewers of the film's content struck some as censorship. In Chapter One I recount the controversy *Planet* engendered.

Dressed to Kill

Whereas government attempts to censor political themes reveal the shifting ideologies of the administration in power, protests against sexual content, ethnicity, religion, and homosexuality, the subjects of Chapters Two through Five, reflect changes in U.S. cultural life. In the 1950s and 1960s, as a series of liberal court decisions freed the movies to treat a wide range of sexually explicit themes, studio and independent producers challenged the powers of the industry's PCA and the Catholic Legion of Decency, both of which disbanded by the late 1960s. Yet the legal climate that had opened the way for more explicit sexual imagery in films changed in the early 1970s when President Nixon appointed four conservative judges to the Supreme Court. Moreover, in the mid to late 1970s, pornography became a major feminist concern. While conservative groups also opposed pornography, feminists for and against its censorship dominated the public debate; 1980 marked both the high point and the end of a brief period during which feminists who wanted pornography censored staged protests in front of movie theatres.

Feminists who viewed pornography as part of the wider system of male hegemony focused their critique on its perceived denigrating effects on women. Unlike other protest groups, some women viewed how they were depicted on screen as more than merely an issue of stereotyping, distortion, or silencing; they argued that pornography was "conduct," not "speech"—not only a matter of representation but a system of oppression in itself—and claimed that it violated women's civil rights and was a primary cause of sexual discrimination in the United States.[29]

In 1977, women in New York and San Francisco formed Women Against Pornography and Woman Against Violence Against Women following the release of a film called *Snuff.* According to Laura Lederer, this film, which purported to show the actual murder or "snuff" of a young woman, was "the powder key that moved women seriously to confront the issue of pornography."[30] When Rochester-area feminists vandalized theatres exhibiting the film, they were arrested. Actions against *Snuff* continued after 1977, but feminist antipornography campaigns did not reach so intense a pitch again until the release of Brian De Palma's *Dressed to Kill* in 1980, when feminist groups in San Francisco, Los Angeles, and Boston demonstrated against the film when it premiered. In New York, an estimated 100–150 protesters carried placards with such sentiments as "Murder of women is not erotic," and chanted such slogans as, "No more profits off our bodies, no more pleasure off our pain."[31] Were these women asking for censorship or merely greater sensitivity? In Chapter Two I examine the controversy.

Year of the Dragon

Although not the first film to draw protests on account of ethnic and racial stereotyping, D.W. Griffith's *The Birth of a Nation* (1915) created the widest such controversy at the time of its release and for many years afterward. As recently as 1992, the NAACP and other African American groups have attempted to halt a planned screening of *Birth*. During the 1970s and early 1980s, other ethnic groups complained about Hollywood's ongoing practices of stereotyping and distortion. Coalitions of Italian Americans, Puerto Ricans, and Cuban Americans launched angry campaigns against the producers of *The Godfather* (1976), *Fort Apache, the Bronx* (1979–1980), *Midnight Express* (1981), and *Scarface* (1983). Several of these coalitions convinced filmmakers to insert disclaimers qualifying the portrayal of a particular ethnic group, yet rarely did the protests produce censorious effects. In 1980, an interracial Committee Against *Fort Apache* (CAFA), consisting primarily of African Americans and Puerto Ricans, staged protests before and after the release of that movie. While CAFA achieved at least one instance of censorship when the Philadelphia City Council prevented all civic venues from showing the movie, Puerto Ricans' participation in protests against racist film imagery practically disappeared during the next decade.

Asian American groups emerged in the 1980s as the most active antagonists to Hollywood's racial stereotyping, claiming that the civil rights movement had influenced mainstream directors to develop "an essentially biracial consciousness (whites and blacks only)."[32] Furthermore, by repeatedly casting white actors in Asian roles and by depicting male Asian characters as villainous and females as sexually demure, filmmakers maintained stereotypes and contributed to Asian Americans' marginalization and oppression. Unlike other racial and ethnic groups during the same period, Asian Americans challenged a series of films rather than just one or two and began to develop a general strategy for resisting the anti-Asiatic imagery produced by Hollywood.

During the late 1970s and 1980s, a group's ability to influence filmmakers' depictions of it corresponded to how powerful the film industry perceived that group to be, how persistent the protest group was, and how it protested. Of all the groups that staged protests during these years, Asian Americans had been perceived by the film industry as one of the least threatening—a perception that was both a sign of inherent racism and evidence that Asian Americans had no significant prior history of challenging filmmakers. In 1977, the Association of Asian/Pacific Artists protested the filming of a Dodge-Aspen commercial that featured the use of "racist" cosmetics. Wider protests greeted *Charlie Chan and the Curse of the Dragon Queen* (1980–1981) and *The Fiendish Plot of Fu Manchu* (1980), feature films that recreated two much-despised stereotypes.

By 1985, Asian Americans had established a network of political and cultural groups determined to fight discrimination and violence not simply by protest but by using to advantage some of the apparatus of mainstream cultural production. The release of Michael Cimino's *Year of the Dragon* galvanized their anger. In Chapter Three I explore the outcome.

Basic Instinct

Gay and lesbian groups' attempts to censor films took Hollywood by surprise, for homosexuals were not only marginalized in society at large but almost completely ignored in films. During the 1950s and early 1960s, while the MPPDA forbade nearly all references to homosexuality, such films as *Cat on a Hot Tin Roof* (1958), *Pit of Loneliness* (1959), *Suddenly Last Summer* (1959), *Devil's Advocate* (1961), *Advise and Consent* (1961), and *The Children's Hour* (1962), each of which contained homosexual characters or themes, challenged the code. Under pressure from Hollywood directors and producers in the post–World War II years, the PCA gradually changed its policies. In 1961, MPPDA president Eric Johnston announced that it would be "permissible under the Code for the PCA to consider approving references in motion pictures to the subject of sex aberrations, provided any references are treated with care, discretion and restraint, and in all other aspects conform to the Code."[33]

As gays and lesbians soon learned, however, screen visibility had its drawbacks: mainstream filmmakers frequently stereotyped homosexuals as psychotic and lonely individuals who could only be "cured" by the "normalcy" of the heterosexual world. In 1969, the Stonewall riots, during which customers of a gay bar in Greenwich Village resisted police brutality, helped to galvanize homosexuals and to focus their anger. The homosexual stereotypes in *The Boys in the Band* (1970), *Fortune and Men's Eyes* (1971), *Death in Venice* (1971), and *The Perfect Couple* (1979) elicited a wave of written criticism and led gay and lesbian groups to demand change. In 1980, *Windows, American Gigolo,* and *Cruising* produced a second wave of activism that included protests in front of theatres. Protests against mainstream movies became one highly visible way of challenging heterosexuals' cultural authority to construct homosexual identity. *Cruising*, which provoked the largest protest among homosexuals to that date, was "the last straw in a long stream of Hollywood horrors," according to film historian Vito Russo. "Coming as it did in company with *Windows* and *American Gigolo*, it acted as a catalyst for a massive nationwide protest of the Hollywood treatment of gays."[34]

In the early 1990s, exasperated with Hollywood, gays and lesbians protested against *Basic Instinct* both before and after its release. While the 1980s had brought a series of AIDS television dramas and a handful of "positive" portrayals of homosexuality in mainstream movies, homosexuals believed that the Hollywood heterosexual hegemony, whether consciously or not, continued to depict them as villains. A media blitz was necessary. In Chapter Five I recount the *Basic Instinct*–centered actions by gay and lesbian groups eager to send Hollywood a message.

The Last Temptation of Christ

While less controversial than sexual, ethnic, and homophobic images, representations of religion have provoked censorship challenges of varying degrees of intensity throughout the history of U.S. film. Most often, censorship of religious content has fallen on Hollywood movies made in the biblical spectacular tradition, including two Cecil B. DeMille films, *King of Kings* (1926) and *Sign of the Cross* (1932), and, more recently, Norman Jewison's *Jesus Christ Superstar* (1973) and Martin Scorsese's *The Last Temptation of Christ* (1988). A second set of films that led to censorship challenges from religious groups is comprised of films either produced in Europe or directed by a European, including Roberto Rossellini's *The Miracle* (1951), Franco Zeffirelli's made-for-television drama *Jesus of Nazareth* (1977), *Monty Python's Life of Brian* (1970–1980), and Jean-Luc Godard's *Hail Mary* (1985). Finally, a third, far smaller, category of films that provoked censorship efforts by religious groups includes those such as *The Callahans and the Murphys* (1927) and *Gone With the Wind* (1939), whose incidental use of religious imagery and "profane" language drew complaints.

In the 1980s, traditionally dominant religious groups sought to reestablish the powerful influence they had wielded during the formative years of the film industry, when many religious leaders helped to establish and operate censorship boards. Attempts to censor increased after Jerry Falwell's Moral Majority emerged as a significant political force in 1979. In that year and the next, conservative religious groups' protests against the comic treatment of the Bible in *Monty Python's Life of Brian* led to censorship in Boston, Cleveland, and other cities. In 1985, Catholic-led protests aimed at censoring Jean-Luc Godard's *Hail Mary* failed to prevent theaters from exhibiting the film. Three years later, Martin Scorsese's *The Last Temptation of Christ* elicited widespread protest.

The religious opposition to and industry defense of *Last Temptation* demonstrated that the larger political struggles between conservatives and liberals over issues such as homosexuality, abortion, AIDS, and prayer in school extended to films as well. With the embarrassing public exposure and subsequent convictions of televangelists Jimmy Swaggart and Jim Bakker, conservative religious groups came to see their campaign against *Last Temptation,* for example, as not just a protest against cinematic transgression but a struggle for the survival of their coalition and for its members' "vision" for America. In Chapter Five I look at the controversy and its aftermath.

The controversies over these five movies show several forms of censorship or attempted censorship in action in the U.S. movie industry today, with group protests emerging as the predominate form. While in each chapter I focus primarily on a single movie released between 1980 and 1995, my larger aim is to view these movies together, as a portrait of fifteen years of conflict. At the very least this book will allow voices of conflict to resonate and contrasting visions of contemporary U.S. society to emerge. For it is through these conflicts over movies—once heralded as the most "democratic" art—that we can better understand the counters of our cultural wars, determine on which side we stand, and assess who, if anyone, has been a winner.

1

Warning—"Political Propaganda"

The Case against
If You Love This Planet (1982)

This whole thing is a joke. It's as though the Reagan administration sat down yesterday and decided to ban films from Canada arbitrarily. This is total distortion.
Roy Cohn

I am outraged. I think the idea of reporting the names of our customers who rent and buy films to the Department of Justice is horrible. It just smacks of everything one ever thought about the year 1984.
Mitchell Block

In March 1983, the Academy of Motion Picture Arts and Sciences awarded Terri Nash, the director of the Canadian documentary *If You Love This Planet,* an Oscar for Best Short Documentary. Clasping the award with pride, Nash thanked the U.S. Justice Department for its role in "advertising" her film (photo 1). She was referring to the department's decision to label *Planet* "political propaganda" and to require its U.S. distributor to give the Justice Department the names of people who had purchased a copy. The academy audience roared with laughter.

During 1982 and early 1983, *Planet* had become a cause

célèbre for environmentalists, liberal journalists, and free-speech advocates. The government's decision to label the film and attempt to restrict its distribution raised questions about free speech under the Reagan administration. Maybe no officials at the Justice Department, as lawyer Roy Cohn suggested on ABC's *Nightline,* had decided to use *Planet* to warn off "subversive" foreign filmmakers. Maybe the labeling had no wider purpose. But shouldn't the long-range implications of such labels be considered? Wasn't it a bad precedent that a branch of the government had routinely

Photo 1. With a little help from the U.S. Justice Department, Terri Nash and Edward LeLorrain received the Best Short Documentary Academy Award for "If You Love This Planet." © Copyright Academy of Motion Picture Arts and Sciences, Los Angeles.

labeled a film propaganda and taken steps to monitor its distribution? As lawyers argued over whether "political propaganda" was a neutral or derogatory label, the media, politicians, and filmmakers considered the broader significance of the labeling. Why is the U.S. government so intimidated by a small Canadian documentary that discusses the medical and social effects of nuclear war? More importantly, what does the government's response to the film reveal about the ideological and cultural agenda of the Reagan administration?

The United States government had been involved with censoring political content from movies in the past, and an overview of past acts of censorship provides a context for the Justice Department's actions against *Planet*. Because such a wide range of films can be called political, the term political content seems to lack precision. But one can't readily enough speak of the overtly political film. But one can readily enough speak of the overtly political film, as Terry Christensen has, as a film focusing on "politicians, elections, government, and the political process" that has at its core "a political message that the viewer can perceive."[1] Films with daring sexual content and other controversial subject matter have been more likely to be censored, but the Hays Office, the Legion of Decency, and a variety of pressure groups as well as city, state, and federal officials have censored political content.

Beginning in 1914, political censorship was most forceful when America was at war and during the McCarthy era, when the fear of communism and communists peaked.[2] In the 1940s and 1950s, nearly all movies censored due to their political content supported 'leftist' causes at a time when such sympathies were unpopular. In 1949, Maryland censors banned a fifty-minute Polish documentary because "they did not believe it presents a true picture of present-day Poland" and it "appears to be communist propaganda."[3] One year later, Memphis censors banned *The Southerner*, a movie that dealt with poverty among tenant farmers, because "[the film] reflects badly on the South."[4] In 1954, the "feminist" film *Salt of the Earth*, produced by blacklisted filmmakers including Herbert Biberman, provoked censorship by local pressure groups and the national projectionists' union. *Salt* tells the story of striking Mexican American zinc miners, many of whom were women; its production involved consulting many local miners and their families. While shooting in the United States, filmmakers were harassed by gun-carrying townspeople, and the Mexican actress playing the lead was deported three times. When the producers tried to market the completed film in the United States, distributors boycotted and the projectionists' union refused to screen it. Finally, the film was exhibited in eleven cities, yet members of the American Legion picketed many of the theatres where it was shown and FBI agents allegedly recorded the license-plate numbers of moviegoers.[5]

That films with controversial political themes went relatively unscathed during the 1950s and 1960s may have encouraged filmmakers to approach politics more boldly. The Supreme Court's *Miracle* decision in 1952, in which films were granted First Amendment protection, coupled with the dissolution of the MPPDA Code in 1968, helped reduce U.S. movie censorship. Terry Christensen writes that "1964 marked the beginning of a period when American filmmakers strongly criticized the dominant values of society."[6] What Michael Ryan and Douglas Kellner call "counterculture filmmaking" reached full swing with such films as Sidney Lumet's *Fail Safe* (1964), Stanley Kubrick's *Dr. Strangelove* (1964), Alfred Hitchcock's *Marnie* (1964), Arthur Penn's *Bonnie and Clyde* (1967), Haskell Wexler's *Medium Cool* (1969), Mike Nichols's *Catch 22* (1970), and Costa Gavras's *Z* (1970).[7] Unlike mainstream movies, politically daring documentaries remained susceptible to censorship. The difference came down to distribution. In 1948 the Justice Department had found the five major studios— Paramount, MGM, Warner Brothers, Twentieth Century Fox, and Walt Disney—in violation of antitrust laws and forced them to abandon their oligarchic control over Hollywood production, distribution, and exhibition; yet many studio movies produced during the 1950s and 1960s still counted on large corporations for distribution.[8] This dependence meant that studios often shaped the political content of their films to suit the ideology of their distributors, many of whom were (and remain) conservative.[9] Because documentaries are often independently funded and exhibited by privately owned theatres, they can avoid depending on the corporations and, arguably, can make more overtly political films than the commercial market generally allows.[10] But they risk government censorship. Actions in 1970 against Fred Wiseman's documentary *Titicut Follies* demonstrated the measures local government would take against independently produced movies it found politically threatening.

Titicut graphically records the mistreatment of inmates in a prison for the criminally insane in Bridgewater, Massachusetts. When Wiseman attempted to show the film in Massachusetts, state legislators banned it outright. Throughout the country, *Titicut* was restricted to "qualified" viewers such as legislators, lawyers, and doctors, who could watch it only in classrooms. Although finally granted commercial release in 1989—with the condition that the subjects' faces were blurred—*Titicut,* Wiseman notes, remains one of the only movies "of any sort in American constitutional history, other than one involving obscenity or national security, that has a partial restraint on its use."[11] Clearly, the government feared this film's effects on the criminal-justice system. Restricting *Titicut's* distribution proved that ideological government censorship endured, even in a liberal cultural climate.

In Hollywood, meanwhile, the profit principle won out. Because studios were able to turn large profits from a slew of liberal-minded features, they managed to avoid skirmishes with some of their conservative corporate backers. *Chinatown* (1974), *The Parallax View* (1974), *Three Days of the Condor* (1974), *All the President's Men* (1976), *The Front* (1976), *Taxi Driver* (1976), *Network* (1976), *Julia* (1977), *The Deer Hunter* (1978), and *Coming Home* (1978) each proved that politics sells.

During the early 1980s, one mainstream movie more than any other, *Missing* (1982), provoked censorial responses by governmental agencies and drew attention to what many critics felt were the government's renewed stakes in controlling films' political content. Directed by Greek filmmaker Costa Gavras and starring Jack Lemmon and Sissy Spacek, *Missing* dramatizes the true-life story of a father's search for his son, U.S. journalist Charles Harmon, who disappeared while working in Chile at the time of the U.S.-sanctioned coup that overthrew Salvador Allende's Socialist government. He was later found dead. The film version of the story, based on Thomas Hauser's 1978 book *The*

Execution of Charles Harmon: An American Sacrifice, was, according to journalist Andrew Kopkind, "deliberately ambiguous" on the question of how Harmon was killed. Kopkind notes that *Missing* "strongly suggests" Harmon was murdered by Chilean police because he had stumbled upon evidence of U.S. involvement in the military coup, and also that the U.S. embassy covered up its knowledge of Harmon's execution. The movie enraged Ambassador Nathaniel Davis and the U.S. State Department. Davis, who along with two other U.S. officials had been stationed in Santiago at the time of the coup, filed suit against the author, film director, and the Hearst Corporation, which published the successful paperback edition of Hauser's book. Commenting on the completed film, Davis charged, "The thrust of the movie essentially is that we were complicit in telling the Chileans to murder Charles Harmon."[12]

On the eve of the *Missing* premiere, the State Department issued a three-page white paper that expressed disapproval of the movie and, according to Rodney Smolla, "declared that after an eight-year investigation, no light was shed upon the circumstances of [Charles Harmon's] death and little upon the circumstances of his disappearance. Furthermore, nothing was discovered to support any charges, rumors, or inferences as contained in the complaint against U.S. government officials." The white paper not only stressed the "official reality" of the government's involvement with Chile, but, in support of the $150 million suit Davis had filed, also favored penalizing the "creators" of the movie. Such a penalty would have violated the First Amendment, which was designed to guarantee artists the freedom to "produce a corrosive political indictment of U.S. policy" if they so choose. "There is nothing evil or unpatriotic," Smolla reminds us, "about a robust skepticism of the American government's behavior and policies."[13] The State Department was clearly censorious in its criticism of *Missing*, but its actions did not ultimately affect the film's exhibition, achieving neither a prior-restraint nor a postrelease cancellation. Still, Kopkind and others saw the broader significance of the *Missing* controversy. For Kopkind, the State Department's actions against the film were evidence less of censorship than of a "cultural battlefield" and an imminent "larger ideological war" in which those favoring the state's imperialist and interventionist rights would fall on one side, those criticizing such rights on the other. "The old dividing line is indeed revitalized," Kopkind declares in the concluding lines of his essay, "and bigger battles are bound to begin."[14]

Critics of the Reagan administration believed that what had been foreshadowed by the *Missing* controversy occurred later in 1982 when the Justice Department applied the "political propaganda" label to three Canadian films—*Acid from Heaven, Acid Rain: Requiem or Recovery?* and *If You Love This Planet.* Of the three, *Planet* drew the most attention because its director most rigorously fought the label, because the film ultimately won an Oscar, and because court cases brought by its U.S. distributor raised questions about an institutional labeling process that harkened back to the 1930s. The U.S. government's initial success was reminiscent of the *Titicut* censorship scenario, where a low-budget documentary was forced to succumb to local censors. The difference lay in the force with which the filmmakers and liberal lawyers defended *Planet*. Whereas the *Titicut* instance had been clear-cut government censorship, *Planet* can be classified as a censorship challenge, with both liberals and conservatives caught in heated dispute over whether censorship had actually occurred.

It started with outrage. Early in 1983, the media, *Planet's* director, Terri Nash, and the film's producer, the National Film Board of Canada (NFB) could hardly believe that the U.S. Justice Department intended to require them to attach "political propaganda" labels to all copies of *Planet* exhibited or distributed in the United States. In the press and in court, the plot thickened: the Left accused the Right of censorship, while the Right accused the Left of distortion and denied that censorship was an issue. The conservative Reagan Justice Department insisted that the term *political propaganda* was a neutral label routinely applied by government officials with no particular ideological agenda and that they were not acting as censors.[15] The Left didn't buy this argument. Despite the political victory of the Right in 1980, or perhaps because of it, the Left—represented by members of the press, environmentalists, and liberal lawyers—attempted to mobilize public opinion, determined to use the controversy as a catalyst for a larger campaign against the Reagan administration. For the Left, the *Planet* labeling suggested an ideological transgression by government and proved that the administration had developed a cultural agenda that warranted silencing speech it did not like to hear (figure 1).

On February 25, 1983, the first day that the story broke in the national press, the ACLU issued a statement condemning the labeling as "one more in a series of recent acts designed to wall off Americans from information which the administration finds embarrassing or distasteful."[16] In the course of the first week, numerous journalists and politicians editorialized and spoke out. CBS TV's *Entertainment*

Figure 1. A print advertisement for *If You Love This Planet,* this photo depicts two young children watching the world blow up in a nuclear holocaust; *Planet* details the environmental and medical consequences of a nuclear war. Courtesy of Mitchell W. Block, Direct Cinema Limited.

Tonight and ABC News's *Nightline* devoted segments of their nightly broadcasts to the *Planet* controversy. Canadian environmental minister John Roberts said, "It sounds like something you would expect from the Soviet Union, not the

United States"; in an open debate on *Nightline,* he exclaimed, "I can't believe that Americans are so feeble in judgment that they need to be protected from slick-talking Canadians going down and discussing issues with them."[17] Other Canadian officials viewed the labeling as evidence of a new McCarthyism, calling is an "extraordinary interference with freedom of speech."[18] U.S. senators George J. Mitchell and Edward Kennedy also complained. "This is an obvious attempt by the Reagan Administration to hinder the expression of views contrary to those of the Administration," Democratic senator Mitchell of Maine said. "It is unworthy of the United States of America." In introducing to the National Press Club Helen Caldicott, the antinuclear activist featured in *Planet,* Senator Kennedy proclaimed: "It is one thing for the right wing to say 'Let Reagan be Reagan.' But it is a very different thing for them to say, 'Let Reagan Be Orwell.'" Robert Rose of the National Clean Air Coalition concurred: "The chilling effect is obvious. This is the Criminal Division of the Justice Department. The film police—I guess that's what you'd call them—and the effect will be to deny American voters one of the few opportunities to learn." And Mitchell Block, the film's U.S. distributor, told *Nightline:* "I am outraged. I think the idea of reporting the names of our customers who rent and buy films to the Department of Justice is horrible. It just smacks of everything one ever thought about the year 1984."[19]

Many of these critics did not realize that the Justice Department, under the Foreign Agents Registration Act (FARA), had been labeling foreign films distributed in the United States for years. The 1930 Tariff Act empowered the Federal Bureau of Customs to approve or bar from importation hundreds of foreign films every year. Eight years later, FARA granted the Justice Department the right to require official labels on films and other audio-visual materials. Conceived as a statute to prevent Nazi and other subversive propaganda from entering the United States, FARA defined political propaganda as "any attempt to influence a segment of the American public with reference to the foreign policy of the U.S., whether pro or con, on behalf of a foreign principal, by written, pictorial or other communication."[20] The statute was enacted on the recommendation of the House Un-American Activities Committee, which claimed to have discovered that hundreds of agents in the United States were disseminating propaganda at the behest of foreign interests.[21]

In 1942, FARA was substantially amended because the initial act did not include people who send materials into the United States. The government added the following introductory statement: "[FARA aims to] protect the national defense, internal security, and foreign relations of the U.S. by requiring public disclosure by persons engaging in propaganda activities and other activities . . . for or on behalf of . . . foreign principals so that the government and the people of the U.S. may . . . appraise their statements and actions in light of their associations and activities."[22] This amendment also required foreign agents to place on file with the Department of Justice two copies of any material considered to be political propaganda and expanded the definition of the term:

> Any oral, visual, graphic, written, or other communication or expression . . . which is reasonably adapted to, or which the person disseminating the same believes will, or which he intends to, prevail upon, in-

doctrinate, convert, induce, or in any other way influence a recipient or any section of the public within the
United States with reference to the political or public
interests, policies, or relations of a government of a
foreign country or a foreign political party or with reference to the foreign policies of the United States or
promote in the United States racial, religious, or social
dissensions.

A section was also added "requiring that all propaganda be
labeled and that the names of its recipients be reported to
the Justice Department" (figure 2). In 1966, the government amended FARA a second time, shifting the act's focus
from the "subversive agent and propagandist of pre-World
War II days to 'agents' acting 'for or in the interests of foreign principals' whose activities are 'political in nature or
border on the political'"—yet Congress did not change the
broad definition of political propaganda offered in 1942.[23]
Since 1966, the Justice Department had been reviewing
about twenty-five foreign films, mostly documentaries, each
year and finding about half of these to require a disclaimer.[24]

Whether critics of the labeling knew about FARA or not,
it was more advantageous for them to focus their criticism
on the controversy over *Planet* than to attack a bipartisan
policy of film labeling. During the first week of the *Planet*
debate, the antilabeling position appeared to dominate.
CBS TV's *Entertainment Tonight* broadcast a news item on a
successful screening in Washington, D.C., held at the request of environmentalists and the film's producers, who
wished to protest the government's label. CBS interviewed
moviegoers as they left the theatre. All were angry. The
same night, ABC TV's *Nightline* featured Mitchell Block,

WHAT MAKES ONE ACADEMY AWARD NOMINEE DIFFERENT FROM ANOTHER?

"registered foreign political propaganda"

"If You Love This Planet"
has been nominated for an Academy Award.

The U.S. Department of Justice has labelled it political propaganda.

Common Sense?

In February, 1983, "If You Love This Planet," along with two other Canadian films on acid rain, was labelled as foreign propaganda, by the U.S. Government.

The Justice Department says it used common sense in deciding that a disclaimer be read that certain films were "materials disseminated by foreign agents."

The government says it used common sense in deciding that only theaters and groups which charge admission for the films turnover their names to the government.

Freedom of Expression

Whenever freedom of expression is threatened, the performing arts community has the greatest amount to lose. Its work depends on a climate of openness, where differences are tolerated and diversity is welcomed. As citizens, the members of the arts community have a special obligation to preserve and protect the future of liberty in America.

The First Amendment is the cornerstone of freedom of expression. It denies government not only the power to ban,

Raise the curtain on the First Amendment. Act with us.

ACLU 633 S. Shatto Place
Los Angeles, CA 90005

☐ I want to act with you. Enclosed is my tax-deductible contribution.*

☐ I want to become involved in the work of the ACLU.

Name _____

Address _____

Figure 2. After the U.S. Justice Department labeled *If You Love This Planet* political propaganda, the ACLU placed this ad in *Variety.* Courtesy of Mitchell W. Block, Direct Cinema Limited.

Bert Neuborne, Dr. Helen Caldicott, and John Roberts, all opponents of the labeling. Only Roy Cohn, a retired former attorney for Joe McCarthy, voiced the prolabel position. Cohn flatly denied that using a "political propaganda" label was anything more than a legitimate exercise of FARA: "This whole thing is a joke. It's as though the Reagan administration sat down yesterday and decided to ban films from Canada arbitrarily. This is total distortion. . . . This all comes under an act passed under the Presidency of F.D.R. in 1938 . . . an act of Congress that requires this procedure to be followed."[25] Cohn's unpopular position continued to be drowned out by numerous voices on the Left calling foul.

From February 25 through about March 5, newspapers like the *Los Angeles Times, Washington Post,* and *New York Times* published the liberal view. A *Los Angeles Times* editorial stated, "The US government has got mixed up in an unseemly little mess by poking its nose into an area where any government presence is always an intrusion. . . . The ruling, an obnoxious form of pollution itself, is an embarrassment and should be rescinded." Similarly, an editorial in the *Washington Post* argued: "Dozens of films, American and foreign, could be characterized as political propaganda of some sort. But this society thrives on free political discourse. It is essential to the democratic form of government we have chosen and are constantly trying to perfect and the taking of names of citizens who express or even choose to listen to unpopular argument is absolutely contrary to the values we hold as Americans." On March 3, *New York Times* op-ed columnist Anthony Lewis passionately expanded these views: "There is more to the film affair than philistine ignorance. It reflects a general and dangerous characteristic of the Reagan Administration. A fear of open debate and information, a fear of freedom. . . . Those who won our independence believed that public discussion is a political duty and that this should be a fundamental principle of the American government. But they were confident people, not little men afraid of contrary ideas, afraid of criticism, afraid of public knowledge."[26]

Although more than a dozen news articles quoted Justice Department explanations, the full prolabel position first appeared in the press on March 6, when the *Washington Post* published an editorial by Thomas P. DeCair, publicity director for the department and its most frequently quoted spokesperson. DeCair took the opportunity to rail against the liberal press: "Contrary to the uninformed hysteria that had developed in some quarters, the Justice Department is not censoring any film in this country. Nor is it trying to curtail the dissemination of any movie. Nor does it seek to intimidate anyone who watches a movie. We are simply enforcing FARA . . . as passed by Congress. The purpose of the label is to notify viewers that the material is being disseminated by a foreign agent. It does not comment on the positions advocated by the film." Four days later, Jody Powell, a journalist who earlier had criticized the Justice Department's labeling, appeared to change sides when he wrote in the *Washington Post:* "Now, more than a week later, it is clear that the real story is that those [anti-label views] cited above, and quite a few others, went off half-cocked. Our rhetoric exceeded our knowledge of the facts by an embarrassing margin. . . . The Justice Department appears to be correct in its original claim that it was simply enforcing the law and that the law itself is less Orwellian than some should have us believe."[27]

Making FARA a sacred cow, DeCair and Powell failed to

question the legitimacy of the Justice Department's employing a law passed fifty years earlier during a period of widespread anticommunism. For them, labeling a movie "political propaganda" was a far cry from censoring it, which in the narrow, classical view, means removing an idea from the marketplace. But liberal critics considered other censorship in a capitalist society. Professor Lawrence H. Tribe of Harvard Law School, for example, told the *New York Times* that labeling was censorship because "it prevents the listeners from hearing the uncensored content of what people have to say."[28] Because the government was altering viewers' reception of *Planet,* Tribe believed, it was in effect being censored.

The real debate over the Justice Department's use of the label sprang from two opposing views of movie censorship. Two lawsuits filed in 1983 claimed that using "political propaganda" to categorize *Planet* and the two other Canadian documentaries was "inherently pejorative, denigrates the films, and stigmatizes those who show them by implying that they are disseminators of distorted information calculated to further the goals of the foreign powers."[29] While the Justice Department held that "political propaganda" is a neutral expression "understood by the 'ordinary individual' to have a non-pejorative meaning," it also claimed that "FARA furthers a compelling national security interest by promoting a free marketplace of ideas and that by requiring disclosure of identifying information . . . guarantees that the marketplace will not be subverted."[30]

Both suits focused, not on the content of the Canadian films, but rather on questions of how to define "political propaganda" and the constitutionality of this phrase. In the first case, filed as *Block v. Smith* by the ACLU and the State of New York on behalf of Mitchell Block, in the U.S. District Court for the District of Columbia, Judge Charles R. Richey dismissed the plaintiff's case for lack of standing, arguing that, "in order to find factually specific injury, the court would have to assume that the public would react negatively to a film labeled 'political propaganda' despite the neutral definition . . . provided by FARA . . . that this 'negative reaction' would cause potential audience members to discount the film's messages or avoid the film completely . . . and finally that . . . the public will lose respect for the plaintiffs because they chose to show the movies." In other words, the court simply did not believe that the 'political propaganda' label would have a negative impact on people who saw the movie. In the second suit, *Keene v. Smith*, California state senator Barry Keene argued that he wished to acquire and exhibit all three Canadian documentaries, "in order to engage in public debate about acid rain and nuclear weapons." Keene's case was successful because he demonstrated that "the government's characterization of [all three films] as 'political propaganda' deterred him" from engaging in such debate. On May 23, 1983, Judge Raul Ramirez of the U.S. District Court for the Eastern District of California found that the State Department's use of 'political propaganda' "reflects a conscious attempt to place a whole category of materials beyond the pale of legitimate discourse." For this reason, Ramirez held that the phrase did in fact abridge Keene's freedom of speech and that those portions of FARA using the term were unconstitutional.[31]

Both suits were soon appealed. While Block's petition was denied by an appellate court in 1986, a year later the Supreme Court reheard Keene's case as *Meese v. Keene,* an appeal of the Ramirez ruling. As in the successful lower court case, the dissenting Supreme Court judges argued that applying FARA, a law aimed at limiting subversive propaganda and discouraging communications by foreign agents acting on behalf of their governments, amounted to "government disparagement of speech" and violated the First Amendment while constituting "blatant" censorship. An affidavit submitted by eminent Yale psychology professor Leonard Dupe was largely responsible for this view. The court's majority decision, written by Justice John Paul Stevens, argued that FARA placed "no burden on protected expression" and that "political propaganda" as defined by Congress "has no pejorative connotation."[32] By denying that the phrase was stigmating, the Supreme Court, by a five to three majority, had in essence declared that the entire incident could not and would not be viewed as censorship. Using the phrase "political propaganda" was now once again constitutional, and the California district court's findings were reversed. Four years after the initial labeling, Block and Keene were back where they started, still feeling that an injustice had been done but unable to prove it in court.

A decade later, Charles Sims, the ACLU lawyer who argued for Block in *Block v. Smith* and *Block v. Meese,* Mitchell Block, and Terri Nash continue to hold strong opinions on the issue. Sims believes that the labeling was "simply the act of a bureaucrat going about his regulatory duties," he told me over the phone in March 1992. He argues that the entire incident ultimately became a "nonevent"—not part of some Reagan "plan," only evidence of a governmental agency in decline: "My gut feeling was that [the decision to label] comes from low-level people, not high-level . . . the government's foreign registration is largely self-executing, that is, people by and large do what the bureaucrats and bureaucratic regulations tell them they should. It's like filing your income tax. People just do it."[33]

Mitchell Block and Terri Nash continue to link the labeling to the ideology of the Reagan administration. In a February 1992 telephone interview, Block called attention to actions by career foreign-service officers in the Reagan administration, who throughout the 1980s, he claims, were systematically trying to stifle dissent: "Any law in the books they could use to go after people, photographers, political activists, they used. I think that *If You Love This Planet* was part of a broader theme to limit distribution of materials coming into the country and going out as well. People in the Reagan and Bush administrations are conservative and they equate criticism with unpatriotic activity such as what Helen Caldicott was saying in 1982–83—that we have too many missiles."[34] Terri Nash agreed, in a telephone interview in March 1992: "What the Reagan administration was trying to do by banning—I don't really mean banning, but by limiting the discussion—was in effect to limit people's choices in terms of ideas. I consider that more propagandistic than what we tried to show. They were the ones with the control."

In testimony before the House of Representatives in May 1990, Nash was more specific. "I can draw no other conclusion than that this was an attempt by the Reagan Administration to intimidate American citizens and to discourage them from having access to the information which these films provide."[35] In our telephone interview, Nash drew attention to Reagan's appointment of Antonin Scalia from the Justice Department to the U.S. Court of Appeals and subsequently to the Supreme Court. Scalia had been the "star" of the Justice Department before he was appointed to the court of appeals, where he heard *Block v. Smith* in 1986.[36] On June 20, 1986, (the day after Reagan appointed him to the Supreme Court), Scalia drafted a twenty-six page decision denying the unconstitutionality of the Justice Department's "political propaganda" label and thereby definitively quashing *Block v. Smith*. While Scalia had not been directly involved in the Justice Department's Registration Unit that had labeled the film in 1983, Nash told me that "the idea that the case was being heard by someone the Reagan administration considered an objective judge was a joke. . . . He wasn't objective at all as far as I was concerned. That was an insidious claim. There's a whole illusion that there's objectivity. There wasn't objectivity on our side either. I was never pretending to say that it was a film that showed both sides. It didn't." Nash's comments raise questions about the labeling that transcend the relatively narrow court debate over whether the term was "neutral" or stigmatizing. For Nash and Block, the issue was not one of semantics, but of whether the Justice Department should have a right to put *any* comment on a film it dislikes. Nash and Block ultimately judged the labeling a self-serving mechanism of an ideological administration aiming to abridge American freedoms as defined by the First Amendment. "Political propaganda," Block said in our telephone interview, "is simply an ideological position that is different than the one you live in. If you plead that the American strategy of producing warheads was wrong, or is wrong, then that is 'political propaganda.'"

Nash and Block presented the view of a vocal and active minority. While mainstream America savored the Reagan revolution, the few remaining Great Society liberals—historians, journalists, and legal scholars—published maga-

zine articles and books charging that the Reagan administration was deliberately ideological in regulating speech.
During Reagan's presidency, they pointed out, attacks on
the Freedom of Information Act (FOIA) drastically increased. Richard O. Curry, for example, finds "the Reagan
Administration the most stridently ideological administration to hold office in the U.S. in decades," while Eugene
Ferguson, Jr., and Diana Autin, among others, document
attacks on the FOIA.[37] Enacted in 1966, the act sought to increase public access to federal government records. Although its main purpose was to "establish a general philosophy of full agency disclosure," Ferguson writes that shortly
after Reagan's election the Reagan administration took
many steps to "limit disclosure under the [FOIA] Act." Both
President Reagan and CIA director William P. Casey proposed amendments that Ferguson suggests seriously "im-
peded the purposes of the Act."[38]

While Congress rejected these changes, a compromise
bill, S.774, was unanimously approved by the Senate Judi-
ciary Committee. As Autin explains, "Under S.774, law enforcement records would receive a broader exemption
and secret service and 'organized crime' information
would be completely exempt. Use of the FOIA would be
restricted to citizens or permanent legal residents, and
requesters would be charged for agency time spent
censoring documents." Several "backdoor" amendments
and executive orders further restricted the FOIA. One
amendment concerned the public announcement of un-
derground nuclear testing. "Since 1975," according to
Autin, "the government policy had been to announce all
such tests: Now, however, only those tests designated as
'large' will be announced. . . . This policy will work to keep

a growing number of such tests secret." This change implies a fear of subverting national security interests. With Executive Order 12356, the Reagan administration revealed the depths of its paranoia. "Executive Order 12356 removed the need to show 'identifiable damage' to national security through release of information, and eliminated the [Jimmy] Carter order's test requiring the balancing of the public's interest in disclosure against the potential harm to national security release." The new executive order lengthened the time for which documents were to remain classified, while "eliminating the automatic declassification of documents after twenty or thirty years and empowering agencies to reclassify and recall previously declassified documents."[39]

Subsequent executive orders allowed federal agencies greater power to deny FOIA requests. Waldman and others have noted a near 40 percent increase in the number of wiretaps from 1983 to 1984 as well as repeated State Department invocations of the McCarran-Walter Act to deny visas to political and literary figures. Many critics of the Reagan administration believe that these were just some of the ways in which the president had redefined the FOIA.[40]

Victor Navasky similarly points to a xenophobic tendency during the Reagan years:

> Reagan's election only reinforced my sense that *Naming Names* involved unfinished business. It was not merely Reagan's anti-communist rhetoric but the omnipresence of the so-called New-Right in his corner that led many to talk of Cold War II, a new McCarthyism. . . . The vocabulary was new, but not the concept—communist propaganda was now disinfor-

mation; where once we had been warned against es-
pionage agents, now we were told to beware of agents
of influence. Terrorist joined communist as a scare
word, the two were not mutually exclusive by a long
shot.[41]

And O. K. Werckmeister draws the thesis of his book, *Citadel
Culture,* from President Reagan's January 12, 1989, Farewell
Address to the American People. Reagan waxed poetic
about a highly defended nation:

> The past few days when I've been at the window up-
> stairs, I've thought a bit of the shining "city upon a
> hill." The phrase comes from John Winthrop, who
> wrote it to describe the America he imagined.
>
> I've spoken of the shining city all my political life, but
> I don't know if I've ever quite communicated what I saw
> when I said it. But in my mind, it was a tall proud city
> built on rocks stronger than the oceans, windswept, God
> blessed, and teeming with people of all kinds living in
> harmony and peace—a city with free ports that
> hummed with commerce and creativity, and if there had
> to be city walls, the walls had doors, and the doors were
> open to anyone with the will and the heart to get here.
>
> That's how I saw it, and see it still.
>
> And how stands the city on this winter night? More
> prosperous, more secure and happier than it was eight
> years ago.

According to Werckmeister, under Reagan America became a "citadel culture," secure yet cut off from the rest of
the world, a society in which "a new artistic and intellectual

culture with official support and with public success has emerged." Further, the country developed an ideology of containment where voices of opposition, if not completely silenced by the dominant culture, were at least robbed of their disruptive capacity.[42]

Even if the Reagan administration had a stridently ideological political agenda, the question remains, Was the Justice Department's decision to label *Planet* part of that agenda? Charles Sims, the ACLU lawyer who argued on behalf of the film, reflected on his defeat in *Block v. Meese* in our 1992 interview:

> A decision like this can have various bad effects. It can contain the seeds for bad things in the future, but beyond that the only harm it can have, I take it, is if it leads to people censoring their own films, or other people censoring films, or smaller audiences for films. I don't know what other bad effects we could be talking about. . . . Did it lead anybody to censor their own films? I would doubt it. Did it lead to any actual censoring of films by anybody else—by producers, or by governmental agents? I don't think so. Did it lead to smaller audiences to films? I think it's probably true that *If You Love This Planet*'s audience was immeasurably increased and I don't think, as a practical matter, that the audience for any other film has been diminished because of this decision.

It is difficult to fault Sims' surprising assessment, for he would seem willing if not eager to cry censorship when he saw it. Yet while *Planet* was not removed from the marketplace of ideas, scholars such as Smith, Smolla, Waldman,

Landsbaum, Dorfman, and Hull convincingly suggest a censorious intent to control not *whether* a political documentary
was shown, but rather *how* the public viewed it. As Smith and
Smolla write, "[The outcome of] *Meese v. Keene* capitulates
to a recurring weakness in American culture, a reflexive
xenophobic tendency to paternalistically shelter Americans
from 'foreign' and alien speech." According to Waldman,
the labeling unmasks the Reagan administration's desire to
"limit public access to oppositional discourse," "not content
to leave the marginalization of oppositional discourse to
market forces." In Landsbaum's view, "The chilling effect
which [the Beirut Agreement and FARA represent] allows
the government to censor films without really trying. . . . The
fear that one might be penalized encourages producers and
distributors to behave as if their film will be subjected to regulation, even if it should not." Dorfman attacks FARA's def-
initional language and scoffs at the government's use of the
"political propaganda" label. "The government claim that
'political propaganda' operates as a neutral term of art," she
writes, "seems disingenuous at best, and fatuous at worst."
Reflecting on the philosophy underlying the First Amendment, Hull concludes that "Americans are capable of sifting
through [any] material, and of judging for themselves what
is and what is not worthwhile, without a paternalistic nudge
from Uncle Sam." Viewed together, such comments convincingly suggest that, although they cannot be called censorship in the classic liberal sense of the word, the Justice
Department's actions *were* censorious.[43]

The government's defeat of the independent filmmakers who brought suit against it provides a final means of relating the labeling incident to broader trends of ideological
and cultural conflict. In the early and mid 1980s, the gov-

ernment's victory proved that an institution with the power to control the use of political content in foreign films distributed in the United States could maintain that power by subtly denigrating the film in question. The incident did not, as Charles Sims noted, result in a wave of government censorship, but still the point had been made: environmental viewpoints critical of those held by the Reagan administration would not be afforded equal status in the marketplace.

While unsuccessful in the courts, Mitchell Block's suit against the Justice Department may be understood in light of the period's culture wars. Viewed in conjunction with the successful case brought by U.S. independent film distributors against the United States Information Agency, Block's challenge represents one among many instances during the 1980s and early 1990s when liberals opposed the "antidemocratic" cultural practices of government and cultural elites.[44] Like protest groups on the Left, opponents of the *Planet* labeling asserted their democratic right to participate in the debate over what speech could be heard in the marketplace and how that speech could be heard.

Murder of Women
Is Not Erotic

Feminists against
Dressed to Kill (1980)

"Dressed to Kill" will probably anger some women a great deal. Finally a filmmaker has come along who is attentive to women's fantasies and he turns out to be a malicious wit. . . . The violence of this
movie, so wildly improbable, leaves one exhilarated rather than
shaken.   *David Denby,* New York *magazine*

From the insidious combination of violence and sexuality in its promotional material, to scene after scene of women raped, killed, or
nearly killed, [Brian de Palma's] *Dressed to Kill* is a master work of
misogyny. . . . If this film succeeds, killing women may become the
greatest turn-on of the Eighties! Join our protest!   *Protest Leaflet*

In late August 1980, almost a month after *Dressed to Kill*
had opened in theatres across the country, feminists
began planning a response to this movie that many felt promoted violence against women. On August 28, members
of Women Against Violence Against Women, of Women
Against Pornography, and of other groups rallied in front
of theatres in Los Angeles, New York, San Francisco, and
Boston, inviting others to join their protest. In the violence

against women it depicted, they argued, *Dressed to Kill* had gone too far.

For many industry executives during the late summer of 1980, these feminist voices might have gone unnoticed and unheard among longer-lived and better organized demonstrations. Hundreds of out-of-work or underpaid actors marched and chanted in front of Disney, Universal, and other studios, demanding revised contracts; gays and lesbians had protested the stereotypes in *Cruising* and *Windows* less than a year earlier; and only the month before, Asian Americans had turned out to protest the racist overtones in *Charlie Chan and the Curse of the Dragon Queen*. It would be easy to suggest that the outcry against *Dressed to Kill* was inspired simply by a climate of protest. But many of the women who acted against *Dressed* had protested against other movies in the late 1970s; they knew the power of protest and the need for it. Though feminists' actions against *Dressed* would not reach the intensity of other groups' actions in ensuing years, they nonetheless helped women protesting against pornography test one method of confronting the misogyny of mainstream movies. More pointedly, they provided women against pornography and women against censorship an opportunity to seize some power, however limited or temporary, from a male-dominated, sexist movie industry at a time when many feared a backlash against feminism.

Recent studies have tended to construe censorship as an act performed by official institutions or dominant social groups.[1] Even those who reformulate film censorship—such as Annette Kuhn, who defends censorship as a "web of force relations" rather than a prohibitive act by a single institution—continue to associate censorship with cultural

dominance.[2] Such scholars overlook the attempts and successes of "minority" pressure groups to force the film industry either to censor its product rigorously or to allow
protesters to do so. As I suggest in the following three chapters, censorship can also be a strategy of empowerment, a
means through which historically marginalized groups can
gain a measure of control over the way they are represented
in dominant media.

The dynamic relationship between those who have held
power and those who have sought to gain it has been more
dramatic and long-lived in the case of sexual words and images than any other type of controversial expression. Until
recently, women have had little opportunity to influence
how their bodies and lives are depicted on screen. This was
the domain of mostly male religious leaders, industry regulators, and state and local officials who fell repeatedly into
heated disputes over the acceptable limits of cinematic
treatments of sexual subjects. Among the most controversial imagery in the intriguing history of such censorship
were the kinetoscope's seductive "Houchi Kouchi" dance
(1894); the peep show *Love in a Hammock* (1896); Theda
Bara's *Cleopatra* (1917); nearly all of Mae West's movies (late
1920s–early 1930s); John Hughes's *The Outlaw* (1943); *A
Streetcar Named Desire* (1950–1951); *The Moon Is Blue* (1953);
and *Lolita* (1962). Two films released in the mid 1960s, *The
Pawnbroker* (1965) and *Who's Afraid of Virginia Woolf?* (1966),
taxed the powers of an aging Production Code Administration (PCA).

The controversy over *The Pawnbroker* centered on a
scene that showed a black prostitute stripping to her waist.
When the PCA refused to give the film an official Seal of Approval unless the scene was excised, the film's producer, Ely

A. Landau, released the film anyway. Landau argued that in his movie the pawnbroker's sight of a naked woman reminds him of his own naked wife being forced to submit to Nazi guards, and that such a memory is crucial to the film's meaning. When Landau brought his case to the MPAA Appeals Board, the board ordered that a Seal be awarded his uncut film; members "recognized," as film historian Alexander Walker notes, "the unique nature of their verdict by passing the word back to the chief censor that one pair of naked breasts did not license a Saturnalia [sic] and he was to continue, as before, turning down scenes of undue exposure."[3] The Legion of Decency, however, who predicted that the *The Pawnbroker* decision would "open the flood gates to a host of unscrupulous operators out to make a quick buck," proved at least partially correct. Subsequent films such as *What's New, Pussycat* (1965) and *Juliet of the Spirits* (1965) reflected a new "morality crisis."[4]

The Pawnbroker's violation of the code's taboo on nudity did not prompt a code amendment, yet in 1966 the profane and blunt sexual language of *Who's Afraid of Virginia Woolf?* did. After optioning the successful Edward Albee stage play for the screen, Jack Warner sent the playscript to the PCA for advice on the adaptation. On March 25, 1966, PCA president Jeffrey Shurlock sent Warner a long list of objections that took exception to such lines as "hump the hostess," "plowing pertinent wives," and "screw, sweety."[5] Warner acknowledged the difficulty of making *Virginia Woolf* as potent on screen as the play had been in the theatre while adhering to the PCA's restrictions on sexually charged language, and when Warner Brothers asked the playwright to change some of the dialogue so as to reduce its shock impact, Albee refused. Shurlock's letter to Warner stated plainly that *Virginia Woolf*, as di-

rected for the screen by Mike Nichols, was "unacceptable under code requirements" and would be denied a Seal. Only
months after the brouhaha over *The Pawnbroker,* Warner appealed Shurlock's ruling to the PCA board. On June 10,
1966, Jack Valenti, newly appointed president of the MPAA,
watched *Virginia Woolf* and deliberated over what to do with
a film that blatantly violated the code yet stood (in many
board members' opinion) an excellent chance for commercial success and an Academy Award. Finally, the MPAA board
decided to grant *Virginia Woolf* a Seal with the proviso that
Warner Brothers agree to several dialogue changes. A month
later, the influence of both *The Pawnbroker* and *Virginia Woolf*
appeals became clear. Valenti issued a streamlined code that,
unlike its predecessor, "cast morality in a supporting—but
not a leading role" and paved the way for the MPAA to develop a movie-rating system.[6] Rating a film had largely depended on its sexual imagery; under the system established
in 1968, the task became increasingly subjective. But one
thing was certain: the new system permitted much more latitude in mainstream movies than ever before.

From the late 1950s through the late 1960s, legal censorship of "obscenity" was also in a state of flux. The controversies over *Lady Chatterley's Lover* (1957), *The Lovers* (1959),
I Am Curious—Yellow (1968), and *Carnal Knowledge* (1972)
forced the courts to define "obscenity" in increasingly per-
missive ways. The groundbreaking 1957 obscenity case *Roth
v. United States,* while it did not concern a motion picture,
would assist lawyers wishing to defend the sexual imagery in
films. In *Roth,* in which the court debated whether to prose-
cute Samuel Roth for publishing allegedly obscene books,
Justice William J. Brennan considered whether obscenity fell
within the areas of protected speech and press. Recalling

that "all ideas having even the slightest redeeming social importance" are considered protected speech, Brennan made a distinction between sex and obscenity:

> Sex and obscenity are not synonymous. Obscene material is material which deals with sex in a manner appealing to prurient interest. The portrayal of sex, e.g. in art, literature, and scientific works, is not itself sufficient reason to deny material the constitutional protection of freedom of speech and press. Sex, a great and mysterious motive force in human life, has indisputably been a subject of absorbing interest in mankind through the ages; it is one of the vital problems of human interest and public concern.

This observation led Brennan to conceive of an obscenity "test": a work could be found obscene if to the average person, applying contemporary community standards, its dominant themes appeal to prurient interest.[7] Brennan upheld the right of the government to enforce an obscenity statute punishing the use of the mails for obscene material and at the same time created a legal means to defend work that did not appeal merely to "prurient" interest.

Late in 1957, when the New York State Board of Censors denied a license to a film adaptation of D. H. Lawrence's *Lady Chatterley's Lover* because it represented adultery "as a desirable, acceptable and proper pattern of behavior," the defense drew on the distinction made in *Roth*. When censorship was lifted, this victory paved the way for prohibitions against censorship of sexual immorality and other instances of ideological obscenity. Movie censorship laws that were found to be forms of prior restraint were soon invalidated in Pennsylvania, Oregon, and Georgia. While other films such as Louis Malle's *The Lovers (Les Amants)* tested the Brennan doctrine, and while censorship based on sexual imagery continued to occur, a predominately liberal Supreme Court made it easier for lawyers to successfully defend many movies against censorship challenges.

In the early 1970s President Richard Nixon appointed four conservative judges to the Supreme Court, which subsequently challenged the Brennan doctrine. The outcome of two cases tried in 1973—*Miller v. California* and *Paris Adult Theatre I v. Slaton*—sent a chill through the movie industry, particularly when a Georgia criminal court found "obscene" the studio-produced movie *Carnal Knowledge* (1972).[8] The conservative Justice Burger persuaded the court to judge the offensiveness of material against local, not national, community standards, thereby increasing the likelihood of municipal censorship. But the waves of censorship foreshadowed by the *Miller* redefinition of obscenity failed to reverse the legal victories of earlier decades.[9] In the 1970s and early 1980s, films of questionable artistic and social value such as *Deep Throat* (1972), *Caligula* (1980), and *Emmanuelle* (1981) were banned locally but ultimately freed from censorship when higher courts invalidated local laws and experts testified to several such films' artistic merits.[10]

In the late 1970s, as pornography mushroomed into a billion-dollar industry, it also became a major feminist concern. While conservative groups opposed pornography, feminists against pornography and feminists against censorship of pornography quickly dominated the public debate. Both groups perceived pornography as a cause for sexual discrimination in the United States, the most blatant evidence of how representation leads to women's oppression in everyday life.[11] While many feminists participated in the prolific written debates over pornography, the more radical "antipornography feminists," as they came to be known, believed direct-action campaigns were the most effective means of publicizing their complaint. The year 1980 marked both the high point and the end of a brief period during which feminists against pornography, or mainstream movies that contained pornographic scenes, staged protests in front of movie theatres.

In what can be viewed as the beginning of a baffling cultural trend that started in the mid to late 1970s and has endured to the present day, two of the most unlikely groups—feminists and conservatives—suddenly had a common target, if not a shared cultural agenda. For conservative writers porn was a moral issue. Irving Kristol, a chief architect of neoconservatism, warned that "what is at stake is civilization and humanity, nothing less." Walter Berns finds porn capable of breaking down the "natural" feelings of shame we associate with sex that he believes are beneficial for a democratic polity because they promote self-restraint. Ernest van den Haag argues for censorship on the grounds that pornography supports "the pure libidinal principal," leads to "loss of empathy for others, and encourages violence and anti-social acts."[12]

The behaviorist suggestion of a causal connection between violence against women in pornography and violence against women in society was championed by antipornography feminists. Robin Morgan, a proponent of this view, suggested that "pornography is the theory; and rape the practice"—an early indication that feminists' and conservatives' positions were closer together than some feminists wanted people to believe. Yet where conservative critiques of pornography were founded on a belief that porn is immoral and evil, antipornography feminists focused on its denigrating effects on women. For them porn promotes antifemale sexuality and therefore sexual inequality.

Gloria Steinem finds misogyny in the roots of the word *pornography,* which she compares to erotica. "Erotica is rooted in 'Eros' or passionate love, and this is the idea of positive choice, free will, the yearning for a particular person. 'Pornography' begins with a root 'porno,' meaning 'prostitution' or 'female captives,' thus letting us know that the subject is not mutual love, or love at all, but domination and violence against women."[13]

Steinem's definition is that reflected in the work of Kathleen Barry, Susan Brownmiller, Mary Daly, Andrea Dworkin, Susan Griffin, Susanne Kappeler, Catherine MacKinnon, Susan Lederer, and Dorchen Leidholdt.[14] Dworkin's views are the most extreme: pornography, she claims, shows women as colonized victims of male aggression and of the "brutality of male history." Specifically, "erotic pleasure for men is derived from and predicated on the savage destruction of women. . . . The eroticization of murder is the essence of pornography, as it is the essence of life."[15] For Leidholdt, along with members of Women Against Pornography (WAP), pornography is also integrally connected to the oppressive misogynist hegemony: "Within the predominant sexual system, articulated and reproduced in pornography, women are defined and acted upon as sexual objects; our humanity is denied and our bodies are violated for sexual pleasure; the bodies of our sisters are literally marketed for profit. We can't think away this system: it is practice as well as ideology, out there as well as inside.

What we can do is analyze it, challenge it, fight it, and ultimately change it."[16]

Such views faced tough challenges from an emerging
group of feminists who sought to distance themselves from
their antipornography sisters. Women who believed in the
liberal soul of feminism, stood firmly against censorship.
But in the late 1970s and in 1980, what the groups of women
shared—a commitment to resist sexism in the media and in
society at large—linked them in struggle and inspired them
to more actively seek change.

The feminist demonstrations against pornographic imagery implied frustration with the ineffectiveness of written
critiques as well as a need to go public with a resentment
toward the producers and exhibitors of specific pornographic works.[17] In 1976, a billboard depicting a bruised
woman in chains with the caption "I'm black and blue from
the Rolling Stones and I love it" triggered a group of California feminists to demonstrate and to organize a national
press conference that ultimately forced Warner Brothers to
remove the offending billboard.[18] Women Against Violence in Pornography and Media (WAVPM) formed
shortly after this success. Members Diane Russell and
Laura Lederer later explained the organization's goals as
follows:

- To educate women and men about the women-
  hatred expressed in pornography and other media violence to women, and to increase understanding of
  the destructive consequences of these images;

- To confront those responsible—for example, the
  owners of pornographic stores and theatres, those

who devise violent images on record covers, newspapers that give a lot of space to advertising pornographic movies, politicians who give out permits for "live shows," pornographic bookstores, etc.;

■ To put an end to all portrayals of women being bound, raped, tortured, killed, or degraded for sexual stimulation or pleasure. We believe that the constant linking of sexuality and violence is dangerous.

WAVPM further viewed pornographic depictions as "sexist lies about women and sex" and rape as one "consequence" of pornography.[19]

The first movie that ignited demonstrations was a low-budget, independently produced film entitled *Snuff*. Released in 1976 not long after the Charles Manson murders, it purported to show the actual murder or "snuff" of a young woman. While many film historians consider *Snuff* less an example of pornography than of the then-popular slasher genre, the subject of this film ignited feminists around the country. Kevin Thomas of the *Los Angeles Times* describes *Snuff*'s plot as follows:

> An American sex picture star goes with her producer to Latin America to make a movie. She has a romantic reunion with the son of a German munitions dealer, winds up pregnant either by him or his father and thus becomes the target of a sadistic Satanist and his equally kinky female followers. . . . The Satanist's girls do a lot of shooting and stabbing, finally catching up with the pregnant sex star. Just as the Satanist starts to stab her we abruptly discover we've been watching a

move-within-a-movie. . . . The director of that movie
becomes so carried away with the stabbing scene he
starts hacking away at his star.[20]

Even though the press reported that the cinematic 'snuff'
was a hoax and that the lead actress was alive and well in
New York City, the film benefited from all the publicity and
premiered to large crowds in New York, Los Angeles, San
Francisco, and other cities.

For its blatant depiction of violence against women,
Snuff raised the ire of antipornography feminists, who took
to the streets in front of many theatres showing the movie.
Not long afterward, women with similar agendas in New
York and San Francisco formed Women Against Porno-
graphy and Woman Against Violence Against Women
(WAVAW). Laura Lederer, who later would edit the well-
known antipornography feminist handbook *Take Back the
Night,* recalls *Snuff* as "the powder keg that moved women
seriously to confront the issue of pornography." Beverly
LaBelle, recounting the butchery depicted in the film's final scene, agrees: "Such graphic bloodletting finally made
the misogyny of pornography a major feminist concern.[21]
Feminists in San Diego, Buffalo, Los Angeles, San Jose, Den-
ver, Philadelphia, and Monticello and Rochester, New York,
among other cities, protested in front of theatres showing
the movie. Demonstrations in the New York area were the
largest and best organized in the country; in addition to
picketing, New York protesters also lodged complaints with
the FBI, the police, the district attorney's office, Mayor Abe
Beame's office, and the United Nations delegations from
Argentina, where the film was allegedly produced. Protesters distributed leaflets that urged: "Stop Snuff. . . . This

movie makes money from the dismembering and murder of women. Is life that 'cheap'? Can we support murder as a business venture? Can we allow the murder of women to be used as sexual entertainment? Can we tolerate such atrocities against human life? Stop Snuff." The leaflet also posed and answered the question, Why are we here?

> We are opposed to the filming, distribution and mass marketing of the film "Snuff." . . .
>
> Whether or not the death depicted in the current film "Snuff" is real or simulated is not the issue. That sexual violence is presented as entertainment, that the murder and dismemberment of a woman's body is commercial film material is an outrage to our sense of justice as women, as human beings.
>
> We—and all are welcomed to join in our efforts— will leaflet, picket, write letters, to do what is necessary to prevent the showing of the film 'Snuff' in New York City. We can not allow murder for profit.[22]

Although the language in this leaflet suggests that these protesters aimed at censorship, other voices encouraged a broader view. Brenda Feigen Fasteau, a feminist lawyer, stated: "I want to emphasize that the First Amendment guarantees the right to view this stuff, but as feminists we have to look at the kind of society that is titillated by the idea of women being murdered. And we have to deal with the possibility that this film is going to create a demand for real snuff films and that real women are going to be murdered." Whatever protesters said, some of their protests did result in censorship. In Baltimore, a judge banned *Snuff* because of the film's so-called "psychotic violence." Responding to feminist protests in Santa Clara, California, Philadelphia, and St. Paul, Minnesota, city officials forced theatres to close down *Snuff*. After a lengthy trial that followed protests in front of a Monticello, New York, theatre, local authorities summoned to court on obscenity charges the theatre owner responsible for exhibiting *Snuff*. In most other places, protests failed to prevent theatres from showing the movie.[23]

In 1977, Rochester-area feminists' protests against *Snuff* was the latest in a short but significant series of militant actions against sexual imagery. According to Martha Gever and Marg Hall, the first action occurred early in 1977, when ten women formed an ad hoc group in response to a billboard advertising a movie entitled *Penetration*. The ad's caption read, "Unbelievably violent . . . graphic . . . a double turn-on. He always hurts the one he loves. Some women deserve it." The women created a counterposter captioned, "The Monroe Theater's Movie Promotes Rape. *No* Women Deserve It." As a result of continued protest, not only was the ad for *Penetration* withdrawn but the movie was never shown. Later in 1977, Rochester-area feminists distributed leaflets that condemned *A Boy and His Dog,* a science fiction film exhibited at the University of Rochester that included such images as the cannibalization of a woman by a boy and his dog. The protest provoked debate within the university, where primarily men accused the leaflet distributors of censorship. That same year, after a local radio station advertised a movie entitled *Nazi Love Camp* using the line "Women beaten, women tortured, and more," Rochester-area feminists picketed in front of the theatre exhibiting the movie until police forced them to leave. Before they were taken away, however, one protester painted onto the side of a building, "Their Profit, Our Blood. This Movie is a Crime Against Women."[24]

In October 1977, poster ads for *Snuff* plastered the city, depicting a woman being cut to pieces by a pair of bloodied scissors and captioned, "The bloodiest thing that ever happened in front of a camera" (figure 3). This time, an-

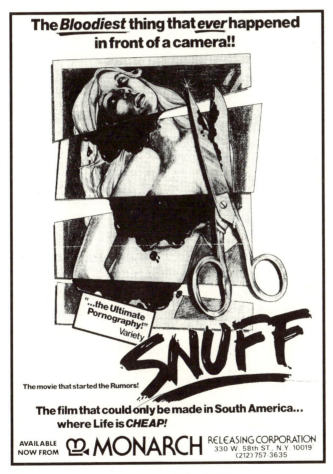

Figure 3. One of several poster ads for *Snuff.*

tipornography feminists were ready, as two of the participants report: "Four of us went to the theatre, spray-painted the doors and chained them shut, put glue in the locks, broke the display window, and ripped up the poster. We were then arrested by plainclothes police, who had been told by a 'confidential informant' that some kind of 'covert action' was going to happen at the theatre."[25]

The women held responsible for the vandalism were fined $100, then released. When the case went to trial, an ad hoc group of Rochester-area feminists attended the proceedings to demonstrate solidarity with the arrested protesters. Soon afterward, another group was formed, Rochester Women Against Violence Against Women. In ensuing years, this group would claim responsibility for disrupting a Rochester porn bookstore and for forcing the University of Rochester to cancel a screening of *The Story of O*.

Actions against *Snuff* and other movies continued after 1977, but feminists' antipornography campaigns did not again reach such an intense pitch until the release of Brian De Palma's *Dressed to Kill* in 1980, when once more the issue was violence against women.[26] This time the movie that ignited their rage was a Grand Guignol drama revolving around a successful male psychiatrist, Robert Elliot (Michael Caine), who by night becomes a vicious killer. Elliot's first victim is Kate Miller (Angie Dickinson), an attractive woman suffering from vivid erotic fantasies that she often can't separate from reality. Nancy Allen plays Liz Blake, a high-class call girl whom Elliott stalks and the police harass once it's known that she witnessed Miller's murder. The movie's intrigue lies in the question, Will Blake provide the key to the mysterious murders before she herself is murdered?

Dressed sparked controversy months before its late sum-

mer release. After the first cut of the movie was submitted
to the MPAA Ratings Board, De Palma was informed that
his movie would probably receive an X rating but not why.
Since he knew that an X—the designation for hard-core
pornography and extreme violence—would almost surely
mean commercial failure, he returned to the edit room, re-
examining the three murder sequences, the nude shower
scenes, and every frame of spurting blood. He carefully
reedited the shower sequence, eliminating all frames showing Angie Dickinson's pubic hair, and dubbed over many
expletives with milder language. The resubmitted film received an R (restricted) rating, meaning moviegoers under
seventeen could be admitted to the theatre accompanied by
an adult. Still not happy, De Palma argued that the controversy over William Friedkin's *Cruising* earlier in the year
(see Chapter Four) had made the ratings board more repressive and tougher on his movie. Jack Valenti, president
of the MPAA, related the board's decision to give *Dressed* an
X to cultural politics: "The political climate in this country
is shifting to the right, and that means more conservative attitudes toward sex and violence. But a lot of creative people
are still living in the world of revolution."[27] While Valenti's
assessment would prove correct not long after Ronald Reagan was elected in November, *Dressed*'s performance at the
box office demonstrated that moviegoers' taste for explicit
sex with violence, no matter what institutional changes were
taking place, had waned not at all.

The film's lurid ad campaign generated excitement and
further controversy. While *Dressed* cost only $6.5 million to
produce, Filmways Pictures, its distributor, spent $6 million
on a poster, print, and television campaign. To test the market, Filmways tried three different print ads, two of which

appeared in the August 4 issue of *New York* magazine. The first, widely used, showed a woman in a shower with the shadow of a man coming toward her cast on the wall beside the shower door. The copy read, "Brian De Palma, the modern master of the macabre, invites you to an evening of extreme terror." The second similarly slick ad displayed a woman peeling off her stockings, while a man lurked in the doorway. Its copy read, "Brian De Palma, master of the macabre, invites you to a showing of the latest fashion . . . in murder." In daily newspapers, a third, bolder ad presented a woman in dark glasses holding a straight razor that reflected a screaming Angie Dickinson. The caption here read, "The second before she screams will be the most frightening moment of your life."[28] Visually, all three ads conflated sex and violence against women. As commentators later noted about the visual power of any poster, the medium operates similarly to most advertising, which aims to construct a pleasure for a viewer and mobilize that pleasure as the desire of a consumer."[29] Filmways's three poster ads were initially thought to excite precisely this type of pleasure, though they targeted distinctly different moviegoer types: the two slick ads aimed at the sophisticated, urban market; the third, more straightforwardly exploitive, ad aimed at Middle America.

The rating controversy, the lurid ads, a high-profile director, a summer film season widely perceived as the dreariest and least lucrative in nearly a decade—each of these factors help explain Filmways's high hopes for *Dressed to Kill* when it opened in 660 national theatres July 25, 1980. While the opening weekend box office was a modest $3.4 million, in the second week the national box office reported a 7 percent increase in ticket sales. One reason for this unusual increase was word-of-mouth advertising; another may have been Filmways's revamped ad strategy. Noting that box office receipts were higher in urban than in rural areas, Filmways had employed only the most exploitive ad outside the major cities that second week. The distributor had realized that for *Dressed* to reach blockbuster status, it needed to bring in "the less demanding audience that would respond to its thrills" rather than to its slick filmmaking technique and repeated homages to Alfred Hitchcock's *Psycho* and other films.[30]

Dressed's box office receipts also increased during its second week in release because of overwhelmingly positive reviews, particularly from the eastern establishment press, including some of the notoriously toughest critics from the *New Yorker,* the *New York Times,* and *New York* magazine. Vincent Canby began his commentary by ruminating on the "two Brian De Palmas," one with a propensity for "anarchic, essentially formless comedies full of low jokes and sometimes inspired satire," the other for "psychological thrillers and horror films executed in the manner of Alfred Hitchcock." He praised De Palma for fusing his two seemingly divergent styles into "a witty, romantic, psychological horror film," *Dressed,* the work of an "unmistakable talent." The *New Yorker*'s Pauline Kael was ecstatic about De Palma's latest exercise in the macabre:

> What makes *Dressed to Kill* funny is that it's permeated with the distilled essence of impure thoughts. De Palma has perfected a near-surreal poetic voyeurism— the stylized expression of a blissfully dirty mind. He doesn't use art for voyeuristic purposes; he uses voyeurism as a strategy and a theme—to fuel his satiric

art. He underlines the fact that voyeurism is integral to
the nature of movies. In the Metropolitan sequence,
we catch glimpses of figures slipping in and out at the
edges of the frame, and there are other almost sub-
liminal images.

David Denby of *New York* magazine began his glowing
but provocative review: "'Dressed to Kill' . . . is the first great
American movie of the eighties. Violent, erotic, and
wickedly funny, 'Dressed to Kill' is propelled forward by
scenes so juicily sensational that they pass over into absur-
dity. De Palma releases terror in laughter: Even at his most
outrageous, Hitchcock could not have been as entertaining
as this." Later in the review Denby accurately forecasted
women's groups' angry responses to the film: "De Palma
may be the first director to use pornography as a way of dra-
matizing the unconscious . . . he flirts more than once with
actual pornography, putting us into a muzzy trance and
then jerking us out of it with a derisive laugh. . . . A bad boy,
that De Palma. If the anti-porn feminists, the pressure
groups, and the more earnest writers at the 'Village Voice'
get hold of him they'll tear him limb from limb."[31] If Denby
was baiting the antipornography feminists, inviting a debate
over free speech and censorship, he would soon get one.
While not every review of *Dressed* was favorable, positive reactions spread by word of mouth, and Filmways spared no
expense in advertising the film's success. During the first
weeks in August, the company purchased full-page ads in
the *Hollywood Reporter* and *Daily Variety*. One read, "Dressed
to Kill': 10 days, 9 million dollars. That's showing your legs!"
To the movie industry, it was clear that the director of the
critically acclaimed *Carrie* had done it again.

But a backlash against the movie was slowly building, reflected at first in a few angry remarks by feminists, then in a
slew of negative reviews by such critics as Richard Corliss in
Time, Dave Kehr in the *Chicago Reader,* Archer Winston in
the *New York Post,* and Rex Reed and Kathleen Carroll in the
New York Daily News. Andrew Sarris of the *Village Voice* attacked *Dressed* in highly opinionated reviews. In the second
and stronger of the two, "Dreck to Kill," Sarris takes pains
to distinguish his criticism of the film from a moral stance
about both film and filmmaker. "That De Palma mucks
about with soft-core porn and hard-edged horror . . . does
not mean in and of itself that he is a raunchy ghoul. Nor
does the fact that he mutilates and murders women on
screen mean that he hates women off screen." It is the film,
Sarris explains, not its effect on viewers, that ought to be under attack: "I do not hold it against De Palma that he imi-
tates Hitchcock, but, rather, that he steals Hitchcock's most
privileged moments without performing the drudgery of
building up to these moments as thoroughly earned cli-
maxes. . . . De Palma is simply cashing in on the current
market for 'grunge,' a term connoting the dispensing of
blood and gore like popcorn to the very young." Taking fel-
low reviewer David Denby directly to task, Sarris ends his review, "coherence, credibility, sense, structure, wit, complexity—are such qualities too much to expect in these
so-far awful '80s?"[32]

Such criticism not only represented a backlash against all
the film's critical acclaim but showed support for the film's
detractors—mainly feminists. Responding to claims that his
movie was misogynist, De Palma told *Newsday*'s Judy Stone:
"I think you should be able to make a film about anything.
Should we get into censorship because we have movies that

are going to upset some part of the community? The ERA people could get a lot more upset about practically anything that comes out of TV and movies in relationship to women. All the media forms are male-dominated."[33] Was De Palma acknowledging and then justifying his misdemeanors because others indulged in them as well, or merely doing what Denby had done: baiting antipornography feminists and inviting a debate over whether pornographic imagery should be censored or celebrated in mainstream films?

Antipornography feminists did not take immediate action. Nineteen days into the release, with the movie's gross at nearly $15 million, there were no protests. None of the published commentary discusses the reason for the slow start. Perhaps antipornography feminists were waiting to see whether the film would score or languish at the box office. Perhaps they were unsure that protesting was the right or necessary response. But it is clear that their decision to protest was fueled by the film's commercial success and high praise by some of the nation's top movie critics. Moreover, they were angry about the content, which they believed was as harmful to women as the worst hard-core pornography. By late August, feminists confronted the critics and public that could find humor in violence done to women—if only, as one protester wrote, "to present an opposing voice in the din of critical acclaim that has helped make *Dressed to Kill* a major box office success."[34] On August 28, feminists staged protests in New York, San Francisco, Los Angeles, and Boston, among other cities (photos 2 and 3). The New York protests were the largest, best organized, and most noticed by the press. Several New York antipornography feminist groups, spearheaded by WAP, banded together in front of the 57th Street Playhouse to picket *Dressed*

Photos 2 and 3 (photo 3 on next page). Members of Women Against Violence Against Women gather in front of the Hollywood Pacific Theatre on Hollywood Boulevard in protest against *Dressed to Kill. Los Angeles Times Photographic Morgue,* Department of Special Collections, University Research Library, UCLA.

Photo 3.

to Kill. An estimated 100–150 protesters carried such placards as "Murder of women is not erotic," "*Dressed to Kill* is a
racist and sexist lie," and "Women's slaughter is not entertainment but terrorism."[35] They chanted, "Murder isn't
sexy, murder isn't funny, but that's how Hollywood makes
its money," and "No more profits off our bodies, no more
pleasure off our pain."[36] The protesters also called on supporters to convey their anger in writing to Brian De Palma,
care of Filmways, and to boycott the film.

A WAVPM protest leaflet distributed in San Francisco
coupled with statements made by WAVAW members
Dorchen Leidholdt and Stephanie Rones suggest that the
intent of antipornography feminists' actions against *Dressed
to Kill* was not to remove the film from theatres. WAVPM's
leaflet details the group's objections to the film:

From the insidious combination of violence and sexuality in its promotional material to scene after scene of women raped, killed, or nearly killed, *Dressed to Kill* is a master work of misogyny. . . . Though Kate Miller [Angie Dickinson] dies and Liz Blake bleeds time and again, three scenes—the rape, the necrophilia, and a slashing scene—were to have happened in women's minds. As if the eroticization of violence were not enough, *Dressed to Kill* asserts that women crave physical abuse; that humiliation, pain, and brutality are essential to our sexuality. . . . If this film succeeds, killing women may become the greatest turn-on of the Eighties! Join our protest![37]

Nowhere in this leaflet does WAVPM state any intention other than to picket. Countering charges made by Andrew Sarris in The *Village Voice,* Dorchen Leidholdt of WAP insisted that none of the three national organizations protesting against *Dressed* had "anti-libertarian overtones":

All are opposed to censorship; all respect First Amendment strictures against the imposition of prior restraints on any form of speech; all are opposed to general prohibitions of the production, distribution, and display of pornographic materials. . . . The demonstrations against De Palma's exercise in misogyny and bigotry were intended only to present an opposing voice in the din of critical acclaim that has helped make *Dressed to Kill* a major box office success. Although we feminists would have preferred to sit back, like Mr. Sarris, and dismiss the film as "unbearably tedious and inept," his brethren would not let us.[38]

Stephanie Rones similarly defended feminists' protests while deriding film critics' reviews: "A movie like 'Dressed to Kill' encourages and perpetuates violence and pairs it with sexuality by having vicious acts instead of loving and caring. Film critics have enormous responsibility and often write about what they see in a very narrow sense, reviewing only the artistic relevance and ignoring the social relevance. . . . Is a woman being slashed in an elevator funny or erotic or entertaining? Critics should look at these films on a broader level." Rones, who works with battered women at the Harriet Tubman Center in downtown Los Angeles, said that "the movie preys off the fear of people who go out at night and women who go out at night alone. . . . The title of the movie itself suggests women can bring on rape by how they dress, that women are dressed to be killed." She dwelled on the film's advertising and the correlation between violence depicted on screen and in everyday life. "The ads come into your home and lay around. . . . Violence becomes fashionable, a vogue. The ads are all attractive; you don't see underneath the real image of a brutalized woman. . . . We simply feel there's a correlation between what people see and how they act. 'Dressed to Kill' is not a documentary. It entices, eroticizes and perpetuates violence." Rones also denied that WAVAW intended to censor *Dressed to Kill:* "We're only asking for responsibility from film critics," she told a *Los Angeles Times* reviewer. "What people see on the movie screen is more than art: its messages influence society."[39]

Far from causing theatre managers to close *Dressed to Kill* or dissuading producers from making similar films, protests against the movie seemed only to increase its box-office profits. During the week when the protests against *Dressed* were largest, the movie rose from third to first place on *Va-*

riety's weekly listing of top-grossing films, ahead of *Airplane* and *The Empire Strikes Back.* When I interviewed Leidholdt over the phone in October 1992, she lamented the fact that feminists' protests had assisted *Dressed* in becoming a commercial success: "After *Dressed to Kill,* we realized that protesting the eroticizing of violence in Hollywood films was not effective. We had been especially scared about *Dressed to Kill* and wanted to educate the public that these movies were doing exactly what so much of violent pornography is doing. We thought Hollywood might listen. But they didn't. They just kept producing one film after another." Leidholdt said that after the protests against *Dressed* had backfired, WAP changed its view of protest campaigns in general. From 1980 on, her organization carried out no further protest in front of theatres. The dearth of feminist protests against the sexual imagery in specific movies during the 1980s confirms her claim.[40]

In the years since 1980, written debates over sexual imagery in mainstream movies such as *Body Double* (1985) and *Fatal Attraction* (1987), and over pornography in general, have come to replace street protests.[41] As strategic attempts of some feminists to gain power over how the media represented women, protests disappeared almost as quickly as they had emerged, but not without antipornography feminists learning that protests do not pay, that they tend to help publicize the movie under attack rather than feminists' complaints against it, and that, to achieve widespread change, efforts would be best spent rewriting the laws governing pornography.

In retrospect, the *Dressed* controversy can be viewed as one among several defining moments in the developing conflict between women against pornography and against its censorship, and, more important here, as a flash point in the emerging culture wars. If women against censorship stood on the sidelines of the controversy, intellectually they were unavoidably caught up in it. In 1980 all feminists shared serious concern for the effects of violent images on women. Debate about sexuality and aggression, feminists would agree, was a good thing, and an explosive debate along those lines would follow at Barnard College in 1982.[42] In later years, however, anticensorship feminists, whose position found articulate expression in the writings of members of Feminists Against Censorship Taskforce (F.A.C.T.), argued that banning pornography "diverts money and attention from programs and services that women really need."[43] These women held the liberal view that censorship is antidemocratic and in fact threatens feminism's fundamental aims: real equality and real power. By mid-decade, the louder voices were those of antipornography feminists, who unabashedly took procensorship positions, Andrea Dworkin and Catherine MacKinnon drafting antiporn legislation in Minneapolis and Indianapolis. In later years, the gap between feminists on the two sides of the debate would grow wider still. But in the late 1970s and in 1980, as neoconservatism began to sweep the country, feminists' collective rallying against several pornographic movies brought cohesion, recognition, and focus to a minority constituency committed to fighting sexism in the male-dominated media, and in society at large.

3

No More Racist Movies Here

Asian Americans against
Year of the Dragon (1985)

There is no way to escape offending someone if you're writing about something important. But it's at the point where you cannot even do that. Nowadays, you cannot make a movie that says anything. It's reached a point of blandness.   *Oliver Stone*

The movie will have a negative effect, especially on people who have been in the Vietnam war and still hate Asians, and for people in areas where they have little contact with Chinese—like in the midwest, the South. . . . The movie provides an excuse to hate.   *Irvin Lai*

On August 22, 1985, Margie Lee, who is Chinese American, entered the women's room at Mann's Village Theatre in Westwood, Los Angeles, after watching *Year of the Dragon*. All conversation among Caucasians stopped. To Lee, the silence was chilling, a reflection of tensions among Caucasians gathered to see the movie and Asian Americans gathered to protest against it.[1] For Asian Americans, these tensions had been mounting for more than a decade, as Hollywood filmmakers continued to release movies containing anti-Asiatic stereotypes. As dozens of protesters chanted, waved placards, and picketed against

Dragon's premiere at the Chinese Mann Theatre on Hollywood Boulevard and in front of New York, San Francisco, and Boston theatres, Asian Americans made plain their refusal to tolerate cinematic racism.

Asian Americans were hardly the first group to protest against negative film images. In 1915, African Americans' large-scale protests against *The Birth of a Nation* set a precedent for all later ethnic-group protests of U.S. films. D. W. Griffith, *Birth's* revolutionary filmmaker, would eloquently argue, "We have no wish to offend with indecencies or obscenities, but we demand, as a right, the liberty to show the dark side of wrong that we may illuminate the bright side of virtue."[2] Yet he had offended many African Americans (and whites) for years to come. African Americans not only succeeded in forcing this powerful film director, who many believed was a racist, to excise some of the most offending scenes in the film but also helped galvanize a constituency. That the NAACP was founded in the wake of the *Birth* controversy reveals how significant African Americans believed moving images were in defining their status in U.S. society. And the NAACP's success would inspire other groups for years to come.

African Americans' victory over film stereotyping in 1915 hardly discouraged the movie industry's propensity to stereotype either them or other minorities. Asians and Mexicans, especially, were victimized in silent films. In one of the earliest instances of resistance to Hollywood Asiatic stereotypes, Sessue Hayakawa, a Japanese actor who had become famous playing stereotyped, diabolical Chinese characters in many U.S. films, complained after appearing in Cecil B. DeMille's *The Cheat* (1915). In this film, Hayakawa plays a sadistic ivory merchant who, rejected by a white woman, brands her on the shoulder in order to "possess" her. The film ends with Hayakawa's character nearly lynched by a Caucasian mob. "Such roles are not true to our Japanese nature," Hayakawa argued. "They are fake and give people the wrong idea of us. I wish to make a characterization which shall reveal us [Japanese] as we really are."[3] That Hollywood ignored Hayakawa's written protest was early proof of how little influence even a leading man, if he was Asian, wielded over Hollywood practices.

During the 1920s, the Mexican government banned U.S. films because they repeatedly portrayed Mexicans as "greasers." In 1921, the MPPDA board unanimously condemned "the occasional and thoughtless practice" of representing Mexican characters as "dictators, bandits, and in other offensive manners" yet took no action on the films already in production that Mexico had banned.[4] The following year, the MPPDA courted the Mexican government and signed an agreement to prevent U.S. producers from using derogatory stereotypes. By 1925, the problem, at least in MPPDA president Will Hays's mind, had been solved. It was not until 1930, however, that the Mexican government agreed with Hays that the ubiquitous "greaser" had in fact faded from the screen.

During the 1930s, the French, Italians, British, and Chinese, among other nations, banned U.S. movies that they claimed depicted their nationals in derogatory ways. In the 1940s, the MPPDA Code's ban on cinematic miscegenation and its warning against misrepresenting the "history, institutions, and prominent citizenry of other nations" still led to frequent tensions, with members of the NAACP or various foreign governments pressuring the MPPDA to administer tougher censorship of racist stereotypes. Some of the most heated disputes over ethnicity occurred during and just after the war. Such films as *A Man on America's Conscience* (1943), *Curley* (1948), *Lost Boundaries* (1949), and *Pinky* (1949) forced the Office of War Information, the MPPDA, the NAACP, and municipal, state, and federal censorship boards to make tough decisions about how the United States would represent specific ethnicities at home and abroad. The Japanese, more than any other group, emerged as the new villains. In a flurry of films made during World War II, Chinese actors invariably played the "villainous" and disposable Japanese militia. During this period, film historian Eugene Wong notes, the Japanese were characterized as "repulsive, sadistic, libidinous little monkeys" determined to "overthrow western civilization." In another set of films produced during the war years, Asian women were depicted as sexually submissive, always available to white men. Such movies as *The World of Susie Wong, South Pacific,* and *Flower Drum Song* and *Dragon Lady* are but a few examples.[5]

During the 1950s and 1960s, when the most popular Asian screen villains shifted from Japanese back to Chinese, the Asian American community still expressed little resistance. According to Wong:

> The new civil rights movement sparked a greater social and filmic emphasis and interest in the upgrading of black and female minorities. The Asians, however, were omitted from what was essentially a biracial consciousness (whites and blacks only) among filmmakers. While certain minorities were able to maximize their political and numerical power against the film industry, the Asians were overlooked as a minority that

had long endured anti-Asiatic racism on all levels of
the industry.

Wong also suggests that the 1960s reinvented screen villains
as Asians, often "substituting [them] for groups that would
have protested violently against negative portrayals."[6] Although the "Yellow Power" movement of that decade raised
Asian Americans' and the country's levels of awareness
about racial injustices against Asians, Hollywood failed to
respond.

Beginning in the 1960s, coalitions of Native Americans,
Mexican Americans, Italian Americans, Cuban Americans,
Puerto Ricans, and African Americans were among the
groups whose protests against specific movies served their
larger goal: combating the ways the dominant culture struc-
tured and maintained their marginalization. By protesting
against stereotypes in the movies, these groups advanced
their struggle against oppression in everyday life, strength-
ened their groups' sense of identity, and raised public
awareness about the effects of ethnic stereotypes.[7]

Native Americans were among the first of these groups
to attack the film industry. In 1960, at the instigation of
many tribes within the state, the Oklahoma legislature
passed a resolution against media stereotyping. Shortly afterward, the Association on American Indian Affairs
(AAIA) launched a follow-up campaign that attempted to
"cause the TV and motion picture industries to drop the vicious stereotype of the Indian as unprofitable business and
to encourage them to show frontier history as the brave if
bloody history shared in common by the Indian and non-
Indian citizens who live in the area today."[8] Within a year,
however, AAIA members lost interest in attacking the me-

dia stereotypes as other struggles—for example, for land rights—grew more urgent. In any case, Hollywood studios did not respond to Native American protests and went on to perpetuate the same stereotypes in such movies as *The Stalking Moon* (1967), *A Man Called Horse* (1970), and *Flap* (or *Nobody Cares for a Dead Indian*) (1970).

Protests by Italian Americans, Cuban Americans, and a coalition of Puerto Rican and African American groups proved more successful than those by Native Americans. When *The Godfather* (1974) was in preproduction, the Italian American Civil Rights League (IACRL) insisted that the producer, Al Ruddy, remove all references to the Mafia. Weeks later, Ruddy, who reportedly received death threats, held a press conference at which he announced that the words *Mafia* and *Cosa Nostra* would be deleted from the script; Ruddy also agreed to give IACRL the profits from the world premiere of *The Godfather*.[9] Ruddy's willingness to make such concessions to the IACRL reveals how much political power the Mafia could wield; it also demonstrates that Hollywood was more responsive to a group of European origin than to newer immigrant groups.

In 1979, Puerto Ricans in New York's South Bronx organized the Inter-Racial Committee Against Fort Apache (CAFA) to combat stereotyped Puerto Rican characters featured in the film *Fort Apache, the Bronx,* as well as a stereotyped and demeaning portrait of the South Bronx. CAFA's protests included on-set demonstrations as well as legislative attempts to suppress *Fort Apache.* The group insisted that David Susskind, the film's executive producer, and Time-Life Films, its distributor, revise the film to reflect a more positive view of the South Bronx. CAFA sued Time-Life Films, charging the company with providing "ideological justification for the neglect of the South Bronx by the rest of the society."[10] William Kunstler, CAFA's lawyer, argued that his clients were suffering group libel and therefore deserved immediate damages of $100 million—$1 billion if the film was completed and released according to the script.[11] The ACLU filed a friend-of-the-court brief on behalf of David Susskind and Time-Life Films and won the case; the producers did not change *Fort Apache*. CAFA later tried and failed to persuade the New York City Council to pass a resolution against the film's depiction of the South Bronx. The only concession that CAFA won came from Time-Life Films and Dan Petrie, the film's director, who agreed to tack onto the final print of *Fort Apache* a twenty-second disclaimer that read, "This film is a portrayal of the lives of two officers and therefore does not dramatize the efforts of people who are struggling to turn the Bronx around."[12] This mild disclaimer did not dissuade viewers from seeing the movie, nor did it pacify the protesters. In ensuing months, CAFA's actions caused the Philadelphia City Council to prevent all civic venues from showing *Fort Apache,* and CAFA's protests in front of one New York theatre, the Gemini, caused United Artists Eastern Theatres to cancel the film's scheduled run. CAFA proved that when film producers were not responsive enough, a broad-based protest by a coalition of ethnic and racial groups could convince a theatre manager to cancel a film.

In 1982, Cuban Americans protested when *Scarface,* a film featuring a "Mariel" gangster and drug dealer from Cuba, was being filmed in Miami. Reportedly, Cuban Americans there threatened the lives of *Scarface* director Brian De Palma and others connected with the film. "They don't play by the same rules as we do," De Palma recalled. "These are crazy, drugged up, South American radicals. The pro-Castro groups threatened us, the anti-Castro groups threatened us, everybody threatened us." Yet because the Cuban Americans' resistance to *Scarface* was supported by civic and city leaders as well as several prominent journalists, it could not be dismissed as the work of a radical fringe. Eduardo Pedron, chief of the Spanish-American League Against Discrimination, explained that the protesters were upset over the stereotypes in *Scarface,* which "would cause damage to the Cuban community in the U.S." Guillermo Martinez of the *Miami Herald* objected to a film that was going "to tell the nation and the world that the prototype of the U.S. gangster of the 1980s is a Mariel [Marielito] refugee." Miami city commissioner Demetrio Perez said that the Al Pacino character, a violent Cuban drug dealer, "would reinforce negative impressions about Miami," a city with a large Cuban American community and a major drug problem.[13] Perez issued a resolution to force the filmmakers to leave Miami, but before he could force them out, the film's producers decided to move production to Los Angeles. While protests continued after the film was released, Cuban Americans' actions against *Scarface* ultimately had no effect on the film's final print, its distribution, or its exhibition. Their result, as with CAFA's protests, was to remind producers of the difficulty of filming in the community where a film is set.

Of all the groups that staged protests during the 1970s and 1980s, Asian Americans—perhaps stereotypically—were perceived by the film industry as one of the least threatening. Asian actors, directors, and producers wielded little power in the industry and, throughout its history, had shown little interest in challenging cinematic stereotypes. But the industry was in for a surprise. More than other ethnic minority groups during the same period, Asian Americans recognized how media stereotypes reinforce existing power relations in America and contribute to a group's subordination and oppression. For Asian Americans, challenging stereotypes became a vital avenue to empowerment.

One of their earliest protests occurred during the production of the film *Charlie Varrick* (1973). Benson Fong, a Chinese American actor, complained to white executives about a black character's use of a racial slur in the line, "That *Chink* son of a bitch burned [cheated] me." The studio suggested the word "Chinaman" as a replacement. When Fong objected again, the scene was cut entirely. Fong later explained why he was so opposed to the word "Chink": "We wanted to let the rest of the American people know that we are Americans, and that we are no longer the ching-chong chinamen who sat on the fence. I don't want to be told I'm Chinese. I know that I'm Chinese. You resent the fact that when you work for the film industry, right away the director or the assistant director treats you like a Chinese person."[14] The same year, a group of Asian American artists criticized the industry's continued practice of casting cosmeticized white actors instead of Asians or Asian Americans as lead Asian characters.[15] Casting John Gielgud as Chang in the remake of *Lost Horizons* (1973) was especially offensive, since Gielgud followed H. B. Warner and Claude Rains, two white actors who had played the part in 1936 and 1960 respectively, signifying that over the course of forty years Asian actors' plight had not changed; this could not be allowed to pass unnoticed.

In 1977, members of the Association of Asian/Pacific American Artists (AAPAA) marched on Los Angeles's Chinatown to protest the filming of a Dodge-Aspen commercial featuring a cosmeticized white actor as Charlie Chan, and a Chinatown setting that was only obliquely suggested. The protesters argued not only that the Chan character was a negative stereotype and a continuation of "racist cosmetology," but that "all roles should be open to all performers, providing experience, talent and other credentials [are] in order."[16] The AAPAA decried negative images of Asian males, of Chinatown communities, and of Asian females depicted as demure and submissive. Despite their efforts, the commercial appeared unchanged on television.

The AAPAA's failure to elicit a response from Dodge-Aspen energized subsequent protests against the Fu Manchu stereotype in *The Fiendish Plot of Fu Manchu* (1980) and the Charlie Chan stereotype in *Charlie Chan and the Curse of the Dragon Queen* (1981). The simple fact that these films had recreated much-despised figures set off an alarm among Asian Americans; in the case of the Chan film, their anger was compounded by the filmmakers' casting white actors as the leads. About seventy-five protesters picketed the Los Angeles studio set where director Clive Donner had begun shooting *Chan*. Before location shooting shifted to San Francisco, Chinese for Affirmative Action (CAA) had convinced the film's producer, Jerry Sherlock, to meet with them. CAA arrived at the meeting with a list of demands, among them "that an Asian American [actor] play Charlie Chan, that he speak in standard—rather than 'chop suey'—English, and that the film not be made in Chinatown." Sherlock's response addressed only one demand: "It would have been nice if we could have cast an Asian American in the part [of Chan], but I just couldn't do it. When you package a film like this, you've got to have box office names."

When the Screen Actors Guild supported the coalition's position, Sherlock responded: "We can't cast an Asian American in the lead. There are no bankable Asian American stars." He considered changing the script but finally did not. Now CAA and AAPAA, among other groups, staged protests in front of the San Francisco *Chan* set. Carrying placards with such slogans as "No More Racism, No More Charlie Chan," the protesters hoped to win a city ban. But Sunri Haru, then president of AAPAA, and others conceded that they really didn't expect the producers to change their production plans. Their hopes were more modest: "Maybe the next time somebody makes Charlie Chan," Haru reasoned, "it will be a little more sensitively made—if it has to be made at all."[17] Despite their actions, *Chan* completed filming in San Francisco's Chinatown. AAPAA and other groups, however, were resolved to protest the film's release.

Before *Chan* premiered, *The Fiendish Plot of Fu Manchu* opened to group protest around the country. In New York, the Organization of Chinese Americans demonstrated in front of the Warner Building. "No more Charlie Chans!" protesters called. "No more stereotypes! No more insults!" When a reporter asked one of the demonstrators, Shubert Hau, what his group wanted, Hau replied, "I want Warner Brothers to withdraw the movie." Other protesters were careful to distinguish their right to free speech from calls to withdraw the movie. "We have a First Amendment right to protest the movie," Robert Wu told an African American reporter. "The movie appeals to base values. How would you like to be called a nigger? That movie debases us."[18] Unlike the demonstrators against *Chan,* however, anti-*Plot* protesters did not make any demands on the film's producer or distributor; their actions were carefully framed to publicize their anger against racism in general and anti-Asian violence in particular.

By the time *Chan* was released on February 11, 1980, a host of protest groups, spearheaded by the playwright Frank Chin, had formed the Coalition of Asians to Nix Charlie Chan—an outgrowth of the earlier Can Charlie Chan.[19] The coalition demanded that Sherlock cancel the movie's first run; it also called on Sherlock to issue a public apology to the Asian American community, to give Asian Americans fairer and broader representation in the media, and to place a ban on stereotyped Asian roles in Hollywood films. Although Sherlock balked at these demands, in the wake of the Chinese community's protests, two Bay Area theatres canceled the movie not long after it opened.[20]

Over the next few years, Asian Americans established a network of political and cultural groups determined to fight discrimination and violence not simply by protest but by using an array of media as forums in which to promote their complaints. Upon learning of Dino DeLaurentiis's plan to produce a film based loosely on Robert Daly's novel *Year of the Dragon,* this network began planning protests far in advance of the film's scheduled release date of August 16, 1985. In New York, a coalition against the movie included nearly a dozen groups, many of whom associated it with other racist and sexist television and film images of Asian Americans and with the increase in anti-Asian violence in America.[21] The producers cast Mickey Rourke as Stanley White, the most decorated cop in the history of the New York Police Department, whose mission is to pursue evil Chinatown criminals; the role of the reporter assigned to investigate a string of Chinatown murders was played by an attractive Asian American model, Ariane. This combination, plus the portrayal of Chinatown as crime infested and the eagerness with which the Asian American reporter submits to the white cop, concerned Asian Americans.

Several months before the film went into production, Janice Sakamoto and Forrest Gok, members of the National Asian American Telecommunications Association (NAATA), warned the Asian American community against any movie based on Daly's racist, "graphically sensationalistic" portrait of Chinatown and Chinese Americans: "Although the film version of 'Year of the Dragon' will be revised somewhat from the book, the basic theme of crime and gang violence in mysterious Chinatown will not change, and it is questionable whether the subject will be treated with any ethnic sensibility." They were equally skeptical about the director-writer team of Michael Cimino and Oliver Stone: "[Michael Cimino] was the director and screenwriter for the five-time Academy Award winner, *The Deer Hunter,* a film on the Vietnam war which glorified US military involvement in that country and portrayed the Vietcong as sadistic murderers with no regard for human life. . . . [Oliver Stone] was the screenwriter for Brian De Palma's ultra-violent Al Pacino starrer, *Scarface,* which raised the ire of Miami's Cuban community."[22] When Henry Der, executive director of Chinese for Affirmative Action, noted that Michael Cimino had not responded to his letter about the upcoming film, Asian Americans grew even more worried. As a result, NAATA and other groups began to monitor Cimino's production plans.

Cimino began filming *Year of the Dragon* on location in New York's Chinatown in early October 1984. During the ensuing weeks, the Chinese Consolidated Benevolent Association (CCBA), the oldest and most powerful association of Chinese in the United States, staged protests at the movie set and criticized the making of the film in its weekly newsletters, objecting to what members viewed as unfair portrayals of Chinese Americans in the Daly novel. One letter of protest reached City Hall, which responded with a note stating that in no circumstances would it "act as a censor."[23] On-location protests continued, but the *Dragon* producers made no concessions to the protesters.

Nearly a year later, on August 13, 1985, Asian Americans attended the preview of *Year of the Dragon* in Los Angeles and New York (photo 4). The following day, thirty-six groups formed the Coalition Against Year of the Dragon and held organizational meetings in San Francisco and New York. The New York coalition, which spearheaded the national protest, issued a press release on August 14 explaining their organization's objections to the film and their reasons to protest:

> Why protest? After previewing "Year of the Dragon," many in the community were outraged by its racist and sexist portrayals of Asians, Blacks, and women characters. One woman, a garment worker from Chinatown and the mother of two boys who appeared in the film, was shocked by the violence and demeaning images on the screen.
>
> We believe that the film grossly distorts the public's perceptions of Chinese Americans during a time of great misunderstanding and anti-Asian sentiment. Chinatown is portrayed as "an exotic foreign world deep within the city" that is dominated by criminals and youth groups—a portrayal that the New York's "Daily News" called the revival of "the oriental villain." Due to the scarcity of accurate and meaningful por-

trayals of Asian Americans in the mass media, there are few realistic images to counter balance the damage done by "Year of the Dragon."

Asian Americans across the country have called for a national boycott of the MGM/UA release, demanding that the company withdraw "Year of the Dragon" from distribution.[24]

Another press release issued by the coalition referred to *Dragon* as "an irresponsible, hostile film that must be stopped." Renee Tajima, a New York–based writer and film-

Photo 4. Asian Americans protested *Year of the Dragon* when it opened at the National Theatre in New York. Photo by Kevin Cohen. Courtesy of *The New York Post.*

maker, told *Variety,* "We know we're going to outreach to other organizations, and we know we're going to demonstrate."[25] It remained to be seen how prerelease picketing, censorious threats, and outreaching would influence the distribution and exhibition of *Dragon.*

When *Year of the Dragon* opened on Friday, August 16, in New York and other cities, an estimated three hundred protesters picketed in front of Loew's Astor Plaza on Broadway. Protesters also greeted the *Dragon* premiere in San Francisco, Los Angeles, and Boston, and at other New York City theatres. Protesters carried signs with such slogans as "No More Racism and Sexism!" "Cimino Exploits Asian Youths!" "No More Suzie Wong's!" and "End the *Year of the Dragon!*" and chanted, "Drive this movie out of town—shut it down! Shut it down!"[26] In New York, a protest rally included a press conference attended by local and national newspaper, television, and radio journalists, with speeches by David Dinkins, Virginia Kee, Miriam Friedlander, and spokespeople from many Asian American groups.

Some of the organizations associated with the coalition issued statements that lay out their group's specific objections to *Dragon* and their intentions in joining the protest. From an Asian CineVision flyer:

> The malevolent Dr. Fu Manchu, the exotic Suzie Wong, and the inscrutable Charlie Chan are the stock Asian images that the film industry has recycled ad nauseum throughout its history. None of these images are realistic, but in many ways they are harmful to the peaceful cohesion of ethnic groups in American life. . . .

[*Dragon*] is a slap in the face to the Chinese American community in which it purportedly is set, taking one negative aspect of Chinatown and irresponsibly blowing it out of proportion. Almost all the major Chinese American characters in the film are murderous gangsters caught in drug dealing, extortion, and assassination, except the Chinese American undercover cop, a token "sidekick" character who makes one meaningless speech about Chinese on the railroads and then is summarily killed off.

The portrayal of Tracy Tzu, the Chinese American newswoman, is as sexist as the rest of the film is racist. Her character reiterates the falsehood that Asian women are submissive, passive sexual objects at the beck and call of domineering white men, and is an insult to independent, thinking women everywhere. . . .

ASIAN CINEVISION urges you to join us in stopping the distribution of this harmful, exploitive film. Boycott YEAR OF THE DRAGON, and help put an end to racist, sexist, exploitive films.

For Asian CineVision, boycotting *Dragon* was a way to challenge the film industry's long history of Asian stereotypes considered "harmful to Asian Americans' peaceful cohesion . . . in American life." Another statement distributed at the protest came from Virginia Kee, a democratic candidate for city council, who focused her criticism on *Dragon* ads: "While the movie itself may be protected under the First Amendment, this right does not extend to the media ads for the movie which depict Chinatown in a bad light. The ads say, 'It isn't the Bronx or Brooklyn, it isn't even New York.

It's Chinatown . . . and it's about to explode.' Chinatown is a community consisting of homes and businesses, not bombs."

A statement issued by the CCBA extends Asian CineVision's and Kee's fear that *Dragon* would produce harmful affects on Asian Americans in Chinatown and elsewhere. "Our community relies on the people who come to eat and shop in Chinatown. People who see this movie will mistakenly believe that Chinatown is unsafe to be in. This will hurt the economic well-being of the community. We plan to boycott the movie and actively work to see that the film is withdrawn." Radical Women and the Freedom Socialist Party linked the Asian Americans' concern over *Dragon* to that of other minorities:

> "Year of the Dragon" is not only over-run with anti-Chinese and anti-woman bigotry, but also grossly misrepresents Blacks, Latinos, Italians, the Polish, the Irish, and immigrants in general. . . . We believe an attack on one is an attack on all. The recently-formed Coalition Against "Year of the Dragon" provides the opportunity for Asian/Pacific Americans to unite with other people of color, feminists, labor, lesbians and gays, and political activists to put an end to the showing of this movie and the production of racist and sexist films.

All of these statements issued on the day of *Dragon's* release highlighted protesters' fears that the film would perpetuate anti-Asiatic violence.[27]

On August 19, the newly formed New York Coalition Against Year of the Dragon held a meeting to assess the success of the protests thus far and to plan future actions. August 24 was designated a national day of protest. Minutes of the meeting suggest that suppressing *Dragon* was no longer considered a possibility or a goal. Attendees agreed that one of their most effective strategies would be informational leafleting. Protest objectives included stopping sales to subsidiary markets (pay-TV, VHS, foreign), attacking MGM/UA, aligning with unions, creating better alternatives for audiences, coordinating a national protest event, creating a task force to organize a letter-writing campaign, and mobilizing city officials and businesses against *Dragon* and similar future films.[28] The coalition also issued a press release stating the new theme for the New York protests—"We saw it, we hate it!"

On August 24, nearly one thousand protesters rallied against *Dragon* in San Francisco, several hundred in New York and Los Angeles, and about thirty in Boston. In a telephone interview on July 10, 1992, Janice Sakamoto, a spokesperson for NAATA in San Francisco, summarized the Bay Area's protest goals, some of which coincided with those of the New York coalition: to educate people about Hollywood stereotyping; to suspend video rights and distribution of *Dragon;* to encourage MGM/UA and Hollywood to create an independent Asian American advisory board; to succeed in having a portion of the film's proceeds go to an Asian community project; and to encourage Hollywood to hire more Asian Americans. In Los Angeles, picketers were organized by an ad hoc alliance, the Asian Pacific American Media Watch. They marched down Sunset Boulevard bearing "a symbolic coffin which they burned in front of Grauman's Chinese Theater," where *Dragon* was showing. One of the protesters, Irvin Lai, the national grand president of Chinese American Citizens, told the *Los Angeles Times,* "We're afraid this film will poison minds. We want people to see our side. We don't like to demonstrate but we must let the people know we are outraged. The racism and sexism are just too prominent to ignore."[29] In Boston, Julian Low, administrative director of the Asian American Resource Workshop, told the *Boston Globe,* "I think it was the most racist [film] I've seen." Marilyn Lee, Mayor Raymond Flynn's liaison to Boston's Asian American community, read a statement condemning "negative stereotyping of any community, regardless of the color of their skin or the cut of their coat." Flynn had met with members of the Asian American community to listen to complaints about increased anti-Asian violence in the Boston area; he supported the Asian Americans' protests: "I find films [like *Dragon*] offensive and insulting. Diversity of our city should be our strength, not our weakness. For some movie to exploit a certain proud segment of our community is just not helpful—whether it be anti-Asian, anti-Catholic, antiminority, antigay."[30]

Although few voices were raised in the film's defense, two of *Dragon's* actors were among its most passionate supporters. Mickey Rourke, who plays Stanley White, the egomaniacal New York policeman on a mission to stomp out Chinatown's Mafia, defended the movie against charges of racism and film industry malpractice: "Dragon employed more Asian actors than any film in years. The Asians who worked on it loved it and support it—and the fact of the matter is it's a film about racism" (photo 5). After attending a successful Hong Kong screening of the film, John Lone, who costars with Rourke as the Chinese Mafia leader and who was himself born in Hong Kong, told a *United Press In-*

ternational reporter: "The criticism of the film in the states came mostly from special interest groups depicted in it [i.e. the Triads]. . . . Prejudice has always been with us. The film lays it in front of you and lets you look at it. It is not a racist film for what it is. It's about a lot of things and one element in the film is racism. . . . The film is not meant to be a documentary and it does not represent all Chinese. It's just an entertaining film." Lone also praised the film for providing Asian Americans work: "Can you remember a film where you've seen so many Asian faces allowed to simply breathe, simply have the dignity and bearing of who we are?"[31] Paul

Photo 5. A duel between New York City's most decorated cop (Mickey Rourke) and Chinatown's most ruthless organized crime leader (John Lone) comes to a climax near the docks of Manhattan. The white cop naturally walks off the victor. "THE YEAR OF THE DRAGON" © 1985 Turner Entertainment Co. All Rights Reserved. Courtesy of the Academy of Motion Picture Arts and Sciences.

Lee, an Asian American businessman hired by MGM/UA to promote the film in the Chinese market, echoed Lone, calling *Dragon* "a landmark picture for Chinese. There are more Chinese actors in one place than in any other major American film." Lone's part, he continued, "is the biggest role ever for an Asian male who is not a Kung Fu star." Such comments, among others, only fueled the anger of the Coalition Against Year of the Dragon.

Most mainstream film reviewers were more critical of Cimino's latest effort than of protesters' actions. The *Los Angeles Times* reported that eighteen national reviews "liked" *Dragon* "with only barely a handful liking it a lot," while twenty-seven disliked it—"but hate might be more like it." Among these, Carrie Rickey wrote in the *Boston Globe,* "Cimino didn't direct a movie, he's choreographed a racist's temper tantrum," and Philip Wuntch of the *Dallas Morning News,* alluding to the film's most violent scene, predicted that the film "could do to Chinese restaurants what 'Jaws' did to beaches."[33]

Despite negative reviews and Asian Americans' protests against the film, *Dragon* seemed at first to be a box-office success. Four days after its national release, *Variety* called *Dragon* "lukewarm" but described as "healthy" its Washington, D.C., opening; the film played in thirty area theatres and earned $220,000 in a weekend, placing it ahead of such other new releases as *Return of the Living Dead, Volunteers, Kiss of the Spider Woman, The Bride,* and *Pee-Wee's Big Adventure.*[34] *Variety* labeled *Dragon* "delightful" in Detroit, "brisk" in Pittsburgh, but only "sleepy" in St. Louis. After three weeks, however, the film was a "disappointing" third on *Variety's* top-grossing films list, having earned only $4 million, well below MGM/UA's expectations. On September 5, three weeks after the film opened, the Coalition Against Year of the Dragon reported in a press release, "[*Dragon*] has closed down in 36 theaters across the country and box office sales dropped 30% in its second week and 9% in its 3rd." It is difficult to say whether Asian American protests helped cause these decreases in profits or whether the drop was the result of negative word of mouth.

On August 29, five days after the national protest, the CCBA in conjunction with the Federation of Chinese Organizations of America filed a $100 million class-action suit against MGM/UA. On the same day, Frank Rothman, CEO and chair of MGM/UA, announced at a meeting of the Los Angeles City Council his decision to attach disclaimers immediately to the nearly two hundred prints of *Dragon* in circulation in Los Angeles and New York–area theatres. Rothman also promised to add disclaimers to all prints of the film in the near future, reading, "This film does not intend to demean or to ignore the many positive features of Asian Americans and specifically Chinese American communities. Any similarity between the depiction in this film and any association, organization, individual or Chinatown that exists in real life is accidental." Rothman told *Variety* that MGM/UA had decided to insert a disclaimer "because we have no desire to offend any group of people."[35]

Rothman's promise of a disclaimer brought credit to Michael Woo, a newly elected city council member and Los Angeles's first Asian American representative, who had been active in the protests against *Dragon*. Rothman stood beside Woo at the city council's meeting while Woo—whom *Variety* described as "beaming with satisfaction"—said, "We are here today to announce an historical event. [Rothman and MGM/UA have] made it clear that 'we will not tolerate people telling them what films to make, but when we have offended groups we will listen.'"[36] Rothman promised that MGM/UA would issue a public apology to the Asian American community and agreed to consider Woo's and the coalition's requests to establish an industry advisory committee composed of Asian Americans assigned to examine scripts relevant to Asian Americans. He also said that he was willing to discuss donating a portion of profits from *Dragon* or a future MGM/UA movie toward an Asian American community project and to hire more Asian Americans at all levels of the film industry.[37]

The media heralded the studio's concession to the protesters as a rare success for community-based pressure. In a September 6 update, the Coalition Against Year of the Dragon stated that MGM/UA's agreement to add a disclaimer indicated that Asian Americans' protests "were working." Some Asian Americans, however, remained skeptical. Writing in the *Asian American Network,* Antonio De-Castro reminded his readers that the roots of their protests against *Dragon* went deep: "The issues that were raised around the movie cannot, as easily as the movie, disappear in the background. . . . The racism underlying [*Dragon* and other films] is a problem that pervades the foundation of American society. And until this problem and its root causes are overcome, the struggle continues."[38]

By the time the Coalition Against Year of the Dragon had organized its August 24 national day of protest, censorious language had practically vanished from its slogans and press releases. The disclaimer itself, a "victory" that boosted Asian Americans' morale, did not constitute censorship, for the film was not removed from the marketplace and no theatres canceled screenings because of subsequent legislative or civil actions (although on September 5, New York City council member Miriam Friedman attempted but failed to pass legislation against *Dragon*). Educational and informational actions had become the campaign's primary strategies. Nevertheless, subsequent demands, such as a plan to disrupt MGM/UA's distribution of *Dragon* in subsidiary markets, as well as Woo's and others' call for Rothman to establish an Asian American committee to screen scripts, reveal that the censorious impulse had not died.

Michael Cimino's *Year of the Dragon* had angered and galvanized the Asian American community as no previous movie had. But what had Asian Americans accomplished through their protests? Did the Coalition Against Year of the Dragon succeed in, as Gina Marchetti writes, "resisting . . . dominant culture's ability to label, limit, and define the racial other"?[39] While MGM/UA's decision to issue an apology to Asian Americans and to insert disclaimers, an action that Rothman said was undertaken at "great expense" to the studio, suggested that the film industry had acknowledged Asian Americans' political power, Rothman's failure to address any of the issues on the coalition's platform undermined the group's claim of empowerment. NAATA spokesperson Janice Sakamoto noted in our 1992 telephone interview that none of the coalition's significant demands had been granted—the suspension of subsidiary rights, the establishment of an Asian American Community Advisory Board, the donation of production profits to an Asian American project. Yet she was hopeful. "With the studios, we always feel we are at point zero. But this is also part of the process of the continued effort of empowering our community. . . . There are many battles in the war. . . . As you know, Hollywood is really about making money. Anything they can exploit to do that, I think they will do. Hopefully, there will be more enlightened directors who will challenge that."

Sakamoto locates the power over ethnic representation in the hands of the studio and the director and implies that, despite occasional responses to protest, Hollywood will remain indifferent to the real issues facing Asian Americans. MGM/UA's response, however, whether a sign of sensitivity or political chicanery, arguably made movie makers and Americans more aware of the "model minority's" rising determination to combat racial stereotypes. And the widespread protests themselves showed that a diverse community had been galvanized. They also indicated that, unlike antipornography feminists, Asian Americans had decided that, however much they desired to censor demeaning stereotypes, their gradual empowerment depended upon structuring demands in noncensorious ways. Their enduring hope was that Hollywood, which they acknowledged to have the final power over representation, might use that power in ways friendlier to their interests.

4

We Are Not Invisible

Gays and Lesbians against
Basic Instinct (1991–1992)

They scribbled "Kill Ray" all over town. We were getting death threats.
Lots of them. They put out fliers showing a woman with a gun in her
hand saying, "Spend your money fast, Ray!"

Ray Chalker
Owner, Rawhide II Bar

We are not about censorship here, we're talking about balance. We
had 2,000 years of one message. We want to have parity.

Tom Amaniano
GLAAD San Francisco

On April 10, 1991, at almost seven o'clock in the morning, several dozen members of the Queer Nation affin-
ity group, Labia, demonstrated in front of a popular country-
western gay bar in San Francisco, Rawhide II, where
the first scenes in *Basic Instinct* were about to be shot. The
protesters were especially angry that a gay-bar owner, Ray
Chalker, would allow filmmakers to shoot a "homophobic"
film in his bar, and that the bar, a symbol of the neighborhood, would be converted into a heterosexual nightclub.
Members of Labia held signs and chanted objections to a

film all believed stereotyped lesbians as psychotic killers. Later that day, they were joined by other gay groups; later that month, at other San Francisco locations, protests mounted and became more confrontational. By the time the movie was due to open nationally, the following spring, no film since *Cruising* (1979–1980) had as greatly enraged and galvanized the gay and lesbian community.

Like that of feminists and Asian Americans, homosexuals' resistance to Hollywood movies sprang from a broader, activist agenda in the 1960s. As homosexuals came to focus on the harm they perceived films had done to their lives and to seek ways to culturally empower themselves, the movie industry itself was changing its long-held views of homosexuality, referred to as "sex perversion" in film's early days. As historian Vito Russo has thoroughly demonstrated, any history of homosexuality in film is as much the story of what was omitted as of what was included. Gay characters and themes were routinely excised from films as early as the 1920s and 1930s. In 1923, a New York censor went after Alla Nazimova's *Salome,* a film made in tribute to Oscar Wilde that reputedly employed an all-homosexual cast. The censor ordered the deletion of several sequences, including shots suggesting a homosexual relationship between two Syrian soldiers. His report stated, "This picture is in no way religious in theme or interpretation. In my judgment, it is a story of depravity and immorality made worse because of its biblical background."[1] With only a few specific references to homosexuality in films from 1923 to 1927, the MPPDA's decision to warn producers against "sex perversion" in 1927 can be explained as a preventive measure to guarantee that producers did not take anything for granted.[2]

The fear of homosexual images was tied not only to

moral campaigns against the movies, but also to attempts to keep the myth of male heroism alive. As Vita Russo explains:

> A nation of immigrants recently mesmerized by the flicker of the nickelodeon seized larger-than-life images of the silent screen to play out its own dream of itself, and there was little room for weakness in the telling. . . . Men of action and strength were the embodiment of our culture, and a vast mythology was created to keep the dream in constant repair. Real men were strong, silent and ostentatiously unemotional. They acted quickly and never intellectualized. In short, they did not behave like women.[3]

According to Russo, filmmakers have always depicted male homosexuality in terms of what is not masculine.

In 1931, two U.S. producers, Clifford Cochron and John Krimsky, attempted to exhibit Leontine Sagan's film *Mädchen in Uniform,* an antiauthoritarian story about a lesbian love affair between a young student and her teacher in a boardinghouse. The movie was released only after complying with a long list of censors' cuts.[4] Even greater censorship challenges greeted Lillian Hellman's screen adaptation of her lesbian-themed play *The Children's Hour* (1936) and the independently produced *Children of Loneliness* (1939).

Rules governing the depiction of homosexuality did not increase during the 1940s, perhaps because the industry so tightly controlled all film content during the war years and there was simply no need to create new rules to curtail imagery that rarely appeared on screen. In the postwar years, however, with homophobia pervasive and filmmakers daring to treat homosexual themes, the screen became an easy target.

Homosexuality became national news after Alfred Kinsey reported that homosexuals could be found "in every age group, in every social level, in every conceivable occupation, in cities and on farms, and in the most remote areas of the country." During the McCarthy era, homosexuality was conflated with communism. Government officials were asked, "Are you or were you once a homosexual and/or a Communist?"[5] In a 1950 *New York Times* story, the Republican National Committee chair Guy George Gabrielson is quoted as saying, "Sexual partners who have infiltrated our government in recent years are perhaps as dangerous as actual communists."[6] In such an atmosphere, it is not surprising that the Production Code Administration tightened its controls over all cinematic implications of homosexuality. The early 1950s, however, were a difficult period for the movie industry. Antitrust suits, attacks by the House Un-American Activities Committee, and the growth of television made producers and directors even more wary of approaching controversial subjects like homosexuality: yet they were also financially strapped and knew they needed controversy to lure audiences back to theatres.

During the mid 1950s, filmmakers' challenges to the code's ban on depictions of adultery, miscegenation, and nudity produced a climate of change that anticipated bolder images of homosexuality. On December 11, 1956, Eric Johnston, chair of the MPAA (MPPDA's replacement since 1951), announced various code revisions "in light of experience and of present-day conditions." The MPAA claimed that the streamlined code rescinded prohibitions against drug addiction, prostitution, miscegenation, child birth, crime, vulgarity, and obscenity, yet controversies continued to arise involving films in each of these subject areas. Playwright Elmer Rice, among others, criticized the MPAA's changes as "trivial" and called the new code "merely a gesture in the direction of those who think the Code is obsolete."[7]

Not only did this new code fail to lift the ban on homosexuality, but during the years following its announcement, restrictions on homosexuality appeared to be even more rigorously enforced.

Rigorous enforcement, however, did not prevent filmmakers from producing *Cat on a Hot Tin Roof* (1958), *Pit of Loneliness* (1959), *Suddenly Last Summer* (1959), and *Devil's Advocate* (1961), each of which contained homosexual characters or themes and challenged the code. In February 1961, in response to these and other films, Otto Preminger directly confronted the PCA, announcing that he intended to release *Advise and Consent,* homosexual theme intact, without the PCA Seal. One month later, William Wyler began production of *The Children's Hour,* complete with the lesbian theme that he had been forced to eliminate twenty-five years earlier from *These Three,* his first version of Hellman's play *The Children's Hour.* Moreover, Gore Vidal's *The Best Man* and Morris West's *The Devil's Advocate* were in production, both with homosexual subplots. In August 1961, *Variety* predicted that *The Children's Hour* couldn't "possibly be approved unless the Code is written to accommodate the producers," and that if "important" producers pressed for another code revision, the MPAA might be inclined to oblige them. The trade paper was correct. In light of the number of projects that treated homosexuality currently in production, PCA president Jeffrey Shurlock requested advice from the board. Two months later he received this response:

It is permissible under the Code for the Production
Code Administration to consider approving reference
in motion pictures to the subject of sex aberrations,
provided any references are treated with care, discretion and restraint, and in all other aspects conform to
the Code.

The ruling in no way opens up the Code to irresponsible or immoral or indecent themes or treatment.

The board feels that, under the Code, the matter may
be handled as acceptably, as morally, as in the other media of expression . . . radio, television, newspaper and
magazines, books and plays . . . all media that appeal, as
do motion pictures, to large and diverse audiences.

Time and again these other media have demonstrated
that the matter can be dealt with responsibly and without offense.[8]

Similar to its earlier treatment of such terms as *propaganda,*
pornography, and *obscenity,* the PCA's revised ruling on homosexuality only offered a general definition of the specific
images that fell under the category "homosexuality." The
PCA never did explain how "sex aberrations" that were
"treated with care," "handled acceptably," and "dealt with
responsibly and without offense" would actually look.

Although a year later a British-producer film, *The Victim,*
would prove that the PCA intended to retain some control
over screen homosexuality, significant changes were un-
derway. As African American and other ethnic and racial
groups had come to understand, gays soon discovered that
representation in movies meant being viewed within the
structures of acceptability established by the majoritarian

culture. A new set of gay stereotypes emerged that tended to represent homosexuality through heterosexual eyes. Gays and lesbians were "nature's tragedy," abnormal, psychotic figures for whom the only remedy was suicide or assimilation into the heterosexual world. Resisting stereotypical depictions, however, fit easily into gay liberationists' larger political project: combating widespread homophobia and violence against gays, and struggling for gay rights. Just weeks after the Gay Liberation Front (GLF) orchestrated the New York Stonewall riots, the group issued this statement of purpose on July 31, 1969:

> We are a revolutionary group of men and women formed with the realization that complete sexual liberation for all people cannot come about unless existing social institutions are abolished. We reject society's attempt to impose sexual roles and definitions on our nature. We are stepping outside these roles and simplistic myths. We are going to be who we are. At the same time, we are creating new social forms and relations, that is, relations based on brotherhood, cooperation, human love, and uninhibited sexuality. Babylon has forced us to commit ourselves to one thing—revolution![9]

This statement, especially the line "We reject society's attempt to impose sexual roles and definitions on our nature," reveals that gay activists were thinking about heterosexual stereotypes and helps explain their bitterness toward the media. In subsequent years, protests against mainstream movies became one highly visible way of challenging heterosexuals' right to construct homosexual identity.

While the GLF and other groups would not engage in direct-action campaigns until the late 1970s, their criticism of Hollywood appeared in an emerging gay press as well as in mainstream publications. Following the 1971 release of MGM's *Fortune and Men's Eyes*, Richard McGuinness, an openly gay film critic for the *Village Voice*, wrote:

> "Fortune" was made under restraint. Psychic restraint. It's unliberated, a duplicitous movie made by the victimized, who sadly believe the only reason the straight powers allow them to make a gay movie is if they pretend to be making a social consciousness movie in which one of the obligatory messages, for the straight audience and to further torment the faggots, is the ingrained moral, "what goes on in prison is a crime," that is, being homosexual itself is a crime. . . . Gay and proud it is not. Elusive, self-destructive, and cruel it is. . . . The straight and the "faggot" can exist together only if the "faggot" hates himself. He is made to be alone and the ones with which he might identify, his kind, are competition or a bone of contention. He must be invisible and alienated, jealous and contemptuous of others of his type, divided and conquered.[10]

Writing in the *New York Times*, Stuart Byron criticized *Fortune*'s depiction of the central gay character as a sex-hungry man whose disgust with his "female" role leads him to murder. Summarizing Byron, Russo writes, "A society that demands that we play one sexual role and one sexual role only is the problem, not the solution." As Russo further observes, "[With *Fortune*] MGM wanted a picture that exploited and condemned homosexuality at the same time." After the re-

lease of *Death in Venice* (1971) and *Some of My Best Friends Are
. . .* (1971), Arthur Bell, a founding member of the Gay Activist Alliance (GAA), lamented in an article in the *New York
Times:* "Our revolution came late in 1969, but our stereotypes continue. Our screen image is alive and sick and in
need of an enthusiastic ending and a liberated beginning."
Bell singled out *The Boys in the Band* (1970) and *Busting*
(1974) as movies that contained especially demeaning
stereotypes and that celebrated homophobia. Robin Wood
similarly noted that "the dominant ideological norms of the
society in which we live are . . . marriage and the nuclear
family . . . between them they offer homosexuals the terms
on which they might be acceptable—the aping of heterosexual marriage and family, complete with poodles as children."[11] Wood criticized gays and lesbians for asking Hollywood producers to accept them. Doing so, he argued, was
"accepting society's terms."[12]

Homosexuals in the 1970s wanted Hollywood not only
to stop creating negative images but to begin producing
positive ones in their place. In 1971, members of the GLF
demonstrated at the premiere of *The Boys in the Band,* as
Morris Knight explained, because "there is not a single
character in the film I don't know. I know the drunk. I know
the pill head. I know the pimply queen. I know every one of
them. They're very real. But they're only a part of this community—and happily they're a dying breed. There are so
many more of us now, proud gay types, who are out there
living and achieving, not worried about pimply skin, not
drinking, and not popping pills."

Two years after GLF's actions against *Boys,* the GAA confronted the Association of Motion Picture and Television
Producers for "false and derogatory depictions of lesbians

and gay men" and suggested ways that the film industry could "put the pros and cons of the gay lifestyle on film with no loss of audience appeal or consequent revenue."[13]

Late in 1973, GAA joined the National Gay Task Force in submitting a list of guidelines to help TV and movie producers present homosexuality on screen, including the following:

> ■ Homosexuality isn't funny. Sometimes anything can be a source of humor, but the lives of twenty million Americans are not a joke.

> ■ Use the same rules you have for other minorities. If bigots don't get away with it if they hate Catholics, they can't get away with it if they hate gays. Put another way, the rights and dignity of homosexuals are not a controversial issue.

> ■ Homosexuality is a natural variant of human sexuality. It is not an illness, nor is it a problem for the majority of gays who are happy to be what they are. . . .

> ■ There is a wide variety of available themes concerning the place of homosexuality in contemporary society and the range of gay relationships and lifestyles. . . . Gays can provide entertainment for a broad, general public. Gays do not want to return to media invisibility.

Through the 1970s, the GAA encouraged the television and film industries to adopt their guidelines. In the case of television, the group achieved a degree of success, but its efforts to change how movies presented gays and lesbians failed. Instead of better portrayals, gay characters were sometimes excised from material just to avoid controversy. In *Marathon*

Man (1976) and *The Turning Point* (1977), both of which contained gay characters in their source material, producers cut the roles in the movie version. At the close of the 1970s, as Russo laments, "not one gay hero [had] emerged on the movie screen."[14]

Three films released in 1980, each containing homosexual stereotypes, galvanized a second wave of opposition against the film industry. "*Cruising* was the last straw in a long stream of Hollywood horrors," according to Russo. "Coming as it did in company with *Windows* and *American Gigolo,* it acted as a catalyst for a massive nationwide protest of the Hollywood treatment of gays."[15] Protests against *Cruising* began during filming in New York in the summer of 1979. Spearheaded by the National Gay Task Force, the protesters (primarily gay men) tried to convince *Cruising* producer Jerry Weintraub and director William Friedkin "to balance the film with portrayals of other sorts of gay women and men." When this request was ignored, gays demonstrated against the production at nearly every one of its eighty New York locations. On July 26, with the film crew scheduled to shoot in Greenwich Village, the heart of the gay community, several hundred activists marched on the local police station. On the same day, the National Gay Task Force filed a request with Mayor Ed Koch's office demanding that the city withdraw Weintraub's and his production team's permit. *Cruising,* the group claimed, would cause "a potentially inflammatory and explosive" reaction from the homosexual community.[16] Mayor Koch issued a statement defending the filmmakers' right to shoot in New York. "To do otherwise," he wrote, "would involve censorship. It is the business of this city's administration to encourage the return of film making to New York City by cooperating to

whatever extent feasible with film makers." Such coopera-
tion, Koch explained, did not mean that the city "accords it
approval or disapproval of film content."[17]

That week Arthur Bell published an article in the *Village Voice* that called upon gays "to give Friedkin and his
production a terrible time if you spot them in your neighborhood. . . . Owners of gay establishments would do well
to tell Friedkin to fuck off when he comes around to film
and exploit." Bell appeared on an ABC morning show
urging callers "to do violence against the movie."[18] The
New York Times and other publications credited him with
inspiring gays to organize a massive and ultimately violent
march on the evening of July 27. Chanting "*Cruising* must
go," approximately one thousand activists stormed
through Greenwich Village, blocking traffic in the Sheri-
dan Square area for nearly thirty minutes. In the process
they managed to "block passage to Friedkin's waterfront
office, blow whistles to disrupt on-the-street filming,
[and] harrass gay men working as extras with name-call-
ing, intimidation, and anonymous telephone threats." As
the film crew shot a scene near the intersection of
Christopher and West Streets, several hundred demonstrators confronted the filmmakers, and at least one activist threw rocks. Friedkin later recalled: "When I looked
into that mob that night, I saw a gang of unruly fanatics;
blowing whistles, throwing bottles and cans at the trucks,
at the actors and at me. . . . So how could I believe that
this group of people were representing the legitimate interests of a very significant minority in this country? A legitimate group, with legitimate interests, does not
threaten to kill you."[19]

Despite this evening of violence and numerous subsequent mass rallies, sit-ins, and marches, Friedkin completed *Cruising* without altering the script.

Gay Rights spokespeople downplayed their petitioning Koch to prevent Friedkin and his crew from shooting *Cruising* in New York, and they continued to pressure Friedkin, Weintraub, and the movie industry in general to exercise self-censorship.[20] Ronald Gold, media advisor for the National Gay Task Force, summarized his group's position: "We are not asking for censorship. We are asking Hollywood to use the same system of self-censorship they apply to other minorities. Nobody would dare to do a film about a group of organized black men whose objective is to rape a white woman. We always find ourselves in a position of having to play civil libertarian to a bunch of bigots who want their constitutional right to express their hatred of us."[21] Bill Kraus, president of San Francisco's Harvey Milk Gay Democratic Club, found it "absurd to argue the First Amendment in this case, because it presumes equality. There's no equality as long as we haven't the power of economic base that Hollywood has to make films on the scale of 'Cruising.' We haven't the means to respond in kind." But civil libertarians such as John Riley, a gay novelist living in Los Angeles, warned that prior censorship of *Cruising* would "reach out to all other films and may ricochet. If the efforts to obstruct *Cruising* succeed, might not that set the stage for anti-homosexual groups to squash pro-gay films?"[22]

In January 1980, with the *Cruising* premiere just one month away, United Artists released *Windows,* another movie homosexuals found offensive due its stereotypes. Gays and lesbians were livid. On January 25, a coalition of groups promoted their complaint against *Windows* and *Cruising,* holding press conferences in New York and Los

Angeles. *Windows,* a lesbian psycho-thriller directed by Gordon Willis, became the coalition's immediate focus. "*Windows,*" declared Mary Jamie Park, director of programs for the Gay Community Services Center in Los Angeles, "is a film that perpetuates and sensationalizes the most pernicious lies about lesbians and rape." The coalition asked United Artists to stop advertising *Windows,* to withhold distribution of the film, and not to sell the movie to television. "We are not advocating censorship," their statement read. "In fact, the only censorship surrounding this controversy is that which the industry has done on its own regarding positive lesbian and gay images in film."[23] When *Windows* opened in New York and other cities on January 18, gays picketed it, the press panned it, and the movie languished at the box office. Fearing protests at the premiere in San Francisco and other northern California cities, Transamerica Company, the parent company of United Artists, announced that the film would not be shown in northern California at all.[24] In New York, the protests and the film's poor box-office showing led several theatres to remove *Windows.*[25] Arthur Bell rejoiced at what he perceived as the protesters' success: "I predict that with *Windows, Cruising, American Gigolo,* we're witnessing the tail end of an era. In six months, our junk food will be less poisonous, more nourishing, and more delightful."[26]

In the light of gays' and lesbians' protests against *Windows* and the brouhaha over *Cruising,* theatre chains and city officials around the country weighed the risks of exhibiting *Cruising* as gay activists completed protest plans. In San Francisco, Mayor Diane Feinstein, concerned for public peace, persuaded United Artists to schedule *Cruising* in the Market Street Theatre rather than at the Ghirardelli

Theatre, where anti-*Cruising* graffiti had been spray painted nearby.[27] General Cinema Corporation canceled plans to open *Cruising* in thirty theatres, claiming that the film deserved an X, not the R that the MPAA had granted it.

While activists such as Morris Kite had warned that gays and lesbians planned large actions that "would go far beyond just demonstrations," Jan Oxenberg, a member of the National Association of Lesbian and Gay Filmmakers and a noted director herself, explained homosexuals' ire: "We're in a real bind here, because United Artists is going to promote 'Cruising' no matter what we say, and we don't want their voice to be the only one that's heard. We're more interested in seeing that the whole issue gets a little more publicity than in seeing 'Cruising' get a little less." In other words, Oxenberg, and others, would be content to educate the public simply by protesting against the film, without demonstrations verging on the type of violence and censorious intent of which Kite warned.[28]

When *Cruising* opened on February 15, 1980, in more than three hundred theatres around the country, picketers in Hollywood shouted such slogans as "Close *Cruising* down" and "Don't support lies," and in New York they unfurled banners and chanted inside the National Theatre on Broadway. While these actions did not cause theatres to remove the film after it had opened, the prerelease protests had perhaps, as Edward Guthmann argues, produced censorious effects: "It has been widely suggested that Friedkin yielded to community pressure, that his final package was far tamer, and less inflammatory, than his original idea."[29] Unlike the Gerald Walker novel on which the film was based, Friedkin's film ended ambiguously; instead of transforming Al Pacino into a psychotic killer, suggesting that exposure to the homosexual world makes one homicidal, Friedkin left the question of who killed Pacino's gay neighbor open. Friedkin also added a disclaimer to the film's final print: "This film is not intended as an indictment of the homosexual world. It is set in one small segment of that world, which is not meant to be representative of the whole."[30] This disclaimer proved that homosexuals had made an impact on the exhibition of at least one mainstream movie.

Exhibitors expected *American Gigolo* to crumble at the box office later in 1980, as *Cruising* eventually had, but the film proved an enormous success. Stuart Byron of the *Village Voice* lamented: "The 'Gigolo' success story is profoundly depressing. One can take no joy in the *Cruising* flop if instead people are attending a movie whose homophobia is simply more subtle. 'Gigolo' posits the pure love of a man (Richard Gere), and a woman (Lauren Hutton), and the human ideal, and against it places a gay world of pimps, madames, and woman-hating sadists—the only gay world it knows."[31] Films released later in the decade, such as *Making Love* (1980), *Personal Best* (1982), *Deathtrap* (1982), *Partners* (1982), *Victor/Victoria* (1982), *La Cage Aux Folles* (1984), *The Color Purple* (1986), *My Beautiful Laundrette* (1986), and *Kiss of the Spiderwoman* (1986), revealed a pattern of greater sensitivity and fewer negative stereotypes. Not only had the mass protests against *Cruising* apparently produced positive results, but when *New York Times* critic Leslie Bennetts proclaimed a "new realism in portraying homosexuals," he seemed to imply that this development was both daring and desirable. Still, many gays and lesbians felt that most of these films represented no real progress, but rather more of the same, again depicting homosexuality through heterosexual eyes.[32]

During the mid to late 1980s, gays and lesbians staged few protests against specific films, preferring to pressure Hollywood in other ways.[33] The decrease in street protests can be explained by the emergence of a more immediate crisis—the AIDS epidemic. Within the course of several years, gay bashing and AIDS phobia soared. The Religious Right stepped up attacks on homosexuals, who directly threatened "family values" (the religious conservatives' catch-all phrase for those undefinable qualities in everyday life that they believed contemporary art and the media threatened to destroy). McCarthyism appeared to be back. Homosexual life and culture became inexorably linked to the "social, political, sexual, and health concerns" of the "Age of AIDS."[34] In 1989, the controversy surrounding Robert Mapplethorpe's photos vitalized gays' and lesbians' struggles in many areas of artistic expression. By attempting to suppress Mapplethorpe's "homoerotic art," the Religious Right challenged gays and lesbians. Art had once again become a site of contestation, and the culture wars were in full spate. By 1990, the Gay and Lesbian Alliance Against Defamation (GLAAD), the activist Queer Nation, the AIDS organization ACT UP, and other groups had again turned their attention to films. Hollywood had omitted the overt lesbianism from *The Color Purple* (1986) and *Fried Green Tomatoes* (1989), and in 1990, director Jonathan Demme planned to direct *Silence of the Lambs,* a blockbuster featuring a psychotic, homosexual serial killer. The old homophobic pattern, it seemed, had reappeared, but this time gays and lesbians were more prepared to fight back.

The release of *Silence of the Lambs* in 1991 generated a debate among gay rights activists, First Amendment advocates, feminists, and writers concerned about the effects of violence on viewers, yet a widespread protest campaign never fully materialized. Ten days before the film's scheduled release on February 14, GLAAD accused Orion Pictures, the film's distributor, of "donating proceeds from a benefit screening of 'Silence of the Lambs' to AIDS Project Los Angeles in order to draw attention away from events in the film that exploit violence against women and perpetuate gay stereotypes." Richard Jennings, executive director of the Los Angeles chapter of GLAAD, criticized *Silence* further because the serial killer, Buffalo Bill, was a psychopathic homosexual: "This film is a continuation of Hollywood's appalling track record of portraying gays in negative ways. [It] could potentially encourage gay bashing . . . [and] also ignores the reality that most violence against women is committed by heterosexual males."[35] Jennings explained that by condemning *Silence,* GLAAD intended to "send a message to Orion and the rest of the film industry that we're tired of being depicted in the movies almost exclusively as villains, murderers, and twisted psychopaths." Michelangelo Signoreli of *Outweek* also predicted that *Silence* would lead to gay bashing, while Ron Rosenbaum of *Mademoiselle* lambasted it as "a sick pornography of butchery . . . a camera infatuated with decayed, mutilated flesh."[36]

In responding to accusations that his movie was homophobic, Jonathan Demme told gay activists, "I think it's really sad that some people with political agendas are trying to stop others from doing some good. . . . I'm sorry the movie is being misunderstood."[37] The *Village Voice*'s C. Carr defended *Silence* in different terms:

> Feminists have been arguing for years now about representation, but this is the first time I've encountered

such disparate male allies of Andrea Dworkin. Does porn cause rape, as Dworkin claims? Does an image cause violence? Yes, insists Michelangelo Signoreli (*Outweek*), who says this film will encourage gay bashing. Yes, asserts Ron Rosenbaum (*Mademoiselle*), who says it will hurt women. Seeing Dworkinism flare up in the gay community just brings bad memories of '70s feminism, while Rosenbaum's twisted paternalism overlooks the fact that women *never* get to have movie heroes like the one played by [Jodie] Foster.[38]

In comparing gay and lesbian criticisms of *Silence* to the "Dworkinism" of antipornography feminists, Carr was in essence accusing the homosexual community of censorious intent. Gays and lesbians who had picketed *Windows* and *Cruising* had distinguished their demands from censorship, but perhaps events of the 1980s had altered homosexuals' perspective. Since *Silence* failed to elicit widespread and unified protests from the homosexual community, maybe censorship was now the only way to change the message being delivered by the film industry, which gays and lesbians believed continued to stereotype, oppress, and marginalize them.

While the 1980s had brought a series of AIDS television dramas and a handful of "positive" portrayals of homosexuality in mainstream movies, when the press reported that Joe Eszterhas had been paid $3 million for a screenplay featuring a bisexual psychopathic killer, to be played by Sharon Stone, being pursued by yet another straight white male cop, gays and lesbians realized that their earlier protests had accomplished nothing.[39] "The fury that has been called up by 'Basic Instinct,'" journalist Michael Bronski wrote in the gay weekly *NYQ* just before the premiere of the film, "is due as much to the realization of our relative powerlessness as it is to the film itself. Twenty-five years after the Stonewall Riots, we are still at war with Hollywood. Only now we are not only smarter and savvier, but closer to our rage than ever before."[40]

In February 1991, immediately after Carolco Pictures announced its plans to film *Basic Instinct* in San Francisco's gay community, GLAAD and Queer Nation—whose members had read a widely circulated early version of Eszterhas's script—began to plan a protest campaign. Letter writing was the first step. Carolco Pictures reported receiving hundreds of requests that the studio cancel its production of *Basic Instinct* or at least shoot the movie outside of San Francisco. A week before the crew was scheduled to begin filming at their first San Francisco location, the Rawhide II bar, Hollie Conley, a member of the local GLAAD chapter, met with a Carolco representative in order to persuade the studio to make script changes. Carolco refused Conley's request and braced for trouble on the set.[41]

Carolco began filming on April 10, and despite their desire to censor the script, gays' and lesbians' earliest on-location protests were legitimate exercises of free speech (photo 6). Protesters passed out leaflets; carried placards that read, "Stop Hate," "Basic Bashing," and "Women Under Attack"; and chanted slogans such as "Hollywood, you stink / Fuck your *Basic Instinct*"—none of which smacked of an intent to censor. During the second week of shooting, however, Queer Nation protesters grew increasingly militant, while GLAAD continued their educational approach. GLAAD activists were especially angered that Ray Chalker, the owner of Rawhide II, had allowed Carolco to use his bar as a shooting location. Chalker claimed that death threats were left on his answering machine, that his Mercedes Benz had been vandalized, and that members of Queer Nation had put glue on the padlocks to his bar. Chalker told the *Washington Post* that death threats against him had appeared in graffiti and fliers all over town.[42] A week after the film crew had begun shooting, Art Agnos, the mayor of San Francisco, issued a press release in which he stated that he agreed with the protesting groups regarding "the negative images" in *Basic Instinct;* Agnos, similar to Koch in the instance of *Cruising,* continued, "No city should be in the position of censoring a movie script. Nor should we be giving a Jesse Helms–like seal of approval to programs or scripts."[43]

Photo 6. Protesters took to the streets of San Francisco at nearly every shooting location for *Basic Instinct.* Courtesy of Marc Geller Photography.

Alan Marshall, the film's producer, agreed to meet with the activists on April 24. Representatives from GLAAD, Queer Nation, ACT UP, and supervisor Harvey Britt's office sat across from him, screenwriter Joe Eszterhas, and director Paul Verhoeven and listed their demands. The activists "wanted Michael Douglas's character to be transformed into a lesbian, and further suggested that Kathleen Turner should be his replacement. They also wanted [the characters] Catherine and Roxy—both of whom murder men in *Basic Instinct*—to murder women as well; that way, they explained, lesbian and bisexual women would not be perceived as man-haters." Eszterhas was the only person connected to the film who appeared receptive to these changes. A week after the meeting, he proposed thirteen pages of script revisions to "reflect a sensitivity to many of the opinions expressed by gay community leaders," among them:

- Several characters' homophobic remarks would be eliminated or such remarks would be countered with pro-gay statements by other characters.

- A scene that may read as a date rape would be transformed into a straightforward love scene.

- Two of the murder victims would be made women instead of men in order to show that the killer is not acting from a man-hating rage but from a psychopathic illness as an individual—her violence is directed at both men and women.

- A precredit disclaimer would be added, reading, "This movie you are about to see is fictional. Its gay and bisexual characters are fictional and not based on reality."

Further, Michael Douglas, who plays the police detective investigating the lesbian murderer, would say, "A lot of the best people I've met in this town are gay."[44] That Eszterhas had suggested these script changes pleased the protesters, but Carolco executives flatly rejected them. "I consider his changes patronizing drivel," Peter Hoffman, president and CEO of Carolco, told *Vanity Fair*. "Joe Eszterhas is a sniveling hypocrite and I have no use for him. Besides, we would never change a script in response to political pressure."[45]

On April 29, after a week of continued pickets, Marshall obtained a restraining order from the city of San Francisco that prevented demonstrators from coming closer than one hundred yards from the filming, being "loud or boisterous," or using lights or "glitter" to distract the filmmakers.[46] For their part, Carolco issued an official response to the April 24 meeting:

> After careful consideration, director Paul Verhoeven, producer Alan Marshall, actor Michael Douglas, along with Carolco and Tri-Star Pictures (the film's distributor) are in agreement that those changes [suggested by the protesters and Eszterhas] undermine the strength of Eszterhas's original material, weaken the characters . . . and lessen the integrity of the picture itself. . . . *Basic Instinct* is a psychological thriller about a police detective investigating a series of brutal, baffling murders. It is not a negative depiction of lesbians and bisexuals. The controversy surrounding the filming of *Basic Instinct* is as much about artistic integrity as it is about the subject matter of the picture. . . . Censorship by street action will not be tolerated. While these groups have a right to express their opinions,

they have no right to threaten First Amendment guarantees of freedom of speech and expression. The filmmakers are men and women of integrity and artistic vision, and we support their work unequivocally. They
are dedicated to the rights of all people and to a life
free of persecution, harassment and discrimination.
We ask only to be accorded the same privilege.

Activists decried the use of the word "censorship" to de-
scribe their demands. "It's really a problem of institutional
censorship that has censored gay men and lesbians for
many years," said Rick Ruvolo, an aide to Harry Britt and
himself a protester. "We're only asking for some balance in
the way we are portrayed on screen." Similarly, GLAAD's
Hollie Conley told the *Bay Area Reporter:*

This is not an issue of their freedom of speech. We
hear that argument dozens and dozens of times. Our
problem is that Hollywood never uses its artistic freedom to make any realistic movies about gays and lesbians. They repeatedly make movies to pander to people's homophobia, and it's time that we demand that
they be more responsible. They have a social responsibility, and we're trying to awaken that social responsibility if it's in there slumbering somewhere.[47]

On the same day that Carolco emphatically rejected Eszterhas's script changes, members of Queer Nation and ACT
UP returned to the streets. An estimated eighty gay activists
blocked traffic at the downtown Moscone Center, blew whistles, and chanted such slogans as "Hey, hey, ho, ho, homophobia has got to go," and "Kiss my ice pick," tactics aimed

at disrupting the filming of a car chase scene. Demonstrators waved U.S. flags and held placards asking motorists to honk in support of U.S. troops and the Forty Niners football team. Several protesters reportedly threw paint bombs at the film crew. According to a *Washington Post* report, these actions were successful: they caused headaches and sound problems on the set. Three nights later came an even more extreme protest. In a deliberate violation of the San Francisco restraining order, members of Queer Nation came within one hundred feet of the set, blew more whistles, and chanted loudly. The production crew was forced to stop filming. Before resuming, producer Alan Marshall convinced the police to arrest some thirty demonstrators. The following night, five more Queer Nationals were arrested.[48]

Gays and lesbians trailed the *Basic Instinct* crew to locations around San Francisco on every evening of filming until May 8, when the production returned to Los Angeles. Although during this period protesters were more subdued, an angry press debate erupted over whether the mainstream media were presenting homosexuals' protests accurately or revealing their own heterosexual and anticensorship biases. The *San Francisco Examiner* inveighed against "storm-trooper tactics" and asserted that "the thought police are at it again. This time it's the thought police of the left. The effort to shoot down the movie is wrong, and it is dangerous to boot. People of minority views—gay activists among them—should be especially careful to protect the freedom of speech and thought."[49] GLAAD found homophobia implicit in such reports: "[They] are trying to fit this issue into a slot they've created about 'political correctness' and 'censorship of the left,'" Hollie Conley told the *Bay Area Reporter*. "I think they're trying to fit it into that mold as a way of creating this ogre of Left-wing thought control which doesn't really exist." A Queer Nation press release stated, "We will not let up until the censorship of our lives ends, and we finally see our richness and complexity as a community reflected back to us on the silver screen."[50]

Charges of "censorship from the left" in *Time* magazine and elsewhere may have influenced protest strategies. In the months leading up to the *Basic Instinct* release date early in 1992, GLAAD San Francisco and the Gay and Lesbian Alliance took a less belligerent stand, as reflected in a joint letter to theatre exhibitors:

> We are writing to you and other film exhibitors to express our concern about the movie "Basic Instinct". . . .
> Our concerns arise from the fact that "Basic Instinct" is the latest example of a long Hollywood tradition of stereotyping lesbians and gays as evil, violent, and psychopathic. This movie's villains are three killers, all of whom are lesbian or bisexual women. The hero is a homophobic, heterosexual man who forces himself sexually on a woman. . . .
>
> We at GLAAD . . . feel we must exercise our First Amendment right to challenge the current consensus, oppose Hollywood's censorship and bigotry, and seek more diverse and accurate representation of lesbians, gays and bisexuals in film.

In a flyer, GLAAD also published a list of "strategies" and "tactics" advising individual protesters on what they could do prior to the release of the film. The group stressed contacting and monitoring the media in order to guarantee "fair" and "accurate" coverage of issues vital to homosexuals' lives. Protesters were urged to "especially challenge loudly and at length any misrepresentation of your views in support of free speech. After all, as victims of centuries of censorship which obliterated all traces of our existence until recently, free dissemination of information is a survival issue of the highest priority to us." GLAAD's use of the word "censorship" to refer to something that heterosexuals in the media had historically done to homosexuals' lives was part of a strategy to reclaim the moral high ground from those who called them censors.[51]

In front of Carolco Studios in Los Angeles, Queer Nation continued protesting the filming of *Basic Instinct*. In August, when the National Gay and Lesbian Task Force succeeded in convincing studio executives to attend a gay rights dinner, it looked as if the combined pressures from GLAAD and Queer Nation had made a difference. Alan Hergott, a leading entertainment industry attorney who helped organize the benefit, told the *Los Angeles Times:* "There are a lot of things going on between the gay community and the motion picture and television industry. Everyone has suffered a huge impact from AIDS and any number of groups have been trying to raise the consciousness of Hollywood about the depiction— and lack of depiction—of gays and lesbians in movies and television. Anyone who goes to the movies and watches TV knows we have a long way to go." On another positive note for gays and lesbians, Richard Jennings, an executive director of GLAAD Los Angeles, was appointed by members of the film industry to direct a new antihomophobia, anti–AIDS discrimination organization called Hollywood Supports.[52]

This 'improvement' in the relations between homosexual groups and Hollywood executives was not enough to persuade homosexuals to drop plans to protest the *Basic Instinct* premiere. As the March 20, 1992, release date approached, a flurry of newspaper and magazine articles informed the public that homosexual activists not only planned to demonstrate at the opening of *Basic Instinct* but also would disrupt the Oscar ceremony, where *Silence of the Lambs* was expected to receive several Academy Awards. On January 16, the *New York Daily News* reported that activists would "give away [*Basic Instinct's*] ending on billboards and via public address systems outside theatres." The *San Francisco Chronicle* suggested that a Los Angeles group "plotted to release moths inside of theatres showing the film, hoping the insects would flock to the projection booth and obscure the screen image." Without revealing specific protest actions, Patt Riese, a member of Queer Nation, told the *Washington Post,* "We plan to be theatrical and colorful and our queer selves."[53]

In the final weeks before the premiere, the militant and educational groups appeared to be growing more unified. "Our effort [will be] to give away crucial information about the film," Alain Klein, a founder of Queer Nation, said, "[in order] to discourage people from seeing it." Rich Wilson, the group's media coordinator, stated an additional goal: "to destroy the first weekend's box-office grosses."[54] In February, a group consisting primarily of lesbians formed "Catherine Did It!"—an organization named after the film's bisexual character who becomes a serial murder suspect. "Our major focus is to keep people from going to the film," Annette Gaudino, a spokesperson for the group, told the *Los Angeles Times.* "We want to tell everyone as much about the movie as possible." Gaudino explained that her group was resorting to protest because many of their proposed script changes were never made. "We know that they went ahead without doing what we asked for," she said. "So

now we're going to do what we have to do to keep the public away from this film." Pam Bates, another "Catherine Did
It!" spokesperson, said, "We're going to actively distribute
leaflets at theatres that give away the whole ending of the
film."[55] In an interview with the *Washington Post*, Phyllis
Burke, the organizer of "Catherine Did It!" explained her
group's decision to reveal the movie's ending: "If the viewer
knows what the ending is, the manipulation of the viewer is
eliminated. We hope the viewer will see more easily what
we're talking about. Our problem is not that we want to see
all perfect images of gays and lesbians. We just want to see
a balance. Unfortunately, there hasn't been one." On
March 1, a letter to the editor responded to the *Los Angeles
Times's* reporting on homosexuals' protest plans by criticizing Queer Nation and "Catherine Did It!":

> [Your report] clearly illustrates why the gay activists in
> our society are, in one significant way, no better than
> its religious fundamentalists, militant feminists and
> other special-interest groups: they are intolerant. The
> gay community's attempts to halt the making of the
> movie "Basic Instinct" . . . are attempts to violate the
> principle of free expression. It's too bad such attempts
> cannot be criminally prosecuted, as is done with
> things like attempted bank robbery and attempted
> murder. . . . Now that the movie has been made (in
> spite of [gay groups'] repressive behavior), they're try-
> ing to keep people from seeing it. If these activities do
> not constitute attempts at censorship, what does?

A spokesperson for "Catherine Did It!" countered: "Please
do not confuse us with those people who censor artists. . . .

Our goal is to bring to your attention Hollywood's consistently defamatory treatment of gays and lesbians." Robert Bray of the Washington, D.C.–based National Gay and Lesbian Task Force similarly addressed the censorship question: "I don't mind a gay villain or two, but I also wouldn't mind a gay or lesbian hero. No one is calling for cultural censorship, but we are asking for diverse representations."[56]

GLAAD continued to emphasize a more educational approach. Chris Fowler, executive director of GLAAD Los Angeles, said in a press release: "[*Basic Instinct*] is based on a stereotype that lesbians hate men. The fact they are lesbians defines their hatred of men, which then lends itself to their murdering of men. This is, in fact, defamatory. This hurts our community. This leads toward hatred against us, which is a very important aspect of hate crimes, the gay bashings and murders that are inflicted in our community." Furthermore, "[GLAAD] plans to use the film's release as a springboard for educational outreach to both the viewing audience and the filmmaking community."[57] In New York, GLAAD organizer Donald Suggs concurred. "The thrust of our effort is educational. . . . We're not telling people, 'we don't think you should be able to see this film.' We think people can make those kinds of decisions themselves. We're just making them aware of the information out there . . . about the way Hollywood has dealt with gay and lesbian issues."[58]

As GLAAD, Catherine Did It! Queer Nation, ACT UP, the Gay Task Force, the National Organization of Women (NOW), and other groups polished their protest plans, it became clear that gays and lesbians had learned to use the mainstream media to their advantage. On March 19, the day before *Basic Instinct* opened, Ellen Carten of GLAAD New York told me in a telephone interview:

[Our campaign] has been a great success already—
there's been more media coverage and the media has
been more fair. It has also been a success because we
have gotten the word out. . . . We are changing the
consciousness around issues—and I don't think anyone could go out and make a movie like this again or
spend three million dollars in optioning a script like
this. . . . The film hasn't opened publicly yet, and we
have been successful in that, with the exception of a
few bad pieces, we've been able to get our point across
in print, radio, TV—and I'd say that that in and of itself spells success for this campaign.

In other words, the groups against *Basic Instinct* were content that their actions had increased public awareness about
one longtime problem in mainstream movies.[59]

During the week before *Basic Instinct*'s scheduled release, Tri-Star Pictures, the film's distributor, began cloak-
ing its screenings in secrecy, proof the studio feared that
protests would adversely affect the opening. On March 11,
gay activists were "disinvited" to a screening after Tri-Star received a copy of a GLAAD press release expressing a strong,
negative opinion about the film. As a Tri-Star spokesperson
explained the studio's decision: "GLAAD representatives
judged the film, based not on its content, but, rather, on
their own public relations agenda." On March 19, Tri-Star
released a statement to the news media: "Freedom of expression covers filmmakers and movie-goers as well as protesters. . . . We hope people will come see 'Basic Instinct'
and make up their own minds. We feel it is a terrific film,
and we expect that most people will agree with us."[60] Like
the Carolco statement, Tri-Star's suggested that homosex-

ual groups had put the company on the defensive. Exhibitors, however, were not perceptibly intimidated. In spite of prerelease protests, letters they had received from protesters, and impending postrelease headaches, theatre chains across the country booked *Basic Instinct* zealously as they would any other potential blockbuster.

Anticipating massive street protests, many theatre managers positioned extra security guards in front of their theatres on the evening of the premiere of *Basic Instinct*. For the most part, however, this precaution proved unnecessary. Protests across the country were smaller and more orderly than expected as homosexual groups and members of NOW demonstrated in front of theatres in Los Angeles, San Francisco, New York, Seattle, Washington, D.C., and other cities (photo 7). The largest protests were staged in San Francisco, where, according to the *San Francisco Chronicle*, one hundred activists "swarmed in front of the Metro Theatre on Union Street, badgering patrons who stood in line and entered the theatre." Demonstrators blew whistles, passed out leaflets, and carried such placards as "Kiss My Ice Pick," "Hollywood Promotes Anti-Gay Violence," and "Save Your Money—The Bisexual Did It." Few protesters tried to dissuade moviegoers from entering the theatre. In Los Angeles the scene was almost identical. The film opened in approximately one hundred theatres in the area, but the coalition of protesting groups focused their actions in front of one threatre—the Westwood Coronet—where some thirty protesters handed out flyers and did not, by and large, attempt to prevent moviegoers from entering.[61]

In Seattle, an estimated forty picketers gathered outside the Cinerama Theatre. Business was slow, but the movie

sparked a heated debate between protesters and ticket buy-
ers. One lesbian activist, Lisa Gay, explained why she was
picketing: "I don't think we are changing anybody's mind,
but I do think it will get people to talk in general. We have
to make some sort of stand." In Washington, D.C., while
protesters were reportedly "tame" in front of one theatre,

Photo 7. On the day the movie opened in New York, a
protester defaces one of the many advertisements for
the film plastered around the city. Photo by William La Force,
Jr. Courtesy of the *New York Daily News.*

filmgoers were forced to wait between reels when a projectionist—presumably a supporter of the protests—began to show the film's second part upside down.[62] The Gay and Lesbian Resource Center spearheaded the protest in Des Moines, Iowa. After attending a matinee screening, a small group gathered in the evening to decide what they wanted to do. Claire Hueholt, a member of the group, described her group's approach to me in a telephone interview on April 10, some weeks later:

> We passed out stickers that said, "Catherine Did It" and flyers that said, Now that you've seen Hollywood's version of a lesbian, we'd like to show you our version of a lesbian. She's someone who wants to have a home, wants to have a partner, wants to be single—and a whole long list of characteristics which basically apply to any human being. We didn't try to block anyone from attending. And then we got asked by the police to move and told that if we came back after the film was over, we'd be arrested.

None of the members of the Des Moines protest group returned to the theatre that night, but on the following day they placed protest flyers on all of the cars in the parking lot near the theatre. Similar to many other actions around the country, theirs was an educational campaign.

In New York, protesters from gay and lesbian groups and from NOW staged their largest actions in front of the Loew's Theatre at Nineteenth Street and Broadway, leafleting, waving placards, chanting, and debating with moviegoers. Some of the people entering the theatre proclaimed their First Amendment right to see whatever they wanted and chastised the protesters for attempting to dissuade them. The protesters, however, were not all giving movie-goers the same message. "What we really want to do is tell [people entering the theatre] not to go tonight," William Meyerhafer of Queer Nation told me in a street interview, while, nearby, Jill Frasca of NOW said to other people: "I'm not telling you not to see this film. I'm telling you that this movie is misogynist and it says queer people are sick. . . . We're both here [homosexuals and women] because if one of us is oppressed, we're all going to be oppressed. If society feels that it's okay to beat up women, then it's going to be okay to beat up queers." In print, activists carefully avoided appearing censorious. A flyer jointly issued by Queer Nation, GLAAD New York, NOW New York, Women's Health Action and Mobilization, and the Bisexual Public Action Committee stated in bold letters: "Basic Instinct=Basic Hatred / Entertainment or Defamation / You Decide." The text continued:

> The movie "Basic Instinct" is Hollywood's latest attack on women and queers. Four out of four lead female characters are man-hating murderers and three are lesbian or bisexual. We think this movie could do us harm, by reinforcing ignorance about homosexuality, and by providing an excuse for an escalating number of assaults on women, lesbians, bisexuals, and gay men. We're not saying that you don't have a right to see films like "Basic Instinct." We're not even asking you to hate it. We would like you to ask yourself whether you support the messages Hollywood sends out.

By all accounts, neither the New York protests nor those in other cities were violent and did not emphasize a censorious approach.[63]

Across the country, many film critics lambasted *Basic Instinct* and refused to take seriously the controversy surrounding its production and release. Al Martinez of the *Los Angeles Times,* for example, chided, "Everyone loves a movie born in hell, and everyone is coming to see it. . . . As a homophobic movie, 'Basic Instinct' is too awkward to be mean. As a dirty movie, it's too obvious to be erotic. I liked 'The Little Mermaid' better. It's about trans-species sexuality. A prince makes love to a fish." In the *Boston Globe,* Diane White similarly mused, "[*Basic Instinct*] offends movie-goers because, as a movie, it doesn't succeed even on its own simple-minded terms. It's so stupid it's difficult to take seriously. The plot is preposterous. The 'surprise' ending is just a cheap trick." Janet Maslin of the *New York Times* found the movie "far too bizarre and singular to be construed as homophobic." Amy Taubin of the *Village Voice,* however, considered the movie progressive in respect to its "feminist" theme.

> What's disturbing is that some queer critics seem determined to read this film as [the character] Nick might; and that reading is sexist. John Weir's piece in the Sunday [*New York*] *Times* a couple of weeks ago—perfect example—describes Catherine pejoratively as "a single woman who likes to have sex with whomever she pleases, and not always for love." Yes! And more power to her. Weir doesn't seem to realize that this is exactly the kind of freedom feminists have aspired to for 20 years.[64]

Views like Taubin's, however, found little support in the mass media, where several talk shows featured guests who decried the film's misogyny. On a CNN News special entitled "Politically Correct Movies," a member of NOW told host Catherine Crier: "I never thought I would live to see the day when Queer Nation and I were on the same side of the issue. . . . When you consider the number of rapes that take place in this society and the violence against women, all of a sudden, you have characters on screen that show women as these sexual predators with these voracious appetites . . . there wasn't a single decent woman in the film. . . . I think it was a profoundly anti-woman film and a sick film."[65]

This statement, directly opposed to Taubin's view, is reminiscent of antipornography feminists' view of *Dressed to Kill;* it also recalls the censorship debate among feminists and, in that sense, places gays and lesbians, Andrea Dworkin, and other women against pornography on the same side.

Everyone who protested against *Basic Instinct* agreed that the film stereotyped a minority group long victimized by the heterosexual majority culture, but GLAAD's educational protests contrasted sharply with Queer Nation's militant actions. During the prerelease period, both groups demanded that Eszterhas change the script according to very specific guidelines. When Carolco rejected these demands and continued to film in San Francisco's gay community, GLAAD issued press releases and asked exhibitors to think twice about the film, but not necessarily to cancel it. Members of Queer Nation, on the other hand, took their anger to the streets and, on at lease one occasion, prevented moviemakers from filming.

Once *Basic Instinct* was playing in theatres, at least one gay activist revealed a censorious impulse, begging moviegoers not to enter the theatre, yet no censorship resulted from any homosexual groups' actions. Theater exhibitors had not refused to show the film, and on no occasion was the movie withdrawn on account of protest or governmental action. The most certain result of gays' and lesbians' protests was that they drew more customers to the film than might otherwise have been inclined to watch it. Tri-Star flatly denied that the demonstrators had raised the public's consciousness about homophobia, while expressing gratitude for the free publicity. Many gay activists, however, proclaimed their actions successful. Although *Basic Instinct* earned close to $15 million its opening weekend—a solid release by practically any movie standards—Judy Sisneros of Queer Nation told the *Los Angeles Times,* "The success of the movie wasn't unexpected—all this publicity about the movie's ratings and the queer community's issues helped to generate interest. But that was a trade-off we had to accept in order to make our point."[66] Sisneros's assessment bears little resemblance to Queer Nation's prerelease goal of "killing" the movie's opening week profits. GLAAD's assessment of their groups' protests more accurately reflected prerelease goals. Hueholt said in our telephone interview: "Our protests were successful. What we wanted to do—we didn't want to discourage people from seeing the film—was to raise awareness that stereotypes of lesbians and the portrayal of women are part of a long history in Hollywood. We wanted to make viewers aware of that problem and, for the most part, the response was very good." Activists agreed that resistance to *Basic Instinct* had increased public awareness of the degrading homosexual stereotypes in movies. And no one disagreed that on the upside, "homophobia ha[d] gotten a lot of ink in the straight media."[67] But the larger question of how the controversy over *Basic Instinct* had affected homosexuals' position within the film industry, and within society at large, drew conflicting responses.

On the militant side, some observers claimed with Michelangelo Signoreli that the protests against *Basic Instinct*, combined with actions like the demonstrations at the 1991 and 1992 Academy Awards, had proven that activism paid off: "The entire two-year period beginning in 1990 seemed like an Academy Awards production in and of itself, a fantasy epic in which an industry begins to deal with an oppressed minority it has continually mistreated. Though they are just a start, the changes are many in comparison to the conditions prevailing only two years before. These events proved what could be done when the system was taken on full force."

Others, among them Michael Bronski, writing in *NYQ*, disagreed. "'Basic Instinct' is a symbol of how deep is popular culture's hatred of queers and women," Bronski wrote, "and its director's and producer's refusal to take seriously our criticism testifies to how little power we wield in this society." Even though he asserts, "direct action works," Bronski finally believes, "we still have little actual influence."[68] Taken together, such opinions demonstrate how hard it is to assess the extent of any protest's influence on the film industry. Not long after *Basic Instinct* was released, however, the industry formed Hollywood Supports, an organization promoting the development of projects with positive images of homosexuals. Perhaps a new era of sensitivity lay ahead.

5

This Film Is Blasphemy

Religious Opposition to
The Last Temptation of Christ (1988)

The key issue, the only issue, is whether or not self-appointed groups can prevent a film from being exhibited to the public, or a book from being published, or a piece of art from being shown. . . . The major companies of the M.P.A.A. support MCA/Universal in its absolute right to offer to the people whatever movie it chooses.   *Jack Valenti*

The issue is not whether "Last Temptation" can be shown, but whether such a film should be shown. . . . With "Last Temptation," Hollywood is assailing the Christian community in a way that it would never dare assault the Black community, the Jewish community, or the gay community.   *Pat Buchanan*

From a mile up, the scene looked like an open-air rock concert, thousands of multicolored moving dots on a large plot of earth. A ground-level view, however, transformed those little dots into not peace-loving hippies but frenzied Fundamentalists. On August 12, 1988, nearly twenty years after Woodstock, about twenty-five thousand Fundamentalist Christians and Catholics stormed Universal Studios in Los Angeles to protest filmmaker Martin Scorsese's "blasphemous" *The Last Temptation of Christ,* a movie many believed to be the filthy cultural by-product of an "open" society. Carrying Bibles and wooden crucifixes, these 1980s groupies, like Christian cheerleaders, chanted "Jesus, Jesus, Jesus."

For many religious groups and spokespeople, *Last Temptation* was the last straw in a series of attacks by the media, pluralists, and liberals on Christian values. The entire brouhaha over *Last Temptation* went far beyond resisting a single movie. Over the course of five years, Scorsese's movie, based on the controversial novel of the same title by Greek novelist Nikos Kazantzákis, would be linked to such cultural evils as AIDS and abortion, the cry for its suppression equated with the survival of family values in a nation considered woefully lacking a spiritual spine. Among the questions that energize this chapter are these: Was the Religious Right, born with Jerry Falwell in 1979 and triumphant over electing Ronald Reagan in 1980, already losing steam? Could religious groups continue to wield the same power that they had called on throughout the history of the film industry?

Religious groups and leaders have played more prominent roles in shaping film content than has any single secular group. Before 1909, the reformers who were the driving force behind a federal censorship movement often represented religious groups and interests.[1] Although some early religious leaders embraced motion pictures as invaluable educational and religious tools for strengthening the cultural life of a community, most were already weary of movies' corrupting influences.

Religious leaders who favored movie censorship stood against not only the evils associated with all motion-picture exhibition but also specific film content and imagery. Although the most widely criticized screen subjects were sex and crime, portrayals of the Bible and of Christ, however insipid, have rarely escaped controversy.[2] In 1913, a spokesperson for the Interchurch World Movement observed, "The element of controversy increases when dogma, theology, or biblical interpretation, or the person of the Deity is presented."[3] Although secondary to the larger issues of decency and morality, how the movies should treat religion would increasingly concern segments of the religious community.

During the 1920s, the power over religious content in movies belonged to industry regulators. In 1922, the MPPDA was organized on account of an increase in pressure from religious reformers. Five years later, the MPPDA's list of "Don'ts and Be Carefuls" included? "pointed profanity," under which such words as "'God,' 'Lord,' 'Jesus,' 'Christ,' (unless they be used reverently in connection with proper religious ceremonies), 'hell,' 'damn,' 'Gawd,' and every other profane and vulgar expression however it may be spelled" were outlawed.[4] The list also warned against ridiculing clergy.

MPPDA president Will H. Hays, a Protestant, courted religious groups, particularly Protestants.[5] His mandate was to bring respectability to an industry plagued by lurid murder, sex, and drug scandals; he knew that one way to achieve this was to strengthen the industry's ties with Protestant America. After establishing a committee on public relations and a network of Better Films Committees, Hays met with members of the International Federation of Catholic Alumnae, the National Catholic Welfare Conference, the Central Conference of American Rabbis, the Council of Jewish Women, the Federal Council of Churches of Christ of America, and other groups, intending to make them all "a friendly rather than a hostile critic of pictures," as he wrote to studio head Albert Warner in 1922, and at first it seemed he was doing just that.[6]

Cecil B. DeMille's *The King of Kings* (1927) was one of the first films to test the influence religious groups had on the presentation of religious subjects. DeMille anticipated their anger over a subject "dear and sacred to them," and despite the presence of a religious advisor on the film, *Kings* especially enraged Jewish groups such as B'Nai B'rith, the Anti-Defamation League, and the Rabbinical Assembly of America.[7] A member of B'Nai B'rith wrote to DeMille: "The picture should never have been made at all but . . . having made it, it should be corrected so as not to give the impression that Jews had anything to do with the crucifixion of Jesus."[8] Although he stopped short of fulfilling all of B'Nai B'rith's demands, DeMille reedited a sequence in which Pilate says, "Crucify him."

Religious pressure against *The King of Kings* was relatively mild compared to Catholics' actions the same year against *The Callahans and the Murphys* (1927). While Catholics had earlier attempted to block the distribution of such films as *Fit to Win* (1918) and *End of the Road* (1921), they had until now opposed censorship and participated actively in Hays's Better Films Committees. But upon reviewing *The Callahans,* Mrs. Thomas A. McGoldrick, chair of the Motion Picture Bureau of the International Federation of Catholic Alumnae, and Father John Kelly, a leader of the Catholic Theatre Guild, recommended deleting "all references to the Catholic Church such as the sign of the cross, crucifixes on the wall ... and the identification of the Picnic of St. Patrick's Day celebration."[9] After the film was released, Catholics convinced censors in Boston to force MGM to reedit it with twenty-three changes, in the process eliminating all explicit references to the Catholic Church. Even with these changes, Catholics and Irish Americans around the country protested against the film. Finally, when Philadelphia's Cardinal Dougherty, one of the nation's most influential prelates, demanded that MGM withdraw all copies of the film in distribution, MGM surrendered; censorship was complete. Such attempts at censorship, as Francis Walsh suggests, can be seen "as a dress rehearsal for the campaign that eventually led to the Legion of Decency," a Catholic pressure group that would have an unprecedented influence on motion picture content for the next thirty years; Hays's courtship had been all too successful.[10]

In 1930, Father Daniel Lord and Martin Quigley refined the MPPDA's "Don'ts and Be Carefuls," adding a section entitled "The Reasons Supporting the Code" that became known as the code's philosophy. Rooted in Catholicism, these reasons included the belief that art affected the moral life of the public and was therefore charged with special obligations. By 1933, however, not even an invigorated code could stem the tide of what many religious leaders believed were morally wayward movies. In October, Archbishop A. G. Cicognani, newly appointed apostolic delegate to the United States, in his address to the Catholic Charities Convention in New York called on all Catholics to boycott motion pictures. "What a massacre of innocence and youth is taking place hour by hour!" he said. "How shall the crimes that have their direct source in immoral motion pictures be measured? Catholics are called by God, the Pope, the Bishops, and the priests to a united and vigorous campaign for the purification of the cinema, which has become a deadly menace to morals."[11]

On April 11, 1934, the Episcopal Committee sent a notice to U.S. bishops outlining a national campaign in which all Catholics would be invited to sign a pledge to join the Legion of Decency.[12] Over the following months, the Legion—whose campaign against the movies was enhanced by radio addresses, newspaper editorials, and several mass demonstrations—received nearly twenty million pledges.

The Legion soon pressured the Hays office to create the Production Code Administration (PCA), a mechanism to enforce the code, and implemented its own system of film classification. Within a matter of a few years, this group had galvanized Catholic pressure against movies containing "offensive" treatments of sex, crime, religion, and other subjects, and it had assured Catholics a loud voice in the collective process of approving screen content.

During the late 1930s and 1940s, amidst widespread political censorship, few movies that treated religious subjects provoked controversy. A famous exception was *Gone with the Wind* (1939), which raised eyebrows and tempers with the "blasphemous" word *damn*.[13] In 1951, however, a small art film, Roberto Rossellini's *The Miracle,* inflamed Catholics and resulted in one of the most significant censorship struggles in the history of the U.S. film industry. The movie, as critic Bosley Crowther summarizes it, is the story of "a poor, simple-minded girl [who] is tending a herd of goats on a mountainside one day, when a bearded stranger passes. Suddenly it strikes her fancy that he is St. Joseph, her favorite saint, and that he has come to take her to heaven, where she will be happy and free. While she pleads with him to transport her, the stranger gently plies the girl with wine, and when she is in a state of tumult, he apparently ravishes her."[14] The seduced peasant woman bears a child whom she imagines she acquired through a miraculous conception. Because the film appeared to question, if not ridicule, Christian dogma, it blatantly violated the MPPDA Code.

U.S. Customs passed *The Miracle,* and in New York State it was licensed twice, without subtitles in 1949 and a year later when it played as part of a trilogy of short films with English subtitles. Twelve days after *The Miracle* opened at the Paris Theatre in New York City, the Legion of Decency officially condemned it as "a sacrilegious and blasphemous mockery of Christian and religious truth."[15] In his movie-review journal, *Motion Picture Herald,* Martin Quigley declared the film an "outrage" and "repugnant to American instincts." He also decried *The Miracle's* "thinly veiled symbolism as an attack not only on Christian faith, but on all religion." Edward T. McCaffrey, the New York City commissioner of licenses and a former head of the Catholic War Veterans in New York, declared *The Miracle* "officially and personally blasphemous" and ordered the Paris Theatre to remove it "on penalty of having the license of the theatre revoked."[16] The Paris closed for five days, the amount of time it took the film's distributor, Joseph B. Burstyn, to win a restraining order in the state court denying McCaffrey's authority to censor a film already licensed by the New York State censors. This order not only forbade McCaffrey from interfering with *The Miracle* on the grounds that he was "not the protector of a large proportion of our citizens or even of all of them"[17] but also challenged the alliance between Catholic leaders and local politicians.

Shortly after *The Miracle* reopened on January 7, 1951, New York's Cardinal Spellman read a mass in St. Patrick's Cathedral calling on Christians "not only of the New York Archdiocese but in all of the U.S." to boycott theatres showing the film. The cardinal proclaimed that the film "blasphemously and sacrilegiously implies a submission to the very inspired word of God"; he also attacked the laws that permitted the film's showing. "If the present law is so weak and inadequate to cope with this desperate situation," he said, "then all right-thinking citizens should unite to change and strengthen the Federal and State statutes so as to make it impossible for anyone to profit financially by blasphemy, immorality and sacrilege."[18] Catholics formed Catholic Action, a coalition of such groups as the Catholic War Veterans and the New York Holy Name Society, and demonstrated in front of the Paris Theatre. The Ancient Order of Hibernians telegraphed Governor Thomas Dewey demanding that he close the movie. The largest demonstration, held on Sunday, January 14, included more than a thousand picketers carrying placards with such sentiments as "This picture is an insult to every decent woman and her mother," "This picture is blasphemous," and "This is the kind of picture the communists want."[19] Protesters also chanted "Don't enter that cesspool!" and "Don't look at that filth!" but they did not physically attempt to prevent anyone from entering the theatre.

Catholics opposed to *The Miracle* convinced the chairman of the Board of Regents of New York State to appoint a three-member committee to review the state censors'process of issuing movie licenses. The Board of Regents unanimously declared *The Miracle* "sacrilegious" and revoked the Paris Theatre's license on grounds that "mockery or profaning of beliefs that are sacred to any portion of our citizenship is abhorrent to the laws of this great state." However, Allen Tate, a Catholic poet and critic, challenged the Board of Regents' ruling in a letter to the *New York Times:*

> The charge against "The Miracle" is sacrilege, a theological category different in kind from that of public morals or public decency. The question then arises: Is there any institution in the United States, civil or religious, which has the legitimate authority to suppress

> books and motion pictures, however disagreeable they
> may be to certain persons on theological grounds? In
> my opinion, there is no such institution under a sys-
> tem that separates church and state.

This statement foreshadowed the larger argument against
any officially sanctioned film censorship whatsoever.[20]

Despite losing an appeal on the New York ruling, in Feb-
ruary 1952 Burstyn succeeded in bringing his case to the
Supreme Court. Three months afterward, Justice Tom C.
Clark drafted the unanimous Court opinion that reversed *The
Mutual Film Corporation v. Industrial Commission of Ohio,* the
1915 case that had declared motion pictures were part of "a
business pure and simple," not "speech" protected by the First
Amendment. Clark found the New York law under which *The
Miracle* had been censored unconstitutional and denied the
Court's right to use "sacrilege" as a legal standard by which to
measure a movie, finding that "the state has no legitimate interest in protecting any or all religions from views distasteful
to them which is sufficient to justify prior restraint upon the
expression of those views. It is not the business of government
in our nation to suppress real or imagined attacks upon a particular religious doctrine, whether they appear in publications, speeches, or motion pictures."[21] This decision crippled
nearly all official censorship; more significant in the context
of this study, it diminished sharply the Legion's ability to ex-
ert any control over movies. As Richard Corliss writes, after
the *Miracle* decision "the Legion had realized that a simple
massing of laity in front of a theatre might not be enough to
force an indepedent-minded exhibitor or distributor to
knuckle under to the pressure that had been successful in
Hollywood."[22] *The Miracle* case changed the course of movie

censorship while demonstrating that religious protesters no longer had the power to censor they had once wielded.

Twenty years later, *Jesus Christ Superstar* (1973), *Godspell* (1973), *Brother Sun, Sister Moon* (1973), and *Nasty Habits* (1976), which all presented liberal interpretations of the Bible, failed to illicit great protest.[23] Actions fizzled even against *Nasty Habits,* a spoof many religious leaders considered blasphemous because it set the Watergate scandal in a cloistered convent. Yet the political, legal, and religious pendulum was about to swing rightward. By 1976, a coalition that became known as the New Christian Right had begun to formalize a cultural agenda and grow more confrontational, and Evangelicals, who had become "a distinct segment of the American religious community," led the charge.[24] A loose coalition of Christians who had in common a traditional gospel message, Evangelicism quickly became one of the largest and fastest-growing religious movements in America, reaching an estimated size of thirty to fifty million by the early 1980s. In 1976, a large part of this growth could be attributed to Jimmy Carter's election to the presidency.[25]

Although Carter, a southern Baptist, was considered by many a liberal Christian, not long after he avowed that he was "born again," *Newsweek* declared 1976 the "Year of the Evangelical" and Evangelicals acted as if Carter was their spokesman. Many conservative Protestant and Catholic Evangelicals would soon use the popularity of the movement to advance their agendas, opposing abortion, pornography, and homosexuality and supporting prayer in schools.[26]

In the late 1970s, the spread of Evangelicalism coincided with and profited from a rapidly expanding network of television ministries, including those of Oral Roberts, Jimmy Swaggart, Pat Robertson, and Jimmy (and Tammy)

Bakker. But the most notable model for hundreds of
emerging conservative Christian organizations was the
Moral Majority, formed in 1979 by the charismatic Jerry Falwell, which embraced "absolute" Christian values and activist politics. When in 1980 Falwell took some credit for the
election of Ronald Reagan to the presidency, it appeared
that the Moral Majority, more than any other religious
group, had succeeded in gaining true political power.[27]

By the mid to late 1970s, the Religious Right came
to view campaigns against movies as extensions of their
broader activism on life-style and other issues. In 1977,
Franco Zeffirelli's *Jesus of Nazareth,* a made-for-television
movie, tested conservatives' commitment to a cultural
agenda. Based on a script by Anthony Burgess, Zeffirelli's
film of the Christ story was intended to absolve Jews of
killing Jesus. "What happened in His passion," Zeffirelli
stated, "cannot be charged against all of the Jews, without
distinction, then alive, nor against the Jews of today." Like
other liberal interpretations of the Bible during the same
period, Zeffirelli wanted his film to explore Christ's human
side and ignore his divinity; Zeffirelli's Christ would be a
man incapable of miracles. He said, "I see Jesus as an ordinary man—gentle, fragile, simple. Of course the public is
going to be annoyed that I am destroying their myths."[28]

Word of Zeffirelli's plan to depict a human Christ spread
among Fundamentalist groups during the months preceding
the movie's scheduled television premiere. Bob Jones III,
president of Bob Jones University in South Carolina, among
others, had concluded from Zeffirelli's prerelease statements
that *Jesus of Nazareth* would deny entirely Christ's divinity.
When Jones urged "good Christians" to boycott all products
produced by the film's sponsor, General Motors, supporters

immediately did so and sent GM nearly twenty thousand letters of protest. As a result, a GM spokesperson, Philip Workman, told the media, "General Motors has decided not to exercise its option to sponsor the TV special, 'Jesus of Nazareth.' This decision reflects our conclusion that commercial sponsorship could be regarded as inappropriate to the subject of the film. We continue to admire its purpose and artistic merit."[29] Procter and Gamble stepped in, and the six-hour film was broadcast on April 3 and 10, as scheduled. Zeffirelli as well as some religious leaders who had seen the movie, however, expressed their anger that GM had been intimidated by the "psychological terrorism" of Fundamentalist protesters, most of whom had not seen the film.

In 1980, the British satire *Monty Python's Life of Brian* provoked protests from an ecumenical mix. When Warner Brothers/Orion Pictures distributed the film in the United States, the Roman Catholic Archdiocese of New York, which had never publicly criticized a movie, condemned *Brian* for its irreverence. Since the movie follows the life of a fictional character, Brian, who is born in a nearby stable at the same time as Christ, the archdiocese deplored the film as a "mockery of Christ's life." Warner Brothers' claim that the movie "is satire, it is a spoof, and it should be viewed in that content" did not deflect protests.[30] The Lutheran Council, the Episcopal Church, and the National Council of Churches condemned the movie. In addition, three Jewish groups representing a thousand Orthodox rabbis formally criticized the film as "blasphemous, sacrilegious, and an incitement to possible violence."[31] During the following months, protests against *Brian* resulted in prior censorship when several exhibitors canceled their plans to show the movie. Theatres in New York, South Carolina, Maine, and

Louisiana, for example, either opened the film, then closed it when faced with protests, or refused to schedule the film at all.

While not as great as the controversy surrounding *Brian,* the U.S. release of Jean-Luc Godard's *Je Vous Salue Marie (Hail Mary)* in 1985 created disturbances in front of several "art" theatres when it opened. As with Rossellini's *Miracle,* nearly all the protests against *Hail Mary* were staged by Catholics. The film, set in contemporary times, features a teenage gas-station attendant and basketball enthusiast named Marie—thought to represent the Virgin Mary—who becomes pregnant without intercourse. Catholic protesters viewed this as a mockery of the Virgin Birth, although many admitted that they had not seen the movie and were basing their views on Pope John Paul II's condemnation, relayed through a Vatican spokesperson. While Godard defended his film, thousands gathered to hear the pope recite the rosary to atone for insults inflicted on the Holy Virgin by *Hail Mary.* Thereupon, Godard asked his Italian distributor, Aldo Addobbati, to withdraw the movie from Rome as soon as possible. Local authorities in Versailles and Rio de Janeiro, both cities in Catholic countries, officially banned *Hail Mary* with varying degrees of success.[32]

In America mass protests were the primary form of pressure against the film. When *Hail Mary* made its U.S. premiere at the New York Film Festival on October 9, 1985, hundreds of Catholics demonstrated in front of Lincoln Center's Alice Tully Hall. Representing numerous Catholic groups, the demonstrators carried placards reading "Hail Mary—Tax-Funded Anti-Catholicism" and "New York State Supplied Vicious Funds for the Vicious Attack on the Catholic Church." They chanted "Shame! Shame!" and "Ave Maria," sprinkled holy water on theatregoers, and marched in circles carrying lit candles.[33] At the same time, many left-wing Catholics nevertheless praised *Hail Mary,* and the film won a prize from the International Catholic Cinema Office at the Berlin Film Festival the year of its release. Still, that protests in New York, Boston, Chicago, Hollywood, Omaha, and Birmingham to varying degrees achieved censorious results showed that conservative religious groups were once again flexing their political muscle in the cultural arena.

No movie housed the collective rage of religious groups as did Martin Scorsese's *The Last Temptation of Christ* which inspired protest and conflict for five years before its release in 1988. When the first draft of the screenplay by Paul Schrader was secretly distributed to several religious leaders in 1983, a group of Protestant women, the Evangelical Sisterhood, and several Fundamentalist groups including the Moral Majority published a newsletter asking people to protest against Gulf & Western, which owned the studio producing the film, Paramount Pictures. Almost immediately, approximately five hundred protest letters a day began pouring into offices at Gulf & Western. Barry Diller, chairman of the G & W Board of Directors, grew anxious not only over the letters, but also because of the film's escalating budget. Diller confronted Scorsese and Harry Ufland, Scorsese's agent at the time. "I don't feel enthusiastic enough [about the film]," Diller reportedly told Scorsese, "to undergo all the problems I would have to undergo."[34] By the time Scorsese and Ufland offered Paramount a scaled-down budget, the studio had decided to abandon the project.

Fear of religious controversy extended from Paramount to the United Artists theatre chain, at the time the second largest in the country. Salah Hassanein, head of United Artists, told

Scorsese: "You people can produce a film, you can act in it, you can direct it, and you can distribute it. But when the audience doesn't like something or when their religious beliefs are offended, they don't find where you are, they go where they saw it last. I don't want it in my theatres. Religious films are just too much trouble."[35] For the next four years, the film industry was unified in its rejection of a potentially big-budget religious film that would certainly stir controversy.

In 1987, Scorcese changed agents from Ufland to the Creative Artists Agency's Mike Ovitz, and a contract with Universal and Cineplex Odeon quickly followed. Finally, *Last Temptation* went into production in October. Anticipating religious pressure, Universal hired Tim Penland, a born-again Christian and head of a marketing company specializing in Fundamentalist interests, to serve as a "religious" liaison between the studio and religious groups. On February 29, 1988, as the principal photography neared completion, Penland coordinated an agreement with Universal, the American Family Association, Bill Bright's Campus Crusade for Christ, and other groups, guaranteeing these groups a private prescreening of the film in June. By midspring, religious leaders, some of whom had read one of the early versions of the screenplay, charged the makers of *Last Temptation* with blasphemy. A newsletter published by Baptist minister John Probst's Media Focus urged other groups to express their concern over *Last Temptation* by writing or calling Tom Pollock, chairman of MCA, Universal's parent company.[36]

Scorsese completed shooting the film but reported that there would be postproduction delays. When Universal announced that the film would not be ready for the scheduled screening, religious leaders exploded and Penland quit his post. Rev. Donald Wildmon reportedly said, "I've waited six

months and I am not waiting any longer." The Campus Crusade urged Christians to increase their letter-writing and tele-
phoning campaigns. Don Beehler, a spokesperson for the
Campus Crusade who had read and objected to the script,
told United Press International, "We'd like to make this the
last temptation of Universal to make a film that is going to de-
fame the name of Jesus Christ."[37] Universal thereupon issued
a statement emphasizing that "delays in the post-production
phase are not uncommon in the motion picture industry,"
and Scorsese offered to screen an unfinished version of the
film for Evangelicals on July 12. Wildmon and other religious
leaders, however, considered Universal's schedule change a
deliberate breach of faith and declined Scorsese's invitation;
they were already preparing for battle.

The prerelease furor over *Last Temptation* escalated on July
12, a day on which, simultaneously, several conservative leaders issued public condemnations of the film, an unfinished
print was screened for mainline religious leaders in New York,
and Evangelicals met in Los Angeles to begin coordinating
their protests. Wildmon called on Universal Pictures to cancel plans to release *Last Temptation* and warned the studio that
it would be committing "financial suicide" if it did not. Basing
his comments on a script that journalists speculated was the
1983 Paul Schrader version, Wildmon told a United Press International reporter, "[The film] is absolutely the most perverted, distorted account of the historical and Biblical Jesus I
have ever read."[38] Wildmon especially objected to a line that
had been deleted from the shooting script: while Scorsese's
Jesus, on the cross, fantasizes that he is making love to Mary
Magdalene, he tells her, "God sleeps between your legs." Wildmon may have not known the line had been excised when he
distributed more than two hundred copies of this early script

to religious leaders around the country along with a letter urging them to send petitions of protest to their local theaters.

In California, more than twelve hundred Christian radio stations condemned the film. Larry Poland's Mastermedia group placed a full-page advertisement in the *Hollywood Reporter,* signed by Christian professionals in the film and television industry and concluding:

> This film maligns the character, blasphemes the deity, and distorts the message of Jesus.
>
> We, the undersigned, professional members of the film and television community, ask that this film not be released.
>
> Whether the gain is a hundred million dollars or thirty pieces of silver makes no difference. Our Lord was crucified once on a cross. He doesn't deserve to be crucified a second time on celluloid.

Poland further urged Christians to boycott the products and services of Universal and MCA. Meanwhile, Mastermedia helped organize a news conference at the Registry Hotel, located near Universal City. There Poland reminded an ad-hoc coalition of southern California religious leaders of Pope John Paul II's entreaty to the industry: "It is in . . . the spirit of the Pope . . .," Poland told the committee and the press, "that we call this meeting today." Finally, he encouraged all Christians to make known their desire to destroy every print of *Last Temptation*.[39]

Religious leaders including Bill Bright, president and founder of Campus Crusade for Christ; Rev. Jude Hayford of the Church of the Way; Rev. Lloyd John Ogilvie of Hollywood Presbyterian Church; and Tim Penland outlined their objections to *Last Temptation*. As Pat A. Broeske recounted in the *Los Angeles Times,* they complained

> that the film portrays Jesus Christ as a mentally deranged and lust-driven man who . . . in a dream sequence, comes down from the cross and has a sexual relationship with Mary Magdalene.
>
> That Universal Pictures violated written agreements to give a select group of Christian leaders a screening "far in advance of the release date," which the religious leaders said would have allowed them to make suggestions to the filmmakers.
>
> That Universal's attempt to profit at the box office at the expense of millions of Christians . . . represents a frightening example of a major film studio's setting aside public responsibility for financial gain.[40]

Attacks against the film grew more grandiose. Bill Bright lamented that "a handful of people with great wealth and depraved minds are corrupting the world," while James Dobson, president of Focus on the Family, decried the film on his weekly radio broadcast as "the most blasphemous evil attack on the Church and the cause of Christ in the history of entertainment."[41] Ministers announced Universal's telephone number to their congregations and provided lists of MCA-owned companies to encourage private boycotts. Meanwhile, Rev. Donald Wildmon had contacted some 170,000 pastors, was mailing 2.5 million "action packets," and had already secured agreements not to show the movie from all the theatres in San Antonio, Texas.

While Evangelicals were campaigning against *Last Temptation* in Los Angeles without having seen the film, many of the liberal, mainline Christians who had watched the movie on July 12 in New York had begun defending it. "Overall, I had a very, very positive reaction," Episcopal bishop Paul Moore of New York said. "I saw nothing blasphemous in it."[42] In a letter published in the *New York Times* two weeks after the screening, Moore elaborated: "In a day and age when fundamentalism of all kinds seems to be growing in the Church, this [film] is a most important and dramatic statement of the traditional teaching of Roman Catholic and Protestant churches, which was originally adopted at the Council of Chalcedon in 451. That Council defined Christ as fully human, fully divine and one person. That so-called christological definition has stood the test of the ages. The movie affirms the classic definition of Christ."[43]

Another attendee, Baptist minister Robert Maddox, said, "The inner struggle [Kazantzákis and Scorsese] portray Jesus having—questioning, the desire for a real life, the lack of desire to die on the cross— really resonated with me. When I was a pastor, I preached that. I felt Jesus really did have those struggles." Rev. William Fore, head of communications for the National Council of Churches, held that the film was "consistent with all important streams of Christian theology" and charged, "It's a shame that some Christians appear to be so unsure of their faith that they can't stand the thought of people seeing something different." Fore also found *Last Temptation* compelling because of the questions it raises about faith and divinity. "How is Jesus man, or is he God?" Fore asked. "Now I think that's an interesting question for a film to raise . . . . He's ambivalent. He's full of anxiety. He's human. And he rises above all that and accepts God's will to be the Savior." Continued widespread criticism of *Last Temptation,* however, far outweighed these favorable responses.[44]

On July 15, Bill Bright, the prominent southern California Evangelical leader, offered to reimburse Universal Pictures for all the money the studio had invested in the making of *Last Temptation* in exchange for all existing prints of the film, which he promised he would destroy. Before Universal responded, another controversy erupted. On July 16, the radical Rev. R. L. Hymers, Jr., led about two hundred members of the Fundamentalist-Baptist Tabernacle of Los Angeles to picket outside of Universal Studios. Four days later, Hymers organized a demonstration outside of MCA chair Lew Wasserman's Beverly Hills home and allegedly said, "These Jewish producers with a lot of money are taking a swipe at our religion." Protesters carried banners reading "Universal is like Judas Iscariot," "The Greatest Story Ever Distorted," "Wasserman Fans Anti-Semitism," and "Wasserman Endangers Israel." During a subsequent protest, an airplane circled Universal trailing a banner that read, "Wasserman Fans Jewish Hatred with 'Last Temptation,'" while protesters chanted, "Jewish Money, Jewish Money," and one of the picketers enacted a movie producer lashing Christ, portrayed by another demonstrator carrying a cross.[45] Referring to Universal as a company whose decision-making body is dominated by non-Christians, Rev. Donald Wildmon appeared to encourage anti-Semitism in a flyer mailed to half a million pastors throughout the United States. Rev. Jerry Falwell weighed in to predict that *Last Temptation* would "create a wave of anti-Semitism."[46] While Archbishop Roger M. Mahony distinguished the U.S. Catholic Conference's moral criticism of the film from others' anti-Semitism, the media bombarded the latest controversy over *Last Temptation* with a barrage of editorials.

On July 21, as the brouhaha over the film itself and Hymers's and others' anti-Semitic remarks continued, Universal Pictures responded to Bill Bright's offer to buy all prints of *Last Temptation* with an open letter published as a full-page ad in *Variety,* the *Hollywood Reporter,* the *Los Angeles Times,* the *New York Times,* the *Washington Post,* and the *Atlanta Constitution:*

> We, at Universal Pictures, have received your proposal in which you have offered to buy "The Last Temptation of Christ" which you would then destroy so that no one could ever see it. While we understand the deep feelings and convictions which have promoted this offer, we believe that to accept it would threaten the fundamental freedoms of religion and expression promised to all Americans under our Constitution. . . . You have expressed a concern that the content of the film be "true." But whose truth? If everyone in America agreed on religious, political and artistic truths, there would be no need for our constitutional guarantees. Only in totalitarian states are all people forced to accept one version of the truth. . . . In the United States, no one sect or constitution has the power to set boundaries around each person's freedom to explore religious and philosophical questions whether through speech, books or film. These freedoms protect all of us. They are precious. They are not for sale.

A spokesperson for Campus Crusade for Christ criticized Universal's letter as "disappointing" because Bill Bright's offer was "sincere." On the same day the ad appeared, an estimated six to seven hundred Christians sponsored by Los Angeles radio station KKLA-FM picketed the MCA head-

quarters. Universal Pictures' letter seemed only to antago-
nize opponents of *Last Temptation.*"[47]

While several entertainment reporters such as Gary
Franklin of KABC-TV opined that Universal should not release *Last Temptation,* most editorials, as Michael Medved
correctly points out in an otherwise biased account of the
protests, supported Scorsese, Universal, and the film. A *Los
Angeles Times* editorial, for example, ended: "In the American tradition the public, by what it reads and views, decides
what ideas prevail. This extraordinary freedom can shelter
abuses and excuses. But the sum of the experience leaves
no doubt about the wisdom of those who drafted these
guarantees and their confidence in the value of an open
competition of ideas. There is no good reason to fear that
test." Roger Ebert asked, "Why is it that censors seem to attack the serious works of art, and ignore the trivial ones?"
He ended his editorial tirade against self-appointed Christian censors: "There is, I believe, a temptation the censors
should honestly ask themselves if they have yielded to. It is
the temptation to commit the sin of pride." In Hollywood,
Jack Valenti, president of the MPAA, issued a statement supported by all of the major Hollywood studios. He attacked
protesters for committing the sin of prior censorship. "Protest whenever and whatever you choose? Of course. But prevent a creative work from being judged by the public? No.
Not now or anytime. No prior censorship, ever." He went
on: "The key issue, the only issue, is whether or not self-
appointed groups can prevent a film from being exhibited
to the public, or a book from being published, or a piece of
art from being shown. . . . The major companies of the
MPAA support MCA/Universal in its absolute right to offer
to the people whatever movie it chooses."[48]

Last Temptation was still scheduled for an August release

and, as far as anyone knew, Scorsese and Universal had made no concessions to the protesters.

Petitions, phone calls, street protests, written criticism, and anti-*Temptation* radio broadcasts increased on all Christian radio and television stations. On July 25 in Waco, Texas, for example, the *Waco Tribune-Herald* reported that fourteen thousand Christians had signed petitions against showing *Last Temptation* in their district, about 8 percent of the county. Pat Buchanan, the nationally syndicated columnist and conservative spokesperson, condemned the film in a *Philadelphia Inquirer* op-ed piece entitled "Anything for a Buck: Hollywood's Sleazy Image of Christ." Buchanan challenged Valenti's and other industry leaders' sensitivity in supporting the film:

> The issue is not whether "The Last Temptation of Christ" can be shown, but whether such a film should be shown. . . . With "The Last Temptation of Christ," Hollywood is assaulting the Christian community in a way it would never dare assault the black community, the Jewish community or the gay community. . . . Christians, America's unfashionable majority, may be mocked; their preachers may be parodied in book and on film; their faith may be portrayed as superstitious folly. And secular society, invoking the First Amendment, will rush to the defense of the defamers, not the defamed. The battle over "Last Temptation" is one more skirmish in the century's struggle over whose values, whose beliefs shall be exalted in American culture, and whose may be derided and disparaged.

Buchanan's article was widely reprinted, admired, and quoted by groups opposed to *Last Temptation,* and it quickened the rising tide of protest.

Despite warnings from Anthony Bosco, a Roman Catholic bishop from Greensburg, Pennsylvania, and many others that protests and public condemnation would only give *Last Temptation* free publicity, religious leaders escalated their campaign.[50] Radio broadcasters Mother Angelica, James Dobson, Pat Robertson, and Paul Crouch urged their approximately eleven million listeners to boycott MCA products and to continue protesting against the film. Mother Angelica, founder and head of the Catholic-oriented Eternal World Network, described *Last Temptation* as "the most satanic movie ever made," declared that it "will destroy Christianity," and warned that "this movie will bring the kind of Chastisement our country has never seen before." Never far from the controversy, Wildmon vented his spleen over Universal's refusal to submit to Fundamentalists' demands. Borrowing a line from Clint Eastwood, he challenged Universal to release the film. "Go ahead," he said, "make my day."[51]

In this "Holy War" or "Culture War," as newspaper articles often referred to the controversy, no matter what anyone on either side wrote, said, or did, victory or defeat depended on what they achieved. For their part, Universal and Scorsese promised to release the film they had spent so much time and money to produce, yet during the first few days of August, the scale appeared to tilt in favor of the protesters. On August 1, several days after Universal affirmed that it and Cineplex Odeon Films would "stand behind the principle of freedom of expression and hope that the American public will give the film and the filmmaker a fair chance," managers of several theatre chains expressed their uneasiness about scheduling the film. Most notably, James Edwards, Jr., owner of 150 Edwards Theaters across the nation, warned that unless "certain changes" were made to *Last Temptation*, which he had heard was a film "demeaning to Christ," he would not show the film in any of his theatres. This statement suggested that religious pressure would in fact produce censorious results.[52]

On August 4, a group called Concerned Women for America placed an advertisement in the *Wall Street Journal* urging stockholders to sell their stock in MCA, as letters continued pouring into Universal Pictures' office, and the press recorded the director Franco Zeffirelli still caught up in a dispute with B'Nai B'rith and other Jewish groups over whether he had uttered anti-Semitic slurs against the producers of *Last Temptation*. Universal Pictures had just received Scorsese's film. Exhausted by the barrage of attacks and allegations, perhaps aware of the upcoming press conference at which Wildmon planned to announce a new wave of actions, the studio went on the offensive, issuing the following statement: "Few motion pictures in recent memory have generated such heated debate, especially when so few people have actually seen the film. Rumors have proliferated. Exaggerations, misconceptions and scenes taken out of context have added fuel to the fire. The best thing that can be done for "The Last Temptation of Christ" at this time is to make it available to the American people and allow them to draw their own conclusions based on fact, not fallacy." The film, originally scheduled for release September 23, would be shown on August 12 in nine selected cities in the United States and Canada. This decision, which allowed the studio to capitalize on the publicity the protests were giving the movie, provoked religious groups once again to step up their attacks.[53]

Angered by the studio's sudden decision to release the film nearly six weeks ahead of schedule, Jerry Falwell publicly "declared war" on Universal Pictures and parent company MCA in an address to the National Press Club. Falwell detailed his objections to the film, beginning with the "sex scene": "Without question, the most obscene part of this film is the 30-minute 'dream sequence' during which Jesus and Mary Magdalene make love on blankets spread over straw." Like many others who had not yet seen a cut of the film, Falwell was basing his remarks on the early Paul Schrader screenplay, not the shooting script. More than any particular scene, however, the film's entire "blasphemous" interpretation of the Bible enraged him: "Neither the label 'fiction' nor the First Amendment gives Universal the right to libel, slander and ridicule the most central figure in world history—and the one whom countless millions have worshipped and served, namely our Lord Jesus Christ. . . . This film is not merely presenting a different slant on theology or a creative, fictitious view of Christ—it is pure blasphemy and morally reprehensive." Falwell listed five ways to boycott MCA, then closed his remarks with a final call to arms: "I am to see the day when Christians and their faith cannot be ridiculed and maligned without consequence. I am confident that blasphemy against God, as is seen in 'The Last Temptation of Christ,' will not go unpunished." MCA/Universal would be punished, Falwell implied, either through some divine intervention or by himself and other Christians.[54]

The events that occurred between August 6 and August 12, the day *Last Temptation* was released, suggest that while in several instances prior restraint was certainly a goal, religious groups were ultimately satisfied simply to demonstrate how consolidated and massive their opposition to Scorsese's "blasphemous" film was. Despite Rev. R. L. Hymers leading a hundred Fundamentalists in another protest outside of a synagogue where he believed Lew Wasserman, then MCA chair, worshipped, and despite Hymers telling *Variety* that Universal "can probably expect violence" and that "we'll stop the showing of the movie," most of the religious groups continuing to protest against *Last Temptation,* it now seemed, had ceased to believe that complete censorship was possible.[55]

Religious leaders issued more condemnations, more calls to arms. Mother Angelica now not only criticized *Last Temptation,* she warned against seeing it. "This movie is the most blasphemous ridicule of the Eucharist that's ever been perpetrated in this world," she told Eternal World Television Network viewers. "This is a holocaust movie that has the power to destroy souls eternally. I don't want to see innocent people losing their souls because some people don't care." On August 9, Rev. Donald Wildmon joined director Martin Scorsese and film critic David Sterritt on ABC TV's *Nightline* and reiterated his opinion that *Last Temptation* was a "blasphemous" film. Confessing that he still had not seen the film, Wildmon admitted that he decried any "human" portrait of Christ, particularly one based on the screenplay he had read: "A major film about Christ, is in essence, by its very nature, a sermon about this Christ. And to present this Christ in a manner in which all scripture and all of history tells us is contradictory to everything we know of him—is rather offensive to millions of people. He's not a weak, insecure, vacillating, mentally unstable person. There's not a picture of him anywhere in scripture of being that kind of person." While Scorsese defended the right to "explore God in our own way," Christians continued to mobilize against the film during the final prerelease days.[56]

One week before the movie opened, religious protesters seemed in several instances to achieve censorious effects. In Orange County, California, Jim Edwards announced that his chain of theatres would not show the film. The United Artists chain, which owned two thousand screens across the country in 1988, and General Cinema Corporation, which owned 1,339, also announced their refusal to show *Last Temptation*. In Hazleton, Pennsylvania, the city council voted unanimously to oppose the film on grounds that it was blasphemous. During a heated argument among residents and the city council, John Ford, the council president, insisted that his resolution did not actually bar the film from being shown locally, although it did "urge residents not to patronize [the film] and to write filmmakers opposing it."[57]

On August 10, two days before *Last Temptation* was due to open, the U.S. Catholic Church joined primarily Protestant opposition to the film by officially rating the film O—morally offensive—and by advising the country's fifty-three million Catholics that the film perverts Christian values. Richard Hirsh, a spokesperson for the U.S. Catholic Conference that had issued the rating, said, "What we saw in the movie was a weak Christ who is a rather mean and nasty person with little compassion and who is self-centered. But even without all that, the sex and violence and gore would have been reason enough to give it an 'O' rating." Bishop Norman F. McFarland and Rev. Robert Schuller, two prominent religious leaders from southern California, each urged their large congregations to boycott the film. McFarland also denied that the national protest was "an attack on freedom of speech or religion. It is a cry of anguish from millions of hurt and offended people whose deepest religious sensibilities and most revered convictions of faith are being assaulted." In a letter issued to viewers of his *Hour of Power* television program, Rev. Schuller said: "I will not walk protest lines. Nor will I take valuable Sunday morning time . . . to speak on such a negative subject. But I personally will not see this film. Neither will my family nor will my close friends. And I will encourage everyone who I can influence not to support this motion picture." As if all this criticism by prominent religious leaders wasn't enough,

Catholics solicited Mother Teresa's views on the film. On August 10, Robert Ziener, National Chairman of Rosaries for Peace, informed the press that Mother Theresa herself believed that if Catholics intensified their prayers, then "Our Blessed Mother [Mary] will see that this film is removed from your land."[58]

On August 11, the day before *Last Temptation's* scheduled opening, Citizens for a Universal Appeal, an ad hoc coalition of religious groups and leaders from Orange County, organized a protest in front of Unversal Studios in Los Angeles that attracted an estimated twenty-five thousand Protestants, Catholics, and some Jews. Carrying wooden crosses and Bibles, many of those who gathered chanted "J-e-s-u-s" and "Boycott MCA." They waved placards reading "Don't Crucify Christ Again," "Some Things Are Sacred," "Stop This Attack on Christianity," "Universal Is Anti-Christian," "Father Forgive Them For They Know Not What They Do," "Don't Distort History," "Don't Trash My Lord," "Jesus Is Not to be Mocked," "Don't Crucify Christ Again," "Lead Us Not into Temptation," "Our Lord Jesus Christ Reigns," "Read the Bible; Know the True Story," "Scripture Not Scripts," and "Holyword Not Hollywood." At a lunchtime rally, the omnipresent Rev. Donald Wildmon, clearly impressed by the turnout, addressed the crowd: "We're unleashing a movement," he beamed. "Christian-bashing is over. . . . We demand that anti-Christian stereotypes come to an end."[59]

In addition to the mass rally, a group called the American Society for the Defense of Tradition, Family, and Property (TFP) placed full-page advertisements in that day's *Los Angeles Times* and *New York Times,* a final and apparently desperate appeal to Universal to stop the release of the film:

One might object that freedom of religion gives everyone the right to say whatever they want about religion. Undoubtedly this is the principle of religious freedom. However, this right does not extend to the point of permitting one to attack the rights of a third party. Hence, if Our Lord is the object of abuse, Christians are also affected. . . . We would like to make a request: Let the TFP and any other like-minded organization see the film's final version and publish an opinion within a few days before its official release. This will create the conditions for a real debate, an honest disagreement and a fair divergence of opinion before the American public, and avert a public blasphemy.

Like Falwell, TFP was accusing Universal of libeling Christ, and once again the tactic did not work.[60]

Universal released *Last Temptation* on August 12 in Los Angeles, New York, San Francisco, Washington, D.C., Chicago, Seattle, Minneapolis, Montreal, and Toronto, as planned, and protesters met the premiere at nearly every theatre in all nine cities (photo 8); no exhibitor canceled the movie. Fearing violence and vandalism, many theatre managers hired uniformed guards to check personal belongings when moviegoers entered the theatre. Before a first showing of the film at the Cineplex Odeon Cinema in Los Angeles, a protester had sprayed yellow paint onto one of the theatre's windows and over a poster advertising the film. At this same theatre, four hundred protesters demonstrated and handed out biblical tracts to moviegoers and passersby. While there was no violence reported, altercations broke out between patrons and protesters. "When one picketer preached to moviegoers," the *New York Times* re-

ported, "many of the 150 patrons . . . yelled back that they
had a right to see the movie if they wanted to." Inside the
theatre, a man who identified himself as Bobby Bible of
Long Beach shouted: "I think it's been a pretty good movie
until now but I feel that I have to say: This is blasphemous!"
Other people in the audience yelled back "Shhh!" and "Be
quiet!" and one man reportedly bellowed, "Well then, go
see it on video." Security personnel escorted "Bobby Bible"
out of the theatre. After this showing, police found glue
spread on the floor of one of the theatre's restrooms. At Los
Angeles's Century Plaza theatre, a man shouted, "That's not
true!" during the scene when Jesus dreams of making love
with Mary Magdalene. After an usher escorted the man
from the theatre, the audience clapped.[61]

Photo 8. An estimated 25,000 protesters amassed in front of Universal Studios, Los Angeles, on the day before *The Last Temptation of Christ* opened in eight cities in the United States and Canada. Courtesy of Michael Tweed/NYT Pictures.

In New York, several hundred protesters who demonstrated in front of the Ziegfield Theatre stood behind a police barricade, yelling and booing patrons waiting on a long line in ninety-degree heat. One protester shouted, "Get off that line before it's too late." In Washington, the *Washington Post* reported that "more than 300 moviegoers circled the block outside the Avalon Theater on upper Connecticut Avenue. . . . About 50 demonstrators marched in their own circle, jeering those who brought tickets. A dozen D.C. police officers from the Special Chemical Weapons unit patrolled the sidewalk between the theatre and Magruder's supermarket, trying to keep the two groups apart." Some of the Washington protesters also handed out an open letter written by Washington Redskins coach Joe Gibbs urging people to boycott *Last Temptation*. Other demonstrators wheeled a mannequin dressed as Christ. As in New York, police officers were positioned inside of the Avalon Theater and a sign posted at the entrance announced: "The theater will be emptied after each showing of 'The Last Temptation of Christ.' We regret that no stayovers will be permitted. Management reserves the right to inspect all carry-in items." Washington police reported a bomb threat after one of the first showings, but when they emptied the theatre between showings they found nothing. In Chicago, a small band of demonstrators that gathered during the midday heat "by late afternoon . . . had swelled to 400 protesters," according to the *Los Angeles Times*, chanting, "Stop the blasphemy!" and "Jesus Christ was not a sinner."[62]

Three hundred protesters staged a peaceful demonstration in a cordoned-off area in front of a Minneapolis theatre. In Seattle, the number of protesters was about one hundred and fifty. In San Francisco, fifty protesters sang and shouted, while some recited the rosary. Still fewer protesters greeted the premiere of *Last Temptation* in Toronto and Montreal.

While protesters waved placards and shouted in front of theatres, fourteen movie directors met at the Director's Guild of America in a show of support for Scorsese and his

Photo 9. Willem Dafoe as Jesus. Fundamentalists particularly objected to the "sex scene" in which Jesus, while on the cross, imagines making love to Mary Magdelene. Copyright © 1988 by Universal City Studios, Inc. Courtesy of MCA Publishing Rights, a Division of MCA, Inc. All Rights Reserved. Courtesy of the Academy of Motion Picture Arts and Sciences.

film, among them Warren Beatty, Peter Bogdanovich, John Carpenter, Martha Coolidge, Randa Haines, Walter Hill, Michael Mann, and Sydney Pollack. They issued a press release that proclaimed "the right of individuals to decide for themselves what they will see and think," and at a press conference, Beatty appealed to theatre owners to join them "in resisting any effort by any pressure group at all to curtail free expression" and called upon studios "to continue to finance and distribute material that is not safe." Pollack said, "Christianity survived for 2,000 years. It will survive Martin Scorsese's $6.5 million movie."[63]

During the weeks that followed *Last Temptation's* successful premiere, the size of the audiences and the number of protesters steadily decreased.[64] When the film opened in an additional thirty-five cities over the next month, protest groups in several towns and cities attempted and achieved censorship. Relatively small protests accompanied *Last Temptation* when it opened in Boston and Philadelphia, two traditionally conservative cities. In Boston, the dozen or more demonstrators outside of the USA Paris Cinema on Boylston Street in the Back Bay were greeted by counterprotesters from an organization called Artists and Writers Against Censorship. Religious leaders in Philadelphia reacted "mildly" to *Last Temptation* when they screened the film the day before it premiered on August 19. Archbishop Bevilacqua, one of the few viewers to raise strong opposition to the film, wrote to MCA chair Lew Wasserman: "It is my intention to urge all the faithful in the Archdiocese of Philadelphia to avoid viewing this film, especially those who might be enticed by publicity to do so. Not viewing this film will help them preserve a more authentic grasp of the true identity of Jesus Christ." When the film opened at the Ritz 5 Theatre, however, the *Philadelphia Inquirer* reported that only eleven protesters greeted it, with banners proclaiming "Christ Never Sinned" and "We Love You, Jesus."[65]

In New Orleans and in Santa Ana, California, city officials passed resolutions to ban *Last Temptation*. In New Orleans, a police jury in two city districts, St. Bernard and Kenner, supported the ban on *Last Temptation* even though those districts had not planned to show the film. Several hundred protesters greeted *Last Temptation* when it premiered at the Main Place Theatre in the Santa Ana shopping mall, and one of them, city councilman John Acosta, threatened to take legislative action against the film. "I really don't think the First Amendment was meant to cover things like this [movie]," Acosta said. "This is stepping over the line. . . . We need to cleanse our souls a little more in this great community of Santa Ana." The showing, however, continued.[66]

In a similar attempt to censor, an insurance company in Montgomery, Alabama, threatened to cancel its coverage of the Capri Theatre, which had said it would show the movie if it could schedule it. Alabama governor Guy Hunt, the city council, the city's mayor, and the publisher of a local newspaper went on record opposing the showing. Hunt said, "Our nation does not need films which persecute those who believe in the values upon which this nation was built." While the movie played, it languished at the box office. In early September in Pensacola, Florida, a federal district judge blocked a county ordinance banning theatres from showing *Last Temptation*. While the film was again allowed exhibition, the attempted censorship clearly affected the box office, for only fifty people attended the opening.[67]

Official bans in Savannah and Oklahoma City were more successful. In Savannah, the Chatham County Commission passed a resolution encouraging citizens "not to participate in any showing of the movie." When the film was due to open at Oklahoma State University (OSU) in late September, the school's regents demanded that OSU administrators first answer legal and ethical questions related to the separation of church and state and the First Amendment. OSU regents further expressed concern that showing the movie could cause "extensive damage to the public interest of the University" and could "highly offend a major segment of the Oklahoma citizenry." This controversial response caused the university to cancel its plans to show *Last Temptation*.[68] Large, peaceful protests followed the film's premieres in Atlanta, Dallas, and Fort Worth.[69]

In contrast, protest manifested as vandalism at least twice more. On August 27, a print of *Last Temptation* due to be shown in the Salt Lake City Cineplex Odeon Center Theater was stolen and the theatre screen slashed. On September 5, vandals at the Los Angeles Cineplex Odeon Showcase Theater—in which the film had not been scheduled to open—spray painted threats against Universal Pictures executives and slashed seats. One message, written below the movie screen, read: "Lew Wasserman: If you release 'The Last Temptation of Christ,' we will wait years and decimate all Universal property. This message is for your insurance company."[70] This kind of scare tactic had proven effective at *Last Temptation* protests in France.[71]

The reactions to the film proved that even in a year when theologically conservative Protestants had been publicly embarrassed by the Jimmy Swaggart and Jim Bakker sex scandals, the influence on public opinion of religious groups such as Rev. Donald Wildmon's American Family Association and James Dobson's Focus on the Family, like the Moral Majority a decade earlier, remained formidable. Moreover, the controversy reveals how much economic power the Religious Right could wield. Universal Pictures' decision to open *Last Temptation* three weeks ahead of schedule and in only nine metropolitan cities was a bow to this power, while protesters' ability to convince three national theatre chains to refuse the film, and their successes in several small cities around the country in 1988 and afterward, confirm it.[72] Using an array of media resources, the Religious Right spread the word about the "blasphemy" in *Last Temptation* to every hamlet in the country. In addition to the national theatre chains, many communities and local theatre managers were therefore predisposed to refuse the film long before it premiered. When Universal managed to schedule *Last Temptation* in such cities as Savannah and Omaha, the combination of protests and official actions caused censorious effects; in both cases, the film was canceled before it was screened. Prior censorship was also achieved in Montgomery and New Orleans and attempted in Pensacola. That a coalition of Evangelical Protestants and orthodox Catholics had prevented several national theatre chains from scheduling *Last Temptation* and had achieved censorship in a number of cities and towns demonstrated convincingly that the Religious Right was still capable of winning significant victories in the ongoing culture wars.

Beyond proving its power to affect the distribution and exhibition of a single film, protests and other actions by the Religious Right proved an effective strategy for galvanizing an ailing constituency and advertising its concerns. Similar to women, Asian Americans and homosexuals, religious groups had managed over the course of one year to communicate to Hollywood, the wider media, and the American public their unwillingness to tolerate films that maligned their most cherished beliefs.

CONCLUSION

Winners and Losers

I am dead set against censorship. Especially when it emanates from special interest groups who have a highly special conception of what is moral. I have faith in the innate taste of all important film artists, and this taste has already been unmistakably displayed.

Tennessee Williams

Since the institution of the rating system in 1968, U.S. movie censorship has become a complex phenomenon. With the exception of Chapter 1, which explored a censorship controversy due to governmental labeling and found the entire action more an instance of ideological intimidation than of censorship, my primary focus here has been on group protests against movies—examining where, if at all, one can say these acts of protest produced censorial results. But as anyone in the movie industry or any careful observer of it knows, censorship also happens in far broader and less overt ways: movie studios' infamous "script notes," self-censorship, market or economic censorship, and movie ratings. Like the censorships described in this book, none of these actions may be legally defined as "censorship," yet each helps produce a different film than the one its creators had in mind.

Creating a film always requires a long negotiation process that finds most writers and directors inevitably compromising their initial vision. To track the pressures for compromise, one has only to speak to a writer offering a script to a movie studio, review a studio's script notes to that writer, or follow a movie's reediting to achieve a desired rating or appease a vain movie star. Many artists make compromises because of the large sums of money involved; in other words, censorship today is part of the business of filmmaking—perhaps more than in any other art in America.

And censorship remains part of the business of politics in this country. Former GOP presidential candidate Bob Dole learned the rhetoric that wins votes, although he took pains to distinguish his hopes for the industry from calls for censorship. In his "Hollywood" speech delivered on May 31, 1995, in Los Angeles to members of the film industry, Dole pleaded:

> Change is possible—in Hollywood, and across the entertainment industry. There are few national priorities more urgent. I know that good and caring people work in this industry. If they are deaf to the concerns I have raised tonight, it must be because they do not fully understand what is at stake. But we must make them understand. We must make it clear that intolerance does not mean neutrality between love and cruelty, between peace and violence, between right and wrong. Ours is not a crusade for censorship, it is a call for good citizenship.

Dole's denial that he was on a "crusade for censorship" played on liberals' fear of the word. Careful analysis of his entire speech, however, shows that like many other cultural conservatives, Dole in fact had a hit list of works that he believed should never have seen the light of day.

> A line has been crossed—not just of taste, but of human dignity and decency. It is crossed every time sexual violence is given a catchy tune. When teen suicide

is set to an appealing beat. When Hollywood's dream
factories turn out nightmares of depravity. You know
what I mean. I mean "Natural Born Killers," "True Ro-
mance." Films that revel in mindless violence and love-
less sex. . . . The mainstreaming of deviancy must come
to an end, but it will only stop when the leaders of the
entertainment industry recognize and shoulder this
responsibility.

Clearly, Dole favored censoring films that fall outside the
bounds of the values he believed ought to be instilled in all
citizens.[1]

Just as Dole posed as a politician against censorship, liberals who have made clear their desire to radically alter a script
or to impose rules on Hollywood have hidden their intentions
behind an almost reverential commitment to the First Amendment. Like conservatives, liberals at times want it both ways—
to appear to favor the U.S. Constitution's most cherished
amendment but at the same time to influence what movies the
film industry produces and Americans watch. For minority
groups, the temptation to censor has often been as strong as
for majority groups, especially since such censorship is generally viewed as a means of balancing scales that have always
weighed against them. In 1915, outraged by the "racism" in
The Birth of a Nation, the brilliant liberal president of the newly
formed NAACP, W.E.B. DuBois, said, "We are aware now as
then that it is dangerous to limit expression; and yet, without
some limitations, civilization could not endure."[2] More recently, the Committee Against Fort Apache, which consisted
of African Americans and Puerto Ricans, sought by judicial in-
junction to prevent filmmakers from shooting *Fort Apache, the
Bronx,* a movie they claimed grossly stereotyped the South

Bronx. That both of these groups, as well as all other Left groups discussed, largely failed in their attempts to censor testifies to the limited powers of minority protesters in a majoritarian industry. Today the successful censor *has* power, while the unsuccessful censors remain mere protesters, forever voicing their complaints.

As movies such as *Kids* (1995) and *Priest* (1995) stir the by-now-familiar debates among liberals and conservatives, one wonders how and whether these culture wars will ever end. Since 1989, when the art of Andres Serrano and Robert Mapplethorpe triggered some of the most heated and widespread debates over culture in decades, the subject of censorship appears to have reached a plateau of intensity, both sides eager to jump into the fray whenever anything controversial is produced, neither side willing to compromise its core positions, to lose any ground. Controversies over movies have finally become inseparable from the larger debates over culture, dynamic forums in which both sides of the cultural divide can complain, and both, at least temporarily, can assure themselves that their values represent the more correct vision for America. Alexis de Tocqueville's image of an America comprised of fiercely antagonistic groups forever vying for power over each other, yet forever neutralizing each others' attempts at control, has proven especially true in recent years. Still, the questions posed by this study remain: From 1980 to 1995, which side of the cultural divide can claim victory? And what does this victory say about the operation of corporate capitalism in the United States?

Debates over film censorship during these years reflected a culture in conflict over sex, race, family values, and homosexuality as political struggles were fought out in a cultural arena and the "cultural divide" (as former vice pres-

ident Dan Quayle referred to the split between conservatives and liberals) widened. Presidents Reagan and Bush
headed stridently ideological administrations; groups on
the Left expressed growing frustration with a film industry
and a majoritarian culture that stereotyped, silenced, and
distorted their lives.[3]

Among the groups that have protested against movies
during these years—antipornography feminists, Asian
Americans, and gays and lesbians on the Left; religious
groups on the Right—those associated with the New Christian Right achieved the most blatant censorship when three
major movie chains decided not to show *The Last Temptation
of Christ* and several small cities around the country canceled the film's engagements.

More recently, Catholic-led protests disrupted release
plans for the controversial *Priest,* a British movie directed
by Antonia Bird that depicts priests having sex with women
and men. Miramax, the producing company, originally
had scheduled the release on Good Friday, but pressure
from the Catholic League, a Roman Catholic lay group,
forced the film company to postpone the general release
to three days after Easter. The protests were especially effective because Miramax is partially owned and many of its
films are distributed by the Walt Disney Company, known
for its family films. Angered to find Disney connected with
a movie like *Priest,* the Catholic League placed a full-page
advertisement in the *New York Times* and other papers urging a major boycott against Disney and its subsidiaries while
highlighting the offense through comparison:

> Everything's gone awry at Disney. The quintessential
> family values company has recently shown a side to the

public that is very disturbing. To be exact, Disney is the force behind a movie that not only casts priests as being depraved, it explains their depravity by blaming the Catholic Church. . . . Think of it this way. How do you think Jews would react if a movie called "Rabbi" portrayed five rabbis in a depraved condition? Would gays tolerate a movie that showed them to be morally destitute? What about a cruel caricature of African-Americans? To top it off, what if it were the cultural heritage or lifestyle of these groups that best explained their behavior? And just think what would happen if those movies had been scheduled to fall on Yom Kippur, Gay Pride Day or Martin Luther King Day?

A week after this statement appeared, Bob Dole, appearing on *Meet the Press,* singled out *Priest* as a reflection of Hollywood's lack of "family values." Again, a movie found itself the center of cultural conflict, and again political figures and a religious group wished to use a film as a means to assert, as Frank Rich wrote, "their own moral authority." That the movie was censored for U.S. audiences long before its general release and that a production entity could be pressured into changing the film's release date demonstrated the considerable political muscle that religious conservatives still wield.[4]

Such results contrast with how women's groups fared when they acted on their concerns over mainstream movies in 1980. As explored in Chapter 2, antipornography feminists found protests ineffective means in combating the sexism in both pornography and Hollywood films; their actions against *Dressed to Kill* had little if any direct impact on Hollywood filmmakers. But protests were catalysts enabling women to organize politically, and some feminists carried their activism to legal arenas. Moreover, during the ensuing years, such movies as *Thelma and Louise* (1991), which presents stronger, more independent portraits of women, and, more recently, *How to Make an American Quilt* (1995), *Boys on the Side* (1995), *Waiting to Exhale* (1995), and *The First Wives Club* (1996) were signs of positive change. Sexually explicit movies such as *Delta of Venus* (1994), *Showgirls* (1995), and *Jade* (1995) floundered at the box office, and the numbers of NC-17 and R-rated films declined; perhaps some of the demands of women for and against the censorship of pornography have begun to be heard.[5]

More encouraging to feminists, women are changing the film industry from the inside. Today, numerous women hold positions as development executives, at least three head major production entities, and many have produced some of the biggest films being made. While men and women are still hardly equal in Hollywood, such change has been promising to feminists angered by the continued sexism in all the media and in society at large.

Asian Americans who protested against *Year of the Dragon* in 1985 almost immediately found Hollywood willing to listen. Asian Americans have since been portrayed favorably in *The Joy Luck Club* (1993), a movie based on the best-selling novel by Amy Tan and directed by Wayne Wang that lyrically recounts the lives of five Asian women and their daughters. A critical and a commercial success, it represents for Asian Americans a welcome change from *Year of the Dragon* and, more recently, *Falling Down* (1992), which, despite efforts by Warner Brothers, angered some Korean Americans. Oliver Stone's *Heaven and Earth* (1993) centers sympathetically on a strong female Asian character. Set during the Vietnam War, it is told from the vantage point of a young Vietnamese woman who, after being raped by a Vietcong soldier and treated like a whore by American GIs, learns to stand up to men—including the American she marries. That Asian-born directors such as John Woo (*Broken Arrow*) and Ang Lee (*Sense and Sensibility*) have emerged on Hollywood's A-list and that Japanese action-hero Jackie Chan (*Rumble in the Bronx*) has become a bankable star at the U.S. box office portends well for Asian American men, at least. But the issue of stereotyping lingers. In 1993, Philip Kaufman's *Rising Run* raised a storm of street protests among Japanese and other Asian Americans, many of whom believed that the film's portrayal of the "burgeoning Japanese economic and political influence on American shores" would lead to increased real-life violence against Asians.[6]

Homosexuals have also been sympathetically depicted in several recent movies. In *The Crying Game,* independently produced and nominated for a Best Picture Academy Award in 1992, a heterosexual Irish nationalist falls for a British, black, gay transvestite, whom he at first believes to be a woman. In Jonathan Demme's *Philadelphia* (1992), Tom Hanks plays a successful lawyer who loses his job at a prestigious law firm when the senior partners discover that he has AIDS; the film sides with Hanks, the victim of homosexual discrimination, in his struggle for legal vindication. A slew of other films in which gay characters have appeared favorably include *The Wedding Banquet; The Incredibly True Adventure of Two Girls in Love; To Wong Foo, Thanks for Everything, Julie Newmar; Home for the Holidays; Boys on the Side; Live Nude Girls;* and *The Birdcage,* all released in 1994, 1995, or 1996. Of these changes, Hollywood Supports' executive director, Richard Jennings, recently noted: "This explosion means that now we have role models, and gay references let us know we are not the only ones. Now we're out there and it's making us look more like a part of the broad tapestry of humanity that people can identify with." But many gays and lesbians lament the continued appearance of stereotypes in some of Hollywood's largest films, such as the Academy Award–winning *Braveheart*. In today's volatile marketplace, it is impossible to predict whether or for how long patterns of sensitivity will continue.[7]

Despite more favorable images, Left groups insist that Hollywood continues to produce negative stereotypes that themselves reflect patterns of social domination in the United States. Some conservatives, however, claim that Left protests have made Hollywood executives and producers cautious about controversial depictions of nearly *any* minority. Invoking the political-correctness debates, they speak of "self-censorship," "censorship from the Left," and a "new McCarthyism," warning that the result will be ideologically correct imagery—an insidious form of censorship. But Left groups ask conservatives to reflect on who really has power over imagery in the United States and claim, as this book suggests, that the forces of corporate capitalism, of patriarchy, and of white supremacy have been and remain truly in the saddle.

The latest protests against and censorship of movies show that having no rules to govern screen imagery is—as Murray Schumach predicted in 1964—as dangerous as having them. During the 1950s and 1960s, a liberal cultural climate assisted in the demise of the MPPDA Production Code, and a liberal Supreme Court led to the near dissolution of legal censorship. But since the 1960s, interest groups with no connection to government or industry have sought to influence movie content and have sometimes succeeded. The First Amendment's right to protest can produce unanticipated effects. Some protests, such as those from the Religious Right, result in recognizable acts of censorship; others, such as those from Left groups, create an environment that legitimizes suppression and encourages self-censorship. Thus, any protest risks some form of censorship. But without protests, some groups are denied the chance to participate in cultural production; their views themselves are censored. Permitting protests from either Right or Left, regardless of their effects, continues to represent a risk worth taking.

Today, activists on both sides of the political divide continue to lash out against specific movies that offend their sensibilities. For conservatives, attacking movies seems forever linked to efforts to instill family values and win votes for political candidates. For leftists, though, a new trend has emerged, one that if continued will ultimately silence the Right's claim that "politically correct" art is censored art. Led by Jesse Jackson and supported by many African American and Hispanic groups, the latest hue and cry has been to change the movie industry from the inside, to attack the structures of power rather than specific movies.[8] Since the film industry has never been democratic, either in terms of the images it produces or among the people responsible for making them, these recent efforts by the Left represent a welcome new direction. If successful, such efforts could turn the days of Left protests into a memory and thereby fully expose the new censors.

NOTES

INTRODUCTION

1. The expression "culture wars" has been popularized in such recent books as William J. Bennett, *The De-Valuing of America: The Fight for Our Culture and Our Children* (New York: Summit, 1992); Richard Bolton, ed., *Culture Wars: Documents from the Recent Controversies in the Arts* (New York: New Press, 1992); Steven C. Dubin, *Arresting Images: Impolitic Art and Uncivil Actions* (New York: Routledge, 1992); Marilyn French, *The War against Women* (New York: Summit, 1992); Patrick M. Garry, *An American Paradox: Censorship in a Nation of Free Speech* (Westport, Conn.: Praeger, 1993); Henry Louis Gates, Jr., *Loose Canons: Culture Wars* (New York: Oxford University Press, 1993); Robert Hughes, *Culture of Complaint: The Fraying of America* (New York: Oxford University Press, 1993); James Davison Hunter, *Culture Wars: The Struggle to Define America* (New York: Basic Books, 1991). The idea of a wide-ranging culture war also figures prominently in the "canon" or "PC" debates over great works on college campuses. See, for example, Paul Berman, *Debating P.C.: The Controversy over Political Correctness on College Campuses* (New York: Bantom Doubleday Dell, 1992).

2. Steven Vineberg, *No Surprises, Please: Movies in the Reagan Decade* (New York: Schirmer, 1993), 21.

3. Sir James Augustus Henry Murray, ed., *The Oxford English Dictionary* (Oxford: Clarendon, 1933), 1466. Quoted in Sue Curry Jansen, *Censorship: The Knot That Binds Power and Knowledge* (New York and Oxford: Oxford University Press, 1988), 14.

4. Thomas I. Emerson, "The Doctrine of Prior Restraint," *Law and Contemporary Problems* 20 (1955): 648. See also Ira H. Carmen, *Movies, Censorship, and the Law* (Ann Arbor: University of Michigan Press, 1966), 6, and Melville Nimmer, "The Constitutionality of Official Censorship of Motion Pictures," *University of Chicago Law Review* 25 (1958): 625.

5. Jansen, *Censorship*, 15.

6. *Mutual Film Corporation v. Industrial Commission of Ohio*, 236 U.S. 230

(1915). Quoted in Garth Jowett, " 'A Capacity for Evil': The 1915 Supreme Court Mutual Decision," *Historical Journal of Film, Radio, and TV,* 9,1 (1989):64.

7. See, generally, Leonard J. Leff and Jerold L. Simmons, *The Dame in the Kimono: Hollywood, Censorship, and the Production Code from the 1920s to the 1960s* (New York: Grove Weidenfeld, 1990).

8. Discussions of the *Miracle* case appear in Bosley Crowther, "The Strange Case of 'The Miracle,' " *The Atlantic,* April 1951, 35–39; Edward De Grazia and Roger K. Newman, *Banned Films: Movies, Censors, and the First Amendment* (New York: Bowker, 1982), 77–86; and Alan F. Westin, *The Miracle Case: The Supreme Court and the Movies,* Inter-University Case Program no. 64 (Tuscaloosa: University of Alabama Press, 1961).

9. See, among a wide range of other articles that appeared in the late 1970s and throughout the 1980s, Irving Howe, "The Decade That Failed," *New York Times Magazine,* December 14, 1982.

10. John Stuart Mill, *On Liberty* (New York: Bobbs-Merrill, 1956 [1859]), 5, 17.

11. Ibid., 20.

12. Alonzo Hamby, *Liberalism and Its Challengers: From F.D.R. to Bush* (New York: Oxford University Press, 1992), xii.

13. Ibid., 300.

14. David Spitz, "A Liberal Perspective on Liberalism and Conservatism," in *Left, Right, and Center: Essays on Liberalism and Conservatism,* ed. Robert A. Goldwin. (Chicago: Rand McNally, 1965), 36–37.

15. Dunham Thorp, *Motion Picture Classic,* December 1928, 63. Quoted in Kevin Brownlow, *Behind the Mask of Innocence* (New York: Knopf, 1990), 210.

16. Quoted in de Grazia and Newman, *Banned Films,* 36.

17. See Murray Schumach, "The Hays Code," *The Face on the Cutting Room Floor: The Story of Movie and Television Censorship* (New York: Morrow, 1964), 242–48. The MPPDA amended the code several times, adding major sections on crime (1938), costumes (1939), profanity (1939), and cruelty to animals (1940). The 1940 revision is reprinted in Leff and Simmons, *The Dame in the Kimono,* 283–92.

18. Richard S. Randall, *Censorship of the Movies: The Social and Political Control of a Mass Medium* (Madison: University of Wisconsin Press, 1968), 100.

19. The social scientists include David Linz, George Comstock, L. Rowell Huesman, and Leonard Eron. See Michael Medved, *Hollywood vs. America: Popular Culture and the War on Traditional Values* (New York: HarperCollins, 1992), 183–86. These studies are reminiscent of the 1933 Payne Studies, the first comprehensive examination of the social effects of motion pictures. Of particular concern to those who did this work was the question of whether

movies caused juvenile delinquency. See Garth Jowett, *Film: The Democratic Art* (Boston: Little, Brown, 1976), 140–46.

20. Medved, *Hollywood vs. America,* 185. Medved also notes that such groups as the National Coalition Against Television Violence, Ted Baer's Christian Film and Television Commission, and Rev. Donald Wildmon's American Family Association, among other television and film watchdog groups, have attacked violent imagery on television rather than movies released in theatres.

21. See "Paramount, USA Cinemas Seek Dismissal of a Lawsuit Centered on 'Warriors,' " *Variety,* April 12, 1987, 24; "Take Heat off 'Warriors': Toning Down Ad Campaign," *Variety,* February 2, 1979, 3; Dan Yakir, "The Gangs Are Back in Town," *New York Post,* March 1, 1979, 27; and Robin Herman, "Ads Resumed for a Gang Movie after Sporadic Violence at Theatres," *New York Times,* February 23, 1979, sec. A.

22. See "Protests and Cancellations Attend Opening of Gang Film 'Colors,' " *Variety,* April 20, 1988, 4; "Gangs: Will Life Imitate a Movie?" *Newsweek,* April 25, 1988, 25; Wanda Coleman, " 'Colors': An End-of-the-80s Bad Rap," *Los Angeles Times,* April 24, 1988, sec. 6; and Brian Moss, "Takin' It to the Street: Officials Fear the Reel Violence in 'Colors' Will Beget Reel Trouble," *New York Daily News,* April 10, 1988.

23. See "Hollywood Speech, Los Angeles, California, May 31, 1995," in "Bob Dole: A Vision for America: Collected Speeches, January–October 1995" (Washington, D.C.: Bob Dole for President, 1996), 32 (pamphlet). Directed by controversial filmmaker Oliver Stone, *Natural Born Killers* can be credited with raising the debate over violence in the media to a new high. While not banned in the United States, the movie faced tough censorship in England, Ireland, and elsewhere.

24. Noting the simultaneous success of Francis Ford Coppola's film *Bram Stoker's Dracula,* Ann Rice's novel *Tale of the Body Thief,* and Madonna's autobiographical *Sex,* Frank Rich editorialized about "the new blood culture" spawned in the age of AIDS. See the *New York Times,* December 6, 1992, sec. 9.

25. In his 1995 year-end essay, Stephen Gallaway quotes one screenwriter, Lionel Chetwynd: "The studios are becoming more sensitive to this issue and are trying to decrease the violence. . . . We have seen 'Jade,' 'Sliver,' 'Assassins,' fail, while films like 'How to Make an American Quilt' are gaining ground. Non-violent films are doing better than violent films, and this will reflect itself once the cycle of production catches up" ("Violence: Body Count," *Hollywood Reporter 65th Anniversary Issue,* December 1995, 38).

26. Clayton Koppes and Gregory Black, *Hollywood Goes to War: How Politics, Profits, and Propaganda Shaped World War II Movies* (New York: Free Press, 1987), 56.

27. De Grazia and Newman, *Banned Films*, 62.

28. See David McCullough, *Truman* (New York: Simon and Schuster, 1992), 551–53].

29. This argument is prominent in much of Catherine MacKinnon's writing. See, for example, *Feminism Unmodified: Discourses on Life and Law* (Cambridge: Harvard University Press, 1987).

30. Laura Lederer, ed., *Take Back the Night: Women on Pornography* (New York: Morrow, 1980), 292.

31. On the protest, see Peter Lester, "Redress or Undress? Feminists Fume While Angie Scores in a Sexy Chiller," *Camera 5*, Fall 1980, 71–72, 81; Andrew Sarris, "Dreck to Kill," *Village Voice*, September 17–23, 1980, 43; and Dorchen Leidholdt, "Women against De Palma," letter to the editor, *Village Voice*, October 1, 1980, 3. The slogan is quoted in Michael Musto, "Drag Stir," *Soho Weekly News*, September 3, 1980.

32. Eugene Wong, *On Visual Media Racism: Asians in the American Motion Picture* (New York: Arno, 1978), 183.

33. Vito Russo, *The Celluloid Closet: Homosexuality in the Movies* (New York: Harper and Row, 1985), 205.

34. Ibid., 239.

CHAPTER 1

1. Terry Christensen, *Reel Politics: American Political Movies from 'Birth of a Nation' to 'Platoon'* (New York, Oxford: Blackwell, 1987), 7.

2. To varying degrees, the following books treat issues of censorship of political content in movies: Christensen, *Reel Politics;* David Culbert, ed., *Film Propaganda in America: A Documentary History,* vol. 1, (New York: Greenwood, 1990); Otto Friedrich, *City of Nets: A Portrait of Hollywood in the 1940s* (New York: Harper and Row, 1986); Clayton Koppes and Gregory Black, *Hollywood Goes to War: How Politics, Profits, and Propaganda Shaped World War II Movies* (New York: Free Press, 1987); and James R. Mock and Cedric Larson, *Words That Won the War: The Story of the Committee on Public Information, 1917–1919* (Princeton, N.J.: Princeton University Press, 1939). A useful discussion of the growth of a communist "popular front" in Hollywood appears in Donald Brownstein, *The Power and the Glitter: The Hollywood-Washington Connection* (New York: Pantheon, 1992), 48–72. Broader works on communism in Hollywood and the actions of the House Un-American Activities Committee include: Larry Ceplair and Stephen Englund, *The Inquisition in Hollywood: Politics in the Film Community, 1930–1960* (Garden City, N.J.: Doubleday, 1980); Walter Goodman, *The Committee: The Extraordinary Career of the House Committee on Un-American Activities* (New York: Farrar, Straus,

Giroux, 1964); Gordon Kahn, *Hollywood on Trial: The Story of the Ten Who Were Indicted* (New York: Boni and Gaer, 1948); Nancy Lynn Schwartz, *The Hollywood Writers' Wars* (New York: Knopf, 1982); and Victor Navasky, *Naming Names* (New York: Viking, 1980).

3. Theodore R. Kupferman and Philip J. O'Brien, Jr., "Motion Picture Censorship—the Memphis Blues," *Cornell Law Quarterly* 36 (1951): 296.

4. "Motion Picture Censorship and the First Amendment," *Yale Law Journal* 60 (1951): 699.

5. See Christensen, *Reel Politics*, 95.

6. Ibid., 113. It is important to note that after the *Miracle* decision movies continued to be banned on state and municipal levels if they could be found "obscene." By 1966, legal censorship for any reason besides obscenity had practically vanished.

7. Michael Ryan and Douglas Kellner, *Camera Politica: The Politics and Ideology of Contemporary Hollywood Film* (Bloomington: Indiana University Press, 1988), 17–48.

8. For an antitrust suit, see *United States v. Paramount Pictures,* 334 U.S. 131 (1948).

9. For an elaboration of this argument, see Michael Parenti, "Preemption, Profits, and Censors," in *Make-Believe Media: The Politics of Entertainment* (New York: St. Martin's, 1988), 182–95.

10. Ibid., 182.

11. See J. Hoberman, "Titicut Follies 'Unbound,'" *Premiere*, March 1992, 41.

12. Andrew Kopkind, "'Missing': Cultural Battlefield," *The Nation*, April 17, 1982, 466, 467.

13. Rodney A. Smolla, *Suing the Press* (New York: Oxford University Press, 1986), 151, 156, 159.

14. Kopkind, " 'Missing,' " 469.

15. In 1986 and again in 1988, independent filmmakers brought similar suits against the United States Information Agency (USIA) and its certifying practices. Under the Beirut Agreement enacted in 1949, the USIA was empowered to certify U.S.-produced films determined to be of "educational, scientific, and cultural character" for overseas distribution. (Roxanne E. Christ, "The Beirut Agreement: A License to Censor?" *Loyola Los Angeles International and Comparative Law Journal* 7 [1985]:258). Since 1966, when congress fully implemented the Beirut Agreement, federal officials have annually awarded "Certificates of International Character" to about five thousand films. The USIA, in concurrence with U.S. Customs, also annually grants certificates to a varying number of international films entering the United States. The USIA certificate guarantees a film lower import and export duties than a film with-

out a certificate. The suits against the USIA attacked the organization for exercising "economic censorship" and violating the First and Fifth Amendments. Argued as *Bullfrog Films v. USIA,* this case was successful both in a Los Angeles city court and when it reached the U.S. Court of Appeals in 1988. The USIA's practices, though rigorously defended by those who exercise them, offer the opportunity to explore tangential instances of attempted governmental censorship, yet the law cases and controversy over such films as *In Our Own Backyards: Uranium Mining in the United States, The Killing Ground, Save the Planet, Cuba and Fidel, Soldier Girls, Ecocide: A Strategy of War, From the Ashes . . . Nicaragua Today,* and *Good-Bye Billy: America Goes to War* represent a narrow debate among government officials and independent filmmakers. The controversy over *If You Love This Planet* was more widespread, particularly because thousands of members of the Academy of Motion Picture Arts and Sciences were obligated to see the film before casting their votes in the documentary—short subject category. Winning the Oscar of course brought even greater attention to the film. For more information on the USIA censorship controversy, see Christ, "The Beirut Agreement," 255–78; Sharon Esakoff, "USIA Censorship of Educational Films for Distribution Abroad," *Cardoza Arts and Entertainment* 3 (1984):377–425; Scott Lewis Landsbaum, "How to Censor Films without Really Trying: The Beirut Agreement and the Foreign Agents Registration Act," *Southern California Law Review* 62 (1989):685–730; and, most importantly, H. L. Rosenberg, "For Our Eyes Only," *American Film* 8 (July/August 1983):40–43.

16. ACLU press release, February 25, 1983, "Censorship-Movies," Archives, ACLU West, Los Angeles.

17. Cass Petersen, "U.S. Calls Three Films Political Propaganda and Restricts Showing," *Washington Post,* February 25, 1983, sec. A. "Canada Propaganda," *ABC News TV,* February 25, 1983, show #470, transcript, 3.

18. Petersen, "U.S. Calls Three Films."

19. Mitchell is quoted in Irvin Molotsky, "Canadian-Films Ruling Assailed in Washington," *New York Times,* February 26, 1983, sec. A. Kennedy is quoted in Cass Petersen, "Canada Asks State Department to Reverse Decision on Three Films," *Washington Post,* February 26, 1993, sec. A; Rose is quoted in Robert D. McFadden, "U.S. Orders Labels on Three Canadian Films," *New York Times,* February 25, 1983; on Block, "Canada Propaganda."

20. Justice Department spokesperson quoted in McFadden, "U.S. Orders Labels." On FARA, see Ann Dorfman, "Neutral Propaganda: Three Films 'Made in Canada' and the Foreign Agents Registration Act," *Communications/Entertainment Law Journal* 7, 3(1985): 439.

21. See Elizabeth Hull, "What's in a Word: The Foreign Agents Registra-

tion Act and Political Propaganda," in *Taking Liberties: National Barriers to the Free Flow of Ideas* (New York: Praeger, 1990), 85.

22. Ibid., 96.

23. Dorfman, "Neutral Propaganda," 436, 441.

24. Molotsky, "Canadian-Films Ruling."

25. "Canada Propaganda."

26. "Political Pollution," *Los Angeles Times,* February 27, 1983, part 4; "Justice Goes to the Movies," *Washington Post,* February 27, 1983, sec. A; Anthony Lewis, "Afraid of Freedom," *New York Times,* March 3, 1983.

27. Thomas P. DeCair, "Justice Is Not Censoring Films," *Washington Post,* March 6, 1983, sec. C; Jody Powell, "It Wasn't Censorship," *Washington Post,* March 10, 1983, sec. A.

28. Molotsky, "Canadian-Films Ruling."

29. Dorfman, "Neutral Propaganda," 447. The first case, *Block v. Smith,* was initiated in March 1983, the second, *Keene v. Smith,* a few months later; neither was resolved until 1987. See Christ, "The Beirut Agreement"; Dorfman, "Neutral Propaganda"; Hull, "What's in a Word"; Landsbaum, "How to Censor Films"; Rodney A. Smolla and Stephen A. Smith, "Propaganda, Xenophobia, and the First Amendment," *Oregon Law Review* 67 (1988):253–85; Lionel S. Sobel, "Rated PP (for "Political Propaganda") by Uncle Sam's Movie Critics: Federal Regulations Concerning the Import and Export of Films that May 'Influence' Public Opinion," *Entertainment Law Reporter* 5, 3 (January 1984): 3–11; and Diane Waldman, "The Justice Department versus the National Film Board of Canada: An Update and an Analysis," *Current Research in Film* 4 (1988):170–87.

30. Dorfman, "Neutral Propaganda," 451, 449.

31. Waldman, "The Justice Department," 181, 182.

32. Stuart Taylor, Jr., "Court Backs 'Propaganda' Label for Three Canadian Films," *New York Times,* April 29, 1987, sec. A.

33. Sims told me that the staff of the Registration Unit, which enforces FARA within the Justice Department, is rapidly decreasing. "If you look at the staff levels from 1950 to the present, you'll see a constant decline." Telephone interview, March 25, 1992.

34. This point finds support in the press. Aric Press and Diane Camper, for example, write: "It would have been a minor tempest except that it fell in the midst of a larger row about censorship by the Reagan Government" ("Keeping the Cats in the Bag," *Newsweek,* April 18, 1983, 92).

35. Terri Nash, testimony, Subcommittee on Courts, Intellectual Property, and the Administration of Justice of the U.S. House of Representatives, March 29, 1990. See also *If You Love Free Speech,* a documentary film produced by Terri Nash for the National Film Board of Canada's Studio D, April 1990.

36. See Press and Camper, "Keeping the Cats in the Bag," 92. When the Supreme Court heard *Meese v. Keene* in 1987, Scalia was not allowed to cast a vote because he had been involved in the earlier appeals court decision on *Block v. Smith.*

37. Richard O. Curry, "Choices: International Education, Civil Liberties, and Domestic Politics during the 1980s," in *Freedom at Risk: Secrecy, Censorship, and Repression in the 1980s*, ed. Richard O. Curry (Philadelphia: Temple University Press, 1988), 194.

38. Eugene Ferguson, Jr., "The Freedom of Information Act: A Time for Change?" *Detroit Law Review* 1 (1983):171, 172, 198. This legal comment provides a thorough legislative history of the FOIA, with information on proposed amendments to the act, 194–98.

39. Diana Autin, "The Reagan Administration and the Freedom of Information Act," in *Freedom at Risk: Secrecy, Censorship, and Repression in the 1980s*, ed. Richard O. Curry (Philadelphia: Temple University Press, 1988) 70, 71, 72. Autin writes, "The administration proposed and lobbied strongly for S. 1730, a full-scale attack on the FOIA. This bill was promoted by the Senate subcommittee on the constitution, chaired by Senator Orrin Hatch, (R-Utah). It would have given the attorney general the power to declare entire categories of records exempt from disclosure under the FOIA, including all files relating to 'counterintelligence,' 'terrorism,' and 'organized crime' " (70). Elsewhere, Diane Waldman notes that the subjects of nuclear weapons and nuclear testing were being hotly debated in 1982. She quotes Joseph F. Clarkson, chief of the Registration Unit in the Criminal Division of the Internal Security Section of the Justice Department, commenting on the decision to label a similar film on the nuclear freeze in 1980. "It was picked because we have an idea of what issues are important as far as Congress is concerned. We know that nuclear disarmament is an issue" (Waldman, "The Justice Department," 177).

40. See Waldman. "The Justice Department," 184. See also Autin, "The Reagan Administration," 76.

41. Navasky, *Naming Names*, 431.

42. Ronald Reagan, "Farewell Address to the American People," January 12, 1989. Quoted in O. K. Werckmeister, *Citadel Culture* (Chicago: University of Chicago Press, 1991), iii, 12.

43. Smolla and Smith, "Propaganda," 255; Waldman, "The Justice Department," 185; Landsbaum, "How to Censor Films," 729; Dorfman, "Neutral Propaganda," 416; Hull, "What's in a Word," 85.

44. In 1988, the independent filmmakers who sued the USIA for "economic censorship" (see note 15, this chapter) were victorious. In upholding an October 1986 ruling by Los Angeles federal judge Wallace Tashima, circuit judge Cecil F. Poole wrote: "The regulations do not pass constitutional

muster: They are neither justified by a compelling government purpose nor narrowly tailored. We also hold that the regulations are void for vagueness under the due process clause of the Fifth Amendment. The regulations are so ambiguous that they provide USIA officials with a virtual license to engage in censorship. In this case, that license has been exercised." Wallace Kendall, "Appeals Court Invalidates U.S. Rules Used to Block Educational Films," *Los Angeles Times,* May 18, 1986, sec. 6.

CHAPTER 2

1. In the field of film censorship studies, see, for example, Lea Jacobs, *The Wages of Sin: Censorship and the Fallen Woman Film, 1928–1942* (Madison: University of Wisconsin Press, 1991), and Leonard J. Leff and Jerold L. Simmons, *The Dame in the Kimono: Hollywood, Censorship, and the Production Code from the 1920s to the 1960s* (New York: Grove Weidenfeld, 1990).

2. See Annette Kuhn, *Cinema, Censorship, and Sexuality, 1909–1925* (London and New York: Routledge, 1988), 7. Broader works on censorship outside of film studies that share this view include Richard O. Curry, ed., *Freedom at Risk: Secrecy, Censorship, and Repression in the 1980s* (Philadelphia: Temple University Press, 1988), Sue Curry Jansen, *Censorship: The Knot That Binds Power and Knowledge* (New York and Oxford: Oxford University Press, 1988), and Michael Parenti, *Make-Believe Media: The Politics of Entertainment* (New York: St. Martin's, 1988).

3. Alexander Walker, *Sex in the Movies: The Celluloid Sacrifice* (Baltimore: Penguin, 1966), 187. For more on the controversies surrounding *The Pawnbroker,* see Leff and Simmons, *The Dame in the Kimono,* 251–54, and Murray Schumach, *The Face on the Cutting Room Floor: The Story of Movie and Television Censorship* (New York: Morrow, 1964), 4–14.

4. *Variety,* April 4, 1965. Quoted in Walker, *Sex in the Movies,* 187, 190.

5. Gerald Gardner, *The Censorship Papers: Movie Censorship Letters from the Hays Office, 1934 to 1968* (New York: Mead, 1987), 199–200.

6. Shurlock to Warner, October 9, 1965, *Virginia Woolf* papers (23B), Lehman Collection. Quoted in Leff and Simmons, *The Dame in the Kimono,* 250, 254.

7. Edward de Grazia and Roger K. Newman, *Banned Films: Movies, Censors, and the First Amendment* (New York: Bowker, 1982), 96. See *Roth v. United States,* 354 U.S. 476, and the companion case, *Alberts v. California,* 354 U.S. 476 (1957). See also de Grazia and Newman, 95–97, 104–7, and Richard S. Randall, *Censorship of the Movies: The Social and Political Control of a Mass Medium* (Madison: University of Wisconsin Press, 1968), 55–58.

8. See *Miller v. California,* 413 U.S. 15 (1973), and *Paris Adult Theatre I v. Slaton,* 185 S.E. 2d 768 (1971); affirmed 413 U.S. 49 (1973). For more on these cases, see Edward de Grazia, *Girls Lean Back Everywhere: The Law of Obscenity and the Assault on Genius* (New York: Random House, 1992), 565–75.

9. See de Grazia and Newman, *Banned Films,* 141.

10. From 1972 to 1981, *Deep Throat* was banned in twenty-one states and resulted in more legal action than any film since *The Birth of a Nation* (de Grazia and Newman, *Banned Films,* 141), yet it grossed more than $25 million. Other commercially successful films originally censored for their sexual content include Bernardo Bertolucci's *Last Tango in Paris* (banned in Montgomery, Alabama, and Shreveport, Louisiana, in 1973), *Caligula* (banned in Atlanta in 1981), and *Emmanuelle* (banned in Covina, California, in 1981). Each of these films, originally rated X by the MPAA, were freed from censorship. The state laws enabling courts to ban *Last Tango* were invalidated; *Caligula* was found obscene after prominent university professors testified to its artistic value; and *Emmanuelle* was freed from legal restraint after an Atlanta zoning ordinance was amended to allow exhibition of X-rated films "so long as [they did not] amount to a preponderance of films whose dominant theme was the depiction of specified sexual activities or anatomical areas" (380). Although the revised ordinance saved *Emmanuelle,* the Supreme Court's decision in *Young v. American Mini Theatres* made like zoning ordinances more popular methods of restricting sexually explicit imagery. For further information, see 143–45.

11. This argument is prominent in much of Catherine MacKinnon's writing. See, for example, *Feminism Unmodified: Discourses on Life and Law* (Cambridge: Harvard University Press, 1987). Other feminist scholars who share this view include Kathleen Barry, *Female Sexual Slavery* (Englewood Cliffs, N.J.: Prentice Hall, 1978); Susan Brownmiller, *Against Our Will: Men, Women and Rape* (New York: Simon and Schuster, 1975); Mary Daly, *Pure Lust: Elemental Feminist Philosophy* (Boston: Beacon, 1984); Andrea Dworkin, *Pornography: Men Possessing Women* (New York: Perigee, 1979); Susan Griffin, *Pornography and Silence: Culture's Revenge against Nature* (New York: Harper and Row, 1981); Susanne Kappeler, *The Pornography of Representation* (Minneapolis: University of Minnesota Press, 1986); Susan Lederer, ed., *Take Back the Night: Women on Pornography* (New York: Morrow, 1980); and Dorchen Leidholdt and Janice G. Raymond, eds., *Sexual Liberals and the Attack on Feminism* (New York: Pergamon, 1990).

12. See Fred Berger, *Freedom, Rights, and Pornography: A Collection of Papers by Fred R. Berger,* ed. Bruce Russell (Boston: Kluwer, 1991), 135, 136.

13. Robin Morgan, "Theory and Practice: Pornography and Rape," in *Take Back the Night,* ed. Lederer, 139. Gloria Steinem, "Erotica and Pornography: A Clear and Present Difference," in ibid., 37.

14. I refer to the books by these authors listed in note 11.

15. Quoted in Williams, *Hard Core,* 68; Andrea Dworkin, "Pornography and Grief," in *Take Back the Night,* ed. Lederer, 289–90.

16. Dorchen Leidholdt, "When Women Defend Pornography," in *Sexual Liberals,* ed. Leidholdt and Raymond, 131.

17. In her attempt to define hard-core pornography, Linda Williams writes, "How can we adequately discuss the pornographic without making some stab at a description of specific pornography?" (*Hard Core,* 29).

18. Lederer, *Take Back the Night,* 15.

19. Diane Russell and Laura Lederer, "Questions We Get Asked Most Often," in ibid., 24, 27.

20. Kevin Thomas, "Controversial 'Snuff' Opens Run," *Los Angeles Times,* March 19, 1976, sec. 4.

21. Lederer, *Take Back the Night,* 292. Beverly LaBelle, "Snuff—The Ultimate in Woman-Hating," in ibid., 274.

22. Leaflet, "Snuff, c. 1976" vertical clipping file, Billy Rose Theatre Collection, Library of Performing Arts, New York City.

23. Fasteau is quoted in "'Snuff' Film Stirs the Wrath of Feminists," *New York Post,* February 21, 1976, sec. C. For more information on the Maryland ban, see Lou Cedrone, "Maryland Bans 'Snuff' Based on Its 'Psychotic Violence,' " *Variety,* April 7, 1976, and "Snuff Ban Is Upheld by Baltimore Judge," *Box Office,* April 5, 1976. On Monticello, see LaBelle, "Snuff," 278. One commentator suggests that distributors of *Snuff* themselves organized protests in front of various theatres around the country to stimulate box-office profits. See "'Snuff' Biz Goes When Pickets Go," *Variety,* March 24, 1976, and Gerald Perry, "Women in Porn: How Young Roberta Findlay Grew Up and Made 'Snuff,' " *Take One,* September 1978, 28–32.

24. Martha Gever and Marg Hall, "Fighting Pornography," in *Take Back the Night,* ed. Lederer, 279, 281, 284. For information on Rochester feminists' resistance to other billboard images and to materials sold in porn bookstores, see 279–85.

25. Ibid., 284, 285. A more widely distributed advertisement for *Snuff* depicts a woman's neck caught between the blades of a film production slate. See "Snuff, c. 1976."

26. When *Snuff* opened in August 1983 at Greenwich Village's Eighth Street Playhouse, for example, WAP and the National Organization of Women (NOW) protested, leafleted, and demanded that the theatre owner, Steven Kirsh, close the film. NOW president Jennifer Brown called the film "especially insidious because its audience was made up primarily of adolescent boys and younger men." Kirsh agreed to close *Snuff* down, stating that "some members of the community have found this film offensive, and we

don't want to offend anybody." See Laurie Johnston and Susan Heller Anderson, "Snuff Is Snuffed," *New York Times*, September 6, 1983, sec. C. In Los Angeles, the Coalition Against Violence Against Women joined homosexual groups in protesting *Windows* (1980), a film that many believed perpetuates pernicious lies about lesbians and rape; they also joined gays in protesting the stereotypes in *Cruising* (1980). See Charles Schreger, "Gays, Feminists Protest Two Films," *Los Angeles Times*, January 25, 1980, sec. V. In a telephone interview on October 7, 1992, WAP founder Dorchen Leidholdt told me that her organization protested against *The Texas Chainsaw Massacre*, among other slasher movies, crediting such protests with the decline of the slasher genre in the early 1980s—a bold claim, to say the least. WAP, WAVAW, and WAVPM, however, are no longer active organizations and the history of their actions against slasher and other movies is largely unrecorded.

27. Peter Wood, "How a Film Changes from an 'X' to an 'R,' " *New York Times*, July 20, 1980, sec. C.

28. See Gerald Laurence, "Dressing 'Dressed' to Sell," *Box Office*, September 1980, 26.

29. Tony Bryant and Griselda Pollack, " 'Dressed to Kill' Window Dressing . . . A Poster Competition," *Framework* 15–17 (1981):28.

30. Gregg Kilday, "Dressing Down," *Los Angeles Herald-Examiner*, August 18, 1980. See also "Filmways Dresses Down Its Ads for 'Dressed to Kill,' " *Variety*, August 4, 1980, and Steven Ginsberg, " 'Countdown' Leads Five Pics Bowing Nationally; 'Kill' up 7% 2nd Weekend," *Variety*, August 5, 1980.

31. Vincent Canby, "Film: 'Dressed to Kill,' De Palma Mystery," *New York Times*, July 25, 1980, sec. C. Pauline Kael, "Master Spy, Master Seducer," *New Yorker*, August 4, 1980, 68. David Denby, "Deep Threat," *New York*, July 28, 1980, 44.

32. Andrew Sarris, "Dreck to Kill," *Village Voice*, September 17–23, 1980, 43–44.

33. Judy Stone, "Interview: Brian De Palma," *New York Newsday*, August 17, 1980.

34. Dorchen Leidholdt, "Women against De Palma," letter to the editor, *Village Voice*, October 1, 1980, 3.

35. See Peter Lester, "Redress or Undress? Feminists Fume While Angie Scores in a Sexy Chiller," *Camera 5*, Fall 1980, 71–72, 81; Sarris, "Dreck to Kill"; and Leidholdt, "Women against De Palma."

36. Michael Musto, "Drag Stir," *Soho Weekly News*, September 3, 1980. More militant protests against *Dressed to Kill* occurred outside the United States. In England, "several hundred Leeds women last month stormed movie houses showing 'The Beast' and 'Dressed to Kill,' horror films in which women are raped and killed. They pummeled men in the audiences and

hurled red paint at the screens before police dragged them out." "Dressed To Kill Protested," *Boston Globe,* December 8, 1980.

37. Reprinted in Chuck Kleinhans, "Dressed to Kill Protested," *Jump Cut,* no. 21, September 1980, 32.

38. Leidholdt, "Women against De Palma." For Andrew Sarris's criticism of WAP and other feminist protests against *Dressed to Kill,* see Sarris, "Dreck to Kill."

39. Lee Grant, "Women vs. 'Dressed to Kill': Is Film Admirable or Deplorable?" *Los Angeles Times,* September 12, 1980, sec. 6.

40. One exception was feminists' protests against *Once Upon a Time in America* in 1984; another came when members of NOW joined gay and lesbian protesters against *Basic Instinct* in 1992.

41. The debates over pornography, *Dressed to Kill,* and De Palma's films are explored in: David Denby, Alan Dershowitz, et al., "Pornography: Love or Death?" *Film Comment* 20, 6 (November–December 1984): 29–47; Marcia Pally et al, "Sex, Violence, and De Palma," *Film Comment* 21, 5 (September-October 1985): 9–13. The first issue features a dialogue between Marcia Pally and Brian De Palma; the second contains articles by legal scholars, antipornography and procensorship feminists, and other figures in the debates. Among the writers included are Alan Dershowitz, Edward Donnerstein, Dorchen Leidholdt, Marcia Pally, Janella Miller, Lois P. Sheinfeld, and Ann Snitow. For information on feminists' objections to *Fatal Attraction,* see Susan Faludi, "Fatal Distortion," *Mother Jones* 13 (February–March 1988): 27–30. Also see Susan Faludi, *Backlash: The Undeclared War against American Women* (New York: Crown, 1991), 126–39.

42. I borrow this idea from Giovanna Asselle and Behroze Gandhy, "Dressed to Kill," *Screen* 23 (September-October 1982):137–43, an article focusing on the controversy *Dressed* aroused in England. For information on the sexuality debates, see Estelle Freedman and Barrie Thorne, "Introduction to 'The Feminist Sexuality Debates,' " *Signs: Journal of Women in Culture and Society* 10 (1984):103–15.

43. Undated F.A.C.T. pamphlet.

CHAPTER 3

1. See Mary Kasdan, "Asians Protest 'Year of the Dragon,' " *Los Angeles Daily News,* August 23, 1985, sec. F.

2. D. W. Griffith, *The Rise and Fall of Free Speech in America* (Hollywood: Larry Edmunds Bookshop, [1916] 1967).

3. Grace Kingsley, "The Splash of Saffron," *Photoplay Magazine,* March

1916, 139. Quoted in Eugene Wong, *On Visual Media Racism: Asians in the American Motion Picture* (New York: Arno, 1978), 74. See also Richard A. Oehling, "The Yellow Menace: Asian Images in American Film," in *The Kaleidoscopic Lens: How Hollywood Views Ethnic Groups,* ed. Randall M. Miller (New York: Ozer, 1980), 189.

4. Helen Delpar, "Good-bye to the 'Greaser': Mexico, the MPPDA, and Derogatory Films, 1922–1926," *Journal of Popular Film and Television* 12 (Spring 1984):36.

5. Wong, *On Visual Media Racism,* 156–57. For a more complete analysis, see Christine Choy, "Images of Asian-Americans in Films and Television," in *Ethnic Images in American Film and Television,* ed. Randall M. Miller (Philadelphia: Balch Institute, 1978), 145–55. See also Richard A. Oehling, "The Yellow Menace: Asian Images in American Film," *The Kaleidoscopic Lens,* 193–200. For a more recent discussion of Asian Americans on-screen, see Diane Carson, "Cultural Screens: Teaching Asian and Asian-American Images," in Diane Carson and Lester D. Friedman, *Shared Differences: Multicultural Media and Practical Pedagogy* (Urbana and Chicago: University of Illinois Press, 1995), 73–97.

6. Wong, *On Visual Media Racism,* 183.

7. Jews protested against and succeeded in censoring several movies containing stereotypes—most notably the British-made *Oliver Twist* (1949). See Gilbert Seldes, *The Great Audience* (New York: Viking, 1950), 100–101. One of the most well documented instances of Irish censorship appears in Francis R. Walsh, "'The Callahans and the Murphys' (MGM, 1927): A Case Study of Irish-American and Catholic Church Censorship," *Historical Journal of Film, Radio, and Television* 10 (1990):33–45.

8. Ralph E. Friar and Natasha A. Friar, *The Only Good Indian . . . The Hollywood Gospel* (New York: Drama Book Specialists, 1972), 260.

9. See Allen L. Woll and Randall M. Miller, *Ethnic and Racial Images in American Film and Television: Historical Essays and Bibliography* (New York: Garland, 1987), 283. When *The Godfather* appeared on NBC television in 1976, Italian Americans were able to convince the network to include the following disclaimer: "*The Godfather* is a fictional account of a small group of ruthless criminals. It would be erroneous and unfair to suggest that they are representative of any particular ethnic group" (Woll and Miller, 285). For more on images of Italians, see Daniel Sembroff Golden, "The Fate of La Famiglia: Italian Images in American Film," in *The Kaleidoscopic Lens,* ed. Miller.

10. "Fort Apache, the Bronx," *American Film,* October 1981, 58.

11. See Nat Hentoff, "O Freedom! Each Neighborhood Its Own Censor," *Village Voice,* April 28, 1980, 24.

12. *New York Times,* February 6, 1981.

13. J. A. Tractenberg, "Fort Apache, the Bronx," *Women's Wear Daily,* September 15, 1983, 20. "Miami 'Scarface,' " *Variety,* September 1, 1982. Enrique Fernandez, "Scarface Died for My Sins," *Village Voice,* December 20, 1983, 73. Marilyn Beck, "Getting Tough with Scarface," *Daily News,* September 9, 1982.

14. Wong, *On Visual Media Racism,* 214, 262.

15. For details about this criticism, see ibid., 46–49, and "Asian Roles for Asian Actors," *Bridge* 3 (June 1974): 4. Other pre-1977 actions were primarily written. In 1975, Japanese groups criticized an NBC production, *Farewell to Manzanar,* which presented an Anglo version of the Japanese experience in the concentration camps in 1941. A group of protesters, the Manzanar Committee, wrote to NBC, "We were greatly disappointed that community input was not sought earlier"; the network did not respond. See Choy, "Images of Asian-Americans," 154. Because *The Deer Hunter* (1978) contained what many Asian Americans viewed as the "sadistic" Asian stereotype, it also was criticized. See Janice Sakomoto and Forrest Gok, "Michael Cimino and the Chinese Mafia," *Asian American Network* (a publication of the National Asian American Telecommunications Association) 2 (Fall 1984): 4.

16. Wong, *On Visual Media Racism,* 119, 261.

17. Richard Goldstein, "Art Beat: The Politics of Culture: The Chan Syndrome," *Village Voice,* May 5, 1980, 32. Cynthia Garney, "Film: A New Charlie Chan: Angry Voices," *Washington Post,* May 4, 1980, sec. H. "Charlie Chan," *American Film,* October 1981, 58. L. Reiko Higa, "Protesters Take to the Streets of San Francisco against 'A Yellow Uncle Tom'—Charlie Chan," *US,* July 22, 1980. Quoted in "Frisco's Chinese Community Seeks City Ban on Chan," *Variety,* April 23, 1980.

18. Allen Wolper, "Fu Manchu and the First Amendment," *Soho Weekly News,* August 27, 1980, 9.

19. Other groups supporting the postrelease protest included the Media Forum, a black group including Roscoe Lee Brown, Lou Gossett, and Sidney Poitier; the League of Black Cinema Artists; Nosotros, an Hispanic actor's group; and the Japanese American Citizens League.

20. " 'Chan' Exhibs Yank Film under Protest," *Variety,* February 24, 1981, 4.

21. See Martha Gever, "Dragon Busters," *The Independent* (October 1988): 8–9. Upon the release of *Dragon,* the protest actually included nearly fifty groups.

22. Sakomoto and Gok, "Michael Cimino," 4.

23. "Statement by the Chinese Consolidated Benevolent Association," August 16, 1985, "Year of the Dragon" file, Asian-CineVision, New York City.

24. "Press Release, Coalition Against Year of the Dragon," August 14, 1985, ibid.

25. Jim Robbins, "Asian-Americans Planning 'Dragon' Boycott Campaign," *Variety*, August 14, 1985, 26.

26. Gene Ruffini, "Big New Film in Reel-Life Drama," *New York Post*, August 17, 1985.

27. "Statement from Asian CineVision Re: Year of the Dragon," signed Peter Chou, Executive Director, August 16, 1985; Virginia Kee, "Year of the Dragon Is Denounced by Chinatown Activist Virginia Kee," press release, August 16, 1985; statement of Chinese Consolidated Benevolent Association, August 16, 1985; Radical Women and the Freedom Socialist Party, statement to the New York City Protest of "Year of the Dragon," August 16, 1985; all in "Year of the Dragon" file.

28. Minutes of Coalition Against Year of the Dragon, August 19, 1985, ibid.

29. Gever, "Dragon Busters," 8. John Horn, "Demonstrators Picket 'Year of the Dragon,' " *Los Angeles Times*, August 26, 1985, sec. 6.

30. Thomas Palmer, " 'Dragon' Protested as Racist Film," *Boston Globe*, August 25, 1985, 26. Guy Livingston, "Mayor of Boston Blasts 'Dragon,' Pickets Converge on Sack House," *Variety*, August 28, 1985, 3.

31. Frank Spotnitz, "Mickey Rourke Fighting Mad over 'Dragon' Reviews," United Press International, August 26, 1985. " 'Year of the Dragon' Opens Huge in Hong Kong," United Press International, November 22, 1985. "Orientals Bristle at Hollywood Stereotype," *Chicago Tribune*, November 22, 1985.

32. Lone is quoted in Robbins, "Asian-Americans Planning." Criticism of the Asian American protests against *Dragon* appeared in many of the press articles covering the film's national release. In a letter to the *Los Angeles Times*, for example, an Italian American wrote: "What is all the fuss about the movie 'Year of the Dragon'? Just because it shows some of the Chinese people in a bad light? We, of Italian descent, have been putting up with this sort of treatment at the hands of the movie and television industry for years" (Beverly Clemence, letter to the editor, *Los Angeles Times*, October 3, 1985. A vice president from a major studio told the *Boston Globe*: "Cimino isn't saying that all Orientals are like criminals in his movie, anymore than Coppola believed that all Italians were like the ones in 'The Godfather.' It's just a movie" (see Michael Blowen, "An Outcry Falls on Deaf Ears," *Boston Globe*, August 25, 1985, sec. 1). MGM/UA defended *Dragon* against anti-Asian charges in a statement issued before the national protest. "Claims made against the film 'Year of the Dragon' and its makers are without validity. . . . Regardless of our opinions, however, we encourage members of the Asian American community to view the film and to make their own judgments" ("MGM/UA Defends Anti-Asian Charges Leveled at 'Dragon,' " *Variety*, August 21, 1985).

33. Pat H. Broeske, "Chop Suey and Other Reactions to Cimino's Latest," *Los Angeles Times,* August 25, 1985, sec. F.

34. "'Volunteers,' 'Dragon,' Bow Well but 'Future' Still Tops Nat. B.O.," *Variety,* August 21, 1985. Dennis Wharton, "'Year' Healthy $220,000 in DC," *Variety,* August 21, 1985.

35. Ray Loynd, "MGM/UA Sending 'Year' Disclaimers out to Exhibitors," *Variety,* September 4, 1985, 3. The suit, filed in the Los Angeles Superior Court, claimed that because MGM/UA's *Year of the Dragon* included a shot of Chinese pictographs that allegedly translated to "CCBA," the filmmakers had implied that members of the CCBA were "trafficking in drugs and otherwise engaged in organized crime" ("Chinese Defamed in Film, Suit Charges," *Atlanta Journal and Constitution,* August 31, 1985). See also John Horn, "The 'Dragon' Wars: Hard-Fought Month," *Los Angeles Times,* September 7, 1985, sec. 5.

36. Loynd, "MGM/UA."

37. See Gever, "Dragon Busters," and Janice Sakomoto, "Communities Unite against 'Dragon,' " *Asian American Network* 3 (Summer–Fall, 1985): 7.

38. See "Coalition Update," the Coalition Against Year of the Dragon, September 5, 1985, "Year of the Dragon" file. Antonio DeCastro, "A Deeper Look into the 'Year of the Dragon' Furor," *Asian American Network* 3 (Fall–Winter 1985): 4–5.

39. Gina Marchetti, "Ethnicity, the Cinema, and Cultural Studies," in *Unspeakable Images: Ethnicity and the American Cinema,* ed. Lester D. Friedman, (Chicago: University of Illinois Press, 1992), 112–39.

CHAPTER 4

1. Vito Russo, *The Celluloid Closet: Homosexuality in the Movies* (New York: Harper and Row, 1981), 29.

2. The warning appeared in the MPPDA list of "Don'ts and Be Carefuls" (Garth Jowett, *Film: The Democratic Art* [Boston: Little, Brown, 1976], 466). As evidence of how few overt representations or implications of homosexuality there were during these years, the New York censors' report of 1928 included not one required deletion in the subject area of homosexuality or "sexual perversion." See Morris Ernst and Pare Lorentz, *Censored: The Private Life of the Movies* (New York: Cape and Smith, 1930), 82–83.

3. Russo, *The Celluloid Closet,* 56.

4. *What Shocked the Censors* (New York: National Council on Freedom from Censorship, 1933). This is a complete listing of New York State censors' cuts from January 1932 to March 1933. Russo states that the Hays Office agreed to the cuts that appear on this list. Although here, as elsewhere, Russo does

not footnote all of his sources, I believe that he refers to the same censorship report cited in my text. See Russo, *The Celluloid Closet,* 57–58.

5. Alfred Kinsey et al., *Sexual Behavior in the Human Race* (Philadelphia: Saunders, 1948), 627. Quoted in Chon Noriega, "Something's Missing Here! Homosexuality and Film Reviews during the Production Code Era, 1934–1962," *Cinema Journal* 30, 1 (Fall 1990): 26.

6. Russo, *The Celluloid Closet,* 99.

7. John Allen Sargent, *Self-Regulation: The Motion Picture Production Code, 1930–1961* (Ph.D. diss., University of Michigan, 1963), 168, 169.

8. Sargent, *Self-Regulation,* 205, 207.

9. John D'Emilio, *Sexual Politics, Sexual Communities: The Making of a Homosexual Minority in the United States, 1940–1970* (Chicago: University of Chicago Press, 1983), 182. On the new stereotypes, see Richard Dyer, "Seen to Be Believed: Some Problems in the Representation of Gay People as Typical," in *Now You See It: Studies on Lesbian and Gay Film,* ed. Dyer (New York and London: Routledge, 1990), 2–19; and Dyer, "Rejecting Straight Ideals: Gays in Film," in *Jump Cut: Hollywood, Politics, and Counter Cinema,* ed. Peter Steven (New York: Praeger, 1985), 286–95.

10. Richard McGuinness, "Gay Yes, but Proud It's Not," *Village Voice,* January 14, 1971, 55.

11. Russo, *The Celluloid Closet,* 98–99, 216. Robin Wood "Responsibilities of a Gay Film Critic," *Film Comment,* January–February 1978, quoted in Russo, *The Celluloid Closet,* 196.

12. Russo, *The Celluloid Closet,* 196.

13. Michelangelo Signorile, *Queer in America: Sex, the Media, and the Closets of Power* (New York: Random House, 1993), 288. Russo, *The Celluloid Closet,* 220.

14. Excerpted from "Some General Principles for Motion Picture and Television Treatment of Homosexuality." Quoted in Russo, *The Celluloid Closet,* 220–21, 226.

15. Ibid., 239.

16. C. F. Brydon and Lucia Valeska, "Wrong 'Background' for a Horror Mystery Movie," letter to the editor, *New York Times,* September 27, 1979, sec. 1. "Protesters Call the Film 'Cruising' Anti-homosexual," *New York Times,* July 26, 1979, sec. C.

17. Les Ledbetter, "1,000 in 'Village' Renew Protest against Movie on Homosexuals," *New York Times,* July 27, 1979, sec. 2.

18. Edward Guthmann, "The Cruising Controversy: William Friedkin vs. the Gay Community," *Cineaste* 10, 3 (Summer 1980), 2–3. Janet Maslin, "Friedkin Defends His 'Cruising,' " *New York Times,* September 18, 1979, sec. C.

19. Guthmann, "The Cruising Controversy," 3. Maslin, "Friedkin Defends His 'Cruising,' " 12.

20. See Fred Ferretti, "Filming of 'Cruising' Goes More Calmly," *New York Times*, August 7, 1979, sec. C.

21. Russo, *The Celluloid Closet*, 240.

22. Guthmann, "The Cruising Controversy," 4.

23. Charles Schreger, "Gays, Feminists Protest 2 Films," *Los Angeles Times*, January 25, 1980, sec. V.

24. See "Windows," *Jump Cut*, May 1980, 197.

25. "Windows Enrages NY Homosexuals," *Variety*, January 23, 1980, 7.

26. Arthur Bell, "Windows," *Village Voice*, June 28, 1980, 30.

27. See Dale Pollack, "Cruising Protests Intensify," *Los Angeles Times*, February 1, 1980, sec. V.

28. Kite is quoted in ibid., Oxenberg in Janet Maslin, " 'Cruising' Defended by Friedkin," *New York Times*, February 6, 1980, sec. C. For information on the rating controversy over *Cruising*, see "Did 'Cruising' Respect Rulings?" *Variety*, June 25, 1980, 4, " 'Cruising' in New Ratings Rumpus; 'R' Taken, Given," *Variety*, June 11, 1980, 4, 30; and Pollack, " 'Cruising' Protests Intensify."

29. Maslin, " 'Cruising' Defended by Friedkin."

30. Russo, *The Celluloid Closet*, 238.

31. Ibid. On *Cruising*'s crumbling, see Pollack, " 'Cruising: Protests on the Picket Lines," *Los Angeles Times*, February 18, 1980, sec. V.

32. Leslie Bennetts, "The New Realism in Portraying Homosexuals," *New York Times*, February 21, 1983, sec. C. See Mary Richards, "The Gay Deception," *Film Comment* 18, 3 (May–June 1982): 15–18, and Andrea Weiss, "From the Margins: New Images of Gays in the Cinema," *Cineaste* 15, 1 (1986):4–8.

33. In 1985, homosexual groups formed the Gay and Lesbian Alliance Against Defamation (GLAAD) in New York. Three years later, this group opened a Los Angeles office and became "the first full-time gay group to put pressure on the film and television industry" (Signorile, *Queer in America*, 289). GLAAD attempted to arrange meetings with Hollywood studios—as other homosexual groups had during the 1970s—and in the late 1980s and early 1990s made headway. Mass protests, however, eventually would prove to be the most effective strategy of confronting Hollywood.

34. Steven Dubin, *Arresting Images: Impolitic Art and Uncivil Actions* (New York: Routledge, 1993), 196. Dubin provides a detailed account of some of the Religious Right's actions against gays, including a useful summary and discussion of the Robert Mapplethorpe controversy.

35. David J. Fox, "Gays Decry Benefit Screening of 'Lambs,' " *Los Angeles Times*, February 4, 1991, sec. F. Elaine Dutka, "'Silence' Fuels a Loud and Angry Debate," *Los Angeles Times*, March 20, 1991, sec. F.

36. Jennings is quoted in Fox, "Gays Decry Benefit Screening." For responses to *Silence* from Signoreli and other writers, see C. Carr, "Sorting Out

the Sexual Politics of a Controversial Film: Writers on the Lamb," *Village Voice,* March 5, 1991, 49. Other writers in this *Voice* debate are Stephen Harvey, Gary Indiana, Amy Taubin, Martha Gever, Larry Kramer, B. Ruby Rich, Jewelle Gomez, and Stuart Klawans. Rosenbaum is quoted in Dutka, " 'Silence' Fuels."

37. David Ehrenstein, "Of Lambs and Slaughter: Director Jonathan Demme Responds to Charges of Homophobia," *The Advocate,* March 12, 1991, 77. See also Caryn James, "Now Starring Killers for the Chiller 90s," *New York Times,* March 10, 1991, sec. 2.

38. Carr, "Sorting out the Sexual Politics," 56.

39. See Nina J. Easton, "Carolco Buys Joe Eszterhas Script for Record 3 Million," *Los Angeles Times,* June 26, 1990, sec. F, and "Eszterhas v. Verhoeven: The Screenwriter Has Left the 'Basic Instinct' Project," *Los Angeles Times,* August 23, 1990, sec. F.

40. Michael Bronski, "Homos v. Hollywood," *NYQ,* March 29, 1992, 28.

41. See David Tuller, "Gay Protest at Movie Location: Filming of Joe Eszterhas' 'Basic Instinct' at South-of-Market Bar," *San Francisco Chronicle,* April 11, 1991.

42. John Boudreau, "Going against 'Basic Instinct'; Film's Negative Portrayal Infuriates Gay Groups," *Washington Post,* June 4, 1991, sec. B.

43. Lynn Hirshberg, "Say It Ain't So, Joe," *Vanity Fair,* August 1991, 81, 82.

44. Bronski, "Homos v. Hollywood," 28, 70, 71.

45. Hirshberg, "Say It Ain't So, Joe," 85. This was quite a different tune than Carolco's official response, quoted later.

46. See David J. Fox and Donna Rosenthal, "Gays Bashing 'Basic Instinct,'" *Los Angeles Times,* April 29, 1991, sec. F, and Keith Clarke, "Film Producers Order Arrest of Protesters," *Bay Area Reporter,* May 2 ,1991, 1, 14.

47. Elaine Herscher, "Film Script Won't Be Changed to Mollify Gays, Lesbians," *San Francisco Chronicle,* April 30, 1991, sec. A. Boudreau, "Going Against 'Basic Instinct.' " Clarke, "Film Producers Order Arrest," 14.

48. See David J. Fox, "SF Gays Defy Court, March on Movie Location," *Los Angeles Times,* April 25, 1991, sec. A; Boudreau, "Going Against 'Basic Instinct'"; and Clarke, "Film Producers Order Arrest." See also Jim Harwood and Claudia Eller, "Citizen's Arrest on 'Basic Instinct' Set," *Variety,* May 6, 1991, 14, and Hirschberg, "Say It Ain't So, Joe," 82.

49. Michael Dorgan, " 'Instinct' Triggers Gay Reflexes," *Daily News,* May 13, 1991, 27.

50. Keith Clarke, "Filming Concludes: 'Instinct' Producer Arrested; Protests Called Major Success," *Bay Area Reporter,* May 9, 1991.

51. Letter to Theater Exhibitors, signed Jesse A. Greenman, Co-Chair, GLAAD-San Francisco, and GLAAD flyer, GLAAD San Francisco files, July 29, 1991.

52. Hergott is quoted in David J. Fox and Victor F. Zonana, "Guess Who's Coming to Gay-Rights Dinner," *Los Angeles Times,* August 5, 1991, sec. F.

53. Marilyn Beck and Stacy Jenel Smith, "Gays Map Out Guerrilla War," *New York Daily News,* January 16, 1992, 45; "The Big Stink over 'Basic Instinct,' " *San Francisco Chronicle,* March 19, 1992, sec. E; Carla Hall, " 'Instinct' Battle Plan: Gay Groups Prepare Assault, Eye Oscars," *Washington Post,* March 19, 1992, sec. C.

54. Andrew Kirtzman, "Gays Bare Film Plot," *New York Daily News,* March 10, 1992, sec. 1.

55. Andy Marx, "Film Clips: A Look inside Hollywood and the Movies: Politically Correct File," *Los Angeles Times,* February 16, 1992, Calendar, 23. Many newspapers reporting on the planned activities of "Catherine Did It!" referred to the group simply as "———Did It!"—in their own blatant act of censorship.

56. Hall, " 'Instinct' Battle Plan." Kent Robinson, letter to the editor, *Los Angeles Times,* March 1, 1992. Steve Murray, "Gay Activists 'Out' Controversial Movie's Killer," *Atlanta Journal and Constitution,* March 10, 1992, sec. E. Lewis Beale, "Lesbian Killers on the Movie Screen: Gay Activists in the Streets," *Newsday,* March 15, 1992, 7.

57. Bob Strauss, " 'Basic Instinct' Sparks Controversy Even Before It Opens," *BPI Entertainment News Wire,* March 5, 1992.

58. Russel Smith, "Gays Outraged at New Film's Portrayal of Homosexuals," *Dallas Morning News,* March 15, 1992, sec. A.

59. On March 19 the National Organization of Women (NOW) formally joined the fray. NOW called *Basic Instinct* "a textbook example of the backlash against women in the media" (Kevin Phinney, "NOW Denounces 'Basic Instinct,' " *BPI Entertainment News Wire,* March 19, 1992). Tammy Bruce, president of NOW Los Angeles, clarified her organization's views vis-à-vis censorship: "We're not suggesting people don't see it. But we want them to think about what they're seeing. Social change doesn't come by waiting for something to go away. At least if people see it, we can cause them to think and debate what they've seen" (Susan Spillman. "A Sexual Shake Down: Challenging Hollywood's Orientation," *USA Today,* March 20, 1992, sec. D).

60. David J. Fox, "Activists Dis-invited to 'Basic' Screening," *Los Angeles Times,* March 11, 1992, sec. F. "Protest Set for 'Basic Instinct' Opening," United Press International, March 20, 1992.

61. Dan Levy, "Gay Rights Protesters Greet 'Instinct' Opening: Demonstrators Assail Homophobic Portrayals," *San Francisco Chronicle,* March 21, 1992, sec. A. Scott Harris, "Opposition to Film 'Basic Instinct' Rises," *Los Angeles Times,* March 21, 1992, sec. B, and David J. Fox, " 'Instinct' Sizzles at the Box Office," *Los Angeles Times,* March 23, 1992, sec. F.

62. Mary Eliza-Cronin, "Plot Twist: Protesters Give Away Film's Ending to Decry Gay-Bashing," *Seattle Times,* March 21, 1992, sec. A. Gary Arnold, "Mixed Up Screening Says It All," *Washington Times,* March 22, 1992, sec. D.

63. Street interviews by the author with William Meyerhafer and Jill Frasca, March 20, 1992; protest flyer handed out in front of Loew's Nineteenth Street Theatre, New York City.

64. Al Martinez, "Don't Read This Column," *Los Angeles Times,* March 24, 1992, sec. B. Diane White, "The 'Instinct' Isn't Basic, Just Base," *Boston Globe,* March 25, 1992. Maslin is quoted in Richard Goldstein, "Base Instinct: Homophobia in Hollywood," *Village Voice,* April 14, 1992, 38. Amy Taubin, "Ice Pick Envy: The Boys Who Cried Misogyny," *Village Voice,* April 28, 1992, 36.

65. "Politically Correct Movies," *CNN,* March 23, 1992, transcript #16.

66. Fox, " 'Instinct' Sizzles at the Box Office."

67. Taubin, "Ice Pick Envy."

68. Signorile, *Queer in America,* 320. Bronski, "Homos v. Hollywood," 28.

CHAPTER 5

1. For a discussion of precode censorship disputes between reformers and progressives, see Nancy J. Rosenbloom, "Between Reform and Regulation: The Struggle over Film Censorship in Progressive America, 1909–1922," *Film History* 1 (1987): 307–25.

2. See "Martin Scorcese vs. Jesus Christ: The Last Judgment?" *The Economist,* August 13, 1988, 77.

3. Interchurch World Movement, "Motion Picture Principles for the Church" (a pamphlet presented for the criticism of the National Religious Advisory Committee to the National Board of Review), National Board of Review Collection, Box 30, Rare Manuscripts Division, Astor, Lennox, and Tilden Foundations, New York Public Library.

4. Edward de Grazia and Roger K. Newman, *Banned Films: Movies, Censors, and the First Amendment* (New York: Bowker, 1982), 31–35. See also Ruth Inglis, *Freedom of the Movies: A Report on Self-Regulation from the Commission on Freedom of the Press* (Chicago: University of Chicago Press, 1947), 115.

5. See Frank Couvares, "Hollywood, Main Street, and the Church: Trying to Censor the Movies before the Production Code," *American Quarterly* 44 (December 1992): 584–616: "In the 1920s . . . it was Protestant America that seemed from the view of the studios most in need of courting" (589). Among the many Protestant organizations that favored federal censorship were the Federal Motion Picture Council, founded in 1925 by several Protestant denominations, and the International Convention of the Disciples of Christ,

which in 1929 adopted a resolution for "federal supervision of motion pictures producing higher standards at the source of production. See *The Public Relations of the Motion Picture Industry* (New York: Federal Council of Churches of Christ in America, Department of Research and Education, 1931), 102–8. A comprehensive list of religious, welfare, civic, professional, and fraternal organizations with which the Hays Office had associations appears in Inglis, *Freedom in the Movies,* 101–3. See also Garth Jowett, *Film: The Democratic Art* (Boston: Little, Brown, 1976), 173–76.

6. Will Hays to Albert Warner, September 5, 1922, 1922 Civic Committee File, American Academy of Motion Picture Arts and Sciences, Los Angeles. Quoted in Richard Maltby, " 'The King of Kings' and the Czar of All the Rushes: The Propriety of the Christ Story," *Screen* 31–32 (Summer 1990): 204.

7. Donald Hayne, ed., *The Autobiography of Cecil B. DeMille* (London: Allen, 1960), 252, quoted in ibid., 93.

8. Maltby, " 'The King of Kings,' " 209.

9. Unsigned letter to W. D. Kelly, July 19, 1927, "The Callahans and the Murphy's" File, American Academy of Motion Picture Arts and Sciences, Los Angeles. Quoted in Francis R. Walsh, "'The Callahans and the Murphys' (MGM, 1927): A Case Study of Irish-American and Catholic Church Censorship," *Historical Review of Film, Radio, and Television* 10, 1 (1990): 37.

10. Walsh, " 'The Callahans and the Murphys,'" 34.

11. Editorial, *America,* October 28, 1933. Quoted in Jowett, *Film,* 248. See also Paul W. Facey, *The Legion of Decency: A Sociological Analysis of the Emergence and Development of a Social Pressure Group* (New York: Arno, 1974), 45.

12. For more information on Catholic bishops involved in the formation of the Legion of Decency, see Facey, *The Legion of Decency,* 81–124; Jowett, *Film,* 248–56; Harold C. Gardiner, *Catholic Viewpoints on Censorship* (Garden City, N.Y.: Image Books, 1961), 80–112; Inglis, *Freedom of the Movies,* 122–23; and Martin Quigley, *Decency in Motion Pictures* (New York: Macmillan, 1937), 75.

13. See Leonard L. Leff and Jerold L. Simmons, *The Dame in the Kimono: Hollywood, Censorship, and the Production Code from the 1920s to the 1960s* (New York: Grove Weidenfeld, 1990), 79–96.

14. Bosley Crowther, "The Strange Case of 'The Miracle,' " *The Atlantic,* April 1951, 35–39. More thorough discussions of the controversy surrounding the U.S. release of *The Miracle* appear in David Giglio, "The Decade of the Miracle, 1952–1962: A Study in the Censorship of the American Motion Picture," Ph.D. diss., Syracuse University, 1964, and Alan F. Westin, *The Miracle Case: The Supreme Court and the Movies* (Inter-University Case Program no. 64, Tuscaloosa: University of Alabama Press, 1961).

15. De Grazia and Newman, *Banned Films,* 79.

16. Martin Quigley, Quoted in Jack Vizzard, *See No Evil: Life inside a Hollywood Censor* (New York: Simon and Schuster, 1970), 215. McCaffrey is quoted in Crowther, "The Strange Case," 37, and in Jowett, *Film*, 415.

17. De Grazia and Newman, *Banned Films*, 79.

18. Crowther, "The Strange Case," 37, 38.

19. See Richard Corliss, "The Legion of Decency," *Film Comment* 4 (Summer 1968): 44.

20. De Grazia and Newman, *Banned Films*, 80. Crowther, "The Strange Case," 38.

21. De Grazia and Newman, *Banned Films*, 82. For information on *Mutual Film Corporation v. Industrial Commission of Ohio*, 236 U.S. 230 (1915), see ibid., 3–5.

22. Richard Corliss, "The Legion of Decency," 44.

23. For more on the controversies surrounding these and other "religious" films, see John Dart, "Age-Old Problem: Portrayals of Christ Tempt Controversy," *Los Angeles Times*, July 30, 1988, sec. 1. Each of these movies, in fact, elicited critical praise. Writing in the liberal journal *America*, Moira Walsh, for example, praised *Jesus Christ Superstar* for its achievement as entertainment and all but excused its scriptural transgressions and use of stereotypes: "The essence, it seems to me, is the attempt of two young agnostics, Tim Rice and Andrew Lloyd Webber, to express their bemused admiration for the life and teachings of Christ in terms that are comprehensible to them. . . . The thrust of the film . . . is benign" (September 1, 1973, 132). In *Christian Century*, James Wall similarly commended *Superstar* as a "surprising film success." Wall said the performers gave their own view of Jesus and "in the process have raised the same questions that have always been raised about him: who is he and what is this strange power that drives him?" (June 27, 1973, 693). Walsh found *Godspell* "an irresistibly engaging show with a high-spirited talented cast . . . you come away convinced that the performers and creative technicians must love one another to have achieved such a joyous, well-balanced collaboration. You even come away temporarily loving your neighbors in the theatre, and maybe that is not such a bad beginning of a Christian message" (April 21, 1973, 379). For more on the written response to *Superstar*, see Gerald E. Forshey, *American Religious and Biblical Spectaculars* (Westport, Conn.: Praeger, 1992), 113–18.

24. Robert Wuthnow, *The Restructuring of American Religion: Society and Faith Since World War II* (Princeton, N.J.: Princeton University Press, 1988), 12.

25. See George Marsden, *Religion and American Culture* (New York: Harcourt, Brace, Jovanovich, 1990), 268.

26. For more on Carter's religion, see Leslie Wheeler, *Jimmy Who?* (New York: Barron's, 1976), 135–60.

27. Marsden, *Religion and American Culture*, 268.

28. Zeffirelli is quoted in Forshey, *American Religious and Biblical Spectaculars*, 165, and in Les Brown, "NBC Spurns Protest; To Show 'Jesus' Film," *New York Times*, March 15, 1977, sec. C.

29. Bill Greeley, "Gospel According to GM: Pull Thy Ad; Won't Sponsor 'Life of Jesus,' " *Variety*, March 16, 1977, 45.

30. Eleanor Blau, "Catholics Deplore New Monty Python Movie," *New York Times*, August 30, 1979, sec. C. "Three Jewish Groups Condemn 'Monty Python's Life of Brian,' " *New York Times*, August 28, 1979, sec. C.

31. "Rabbinical Alliance Pours on Condemnation of 'Life of Brian,' " *Variety*, August 29, 1979, 7.

32. In Versailles, conservative Catholics invaded the theatre where *Hail Mary* was playing and mutilated two reels described as "shocking and profoundly blasphemous." Local authorities subsequently banned the film to avoid public disorder, but when a court appeal was made for a national ban, a Paris judge upheld "spectators rights to choose and the liberty of expression" and the same day reversed the Versailles ban (see Susan Barrowclough, "Godard's 'Marie' ": The Virgin Birth and a Flurry of Protest," *Sight and Sound*, Spring 1985, 80). In Brazil, President José Sarney, under pressure from the Roman Catholic Church, banned *Hail Mary*. When this decision was attacked by, among others, author-politician Fernando Marais, Brazil's Conference of Bishops issued a statement insisting that there was "a difference between 'political and ideological censorship,' which cannot be accepted and caused so much ill during the military government, and 'censorship of a moral nature,' which can be necessary in defense of the common good" (Alan Riding, "Film about Mary Banned in Brazil," *New York Times*, February 10, 1986, sec. A).

33. See Harlan Jacobson, "Hail Mary," *Film Comment*, November–December 1985, 61–65, and John Water, "Flock Shock," *American Film*, January–February 1986, 38–41. Among the groups protesting the Lincoln Center premiere were Knights of Lithuania; Greater New York Chapter of the Catholic League for Religious and Civil Liberties; National Coalition for Clergy and Laity; Knights of Columbus; Holy Name Society; American Society for the Defense of Tradition, Family, and Property; and Morality Action Committee of Jackson Heights.

34. Mary Pat Kelly, *Martin Scorsese: A Journey* (New York: Thunder's Mouth, 1991), 178.

35. Ibid., 180.

36. Pat H. Broeske, " 'Last Temptation': Is It Already Bearing Its Cross?" *Los Angeles Times*, April 17, 1988, sec. 6.

37. John Dart, "Church Leaders Upset at Delay in Film Screening," *Los*

Angeles Times, June 18, 1988. "Church Leaders Upset at Film on Jesus," United Press International, June 18, 1988.

38. "Minister Blasts Universal Movie as 'Perverted,' " United Press International, July 12, 1988.

39. "Evangelists Intensify Struggle to Stop Film," *Los Angeles Times,* July 12, 1988, sec. 6.

40. Pat A. Broeske, "Universal Asked to 'Destroy' Scorsese's Film about Christ," *Los Angeles Times,* July 13, 1988, sec. 6.

41. Aljean Harmetz, "New Scorsese Film Shown to Religious Leaders," *New York Times,* July 13, 1988, sec. C. "Evangelists Intensify Struggle to Stop Film," *Los Angeles Times,* July 12, 1988, sec. 6.

42. Harmetz, "New Scorsese Film."

43. Paul Moore, Jr., " 'Last Temptation' Dwells on Humanity of Jesus," *New York Times,* July 24, 1988, sec. C.

44. John Dart, "Some Clerics See No Evil in 'Temptation,' " *Los Angeles Times,* July 26, 1988, sec. 6. Fore is quoted in Harmetz, "New Scorsese Film," and in Cynthia Gorney, "The 'Temptation' Furor: Studio Ads Defend Scorsese's Controversial Film about Christ," *Washington Post,* July 22, 1988, sec. D.

45. John Dart, "Church Likely to Condemn 'Temptation,' Mahony Says," *Los Angeles Times,* July 20, 1988, sec. 1; John Dart, "2 Step Back from Film Protest over Anti-Jewish Tone," *Los Angeles Times,* July 23, 1988, sec. 2.

46. Aljean Harmetz, "Film on Christ Brings Out Pickets, and Archbishop Predicts Censure," *New York Times,* July 21, 1988, sec. C. The accusations of anti-Semitism spread to Rome, where Franco Zeffirelli allegedly said the film was the product of the "Jewish cultural scum of Hollywood." While Zeffirelli vehemently denied making this comment, claiming "I have always been a friend of the Jews," the dispute over whether or not he did added to the larger controversy over the movie.

47. Universal Pictures, "A Letter to Bill Bright, Campus Crusade for Christ," *New York Times,* July 21, 1988, sec. C. Nina J. Easton, "Studio Fires Back in Defense of 'Temptation,' " *Los Angeles Times,* July 22, 1988, sec. 2.

48. See Michael Medved, *Hollywood vs. America: Popular Culture and the War on Traditional Values* (New York: HarperCollins, 1992), 46–48. While I agree with Medved's general assessment of the media's reporting of the *Last Temptation* controversy, his account is tendentious and suffers from a lack of substantive citations from the numerous news articles and television programs covering the events. "The Test of 'The Last Temptation of Christ,' " *Los Angeles Times,* July 23, 1988, sec. 2. Roger Ebert, "Censors Should Resist 'Temptation,' " *New York Post,* July 22, 1988, sec. D. Valenti is quoted in "MPAA Supports Universal's 'Temptation,' " *Variety,* July 27, 1988, 3, and in Aljean Harmetz, "Top Studios Support 'Christ' Film," *New York Times,* July 25, 1988, sec. C.

49. Letter, Sandra Gines, religion writer for the *Waco Tribune-Herald,* to Leanne Katz, Executive Director of the National Coalition Against Censorship (NCAC), July 25, 1988, "Last Temptation of Christ," Movie Censorship File, NCAC Archives, New York City. Pat Buchanan, "Anything for a Buck: Hollywood's Sleazy Image of Christ," *Philadelphia Inquirer,* July 27, 1988, sec. A.

50. John Dart, "Bishop Decries Free Publicity for 'Temptation' Movie," *Los Angeles Times,* July 27, 1988, sec. 1.

51. "MPAA Supports Universal's 'Temptation,' " *Variety,* July 27, 1988, 26.

52. *Orange County Business Journal,* August 1, 1988, 3. Tim Robbins, et al., " 'Last Temptation' War Rages On; Exhibs Pressured, Italy Quakes," *Variety,* August 3, 1988, 6.

53. See Aljean Harmetz, " 'Temptation' Gets Early Release," *New York Times,* August 5, 1988, sec. C.

54. "Obscenity and Blasphemy on Film: Statement by Jerry Falwell on 'The Last Temptation of Christ,' August 5, 1988," *Liberty Report,* September 1988, 1, 5, "The Last Temptation of Christ: Clippings File," Academy of Motion Picture Arts and Sciences Library, Los Angeles.

55. Hymers is quoted in Kim Masters, "The Careful Strategy of 'Temptation'; Limited Release, Avoidance of TV Ads Planned," *Washington Post,* August 10, 1988, sec. D. For more information on the Hymers controversy, see Dart, "2 Steps Back."

56. Mother Angelica is quoted in Russell Kishi, "Religious Leaders Damn 'Last Temptation of Christ,' " United Press International, August 9, 1988, and Wildmon in "Last Temptation Controversy," ABC-TV *Nightline,* August 9, 1988, show #1882, transcript, 6.

57. On Edwards, see Aurelio Rojos, "Fundamentalists Demonstrate against Controversial Film," United Press International, August 6, 1988, and "Edwards Cinema Chain Won't Run 'Last Temptation,' " *Los Angeles Times,* August 7, 1988, sec. 6. On UA and GCC, see David Grogan, et al., "In the Name of Jesus," *People,* August 8, 1988, 40. On Hazleton, see "Catholics Urged to Shun Film," *Philadelphia Inquirer,* August 19, 1988, and for quote, "Actress's Kin and Others Protest Council's Stand on Film," *Scranton Times,* August 10, 1988.

58. Hirsh is quoted in Geraldine Baum, "Bishops: Christ Film 'Offensive,'" *Newsday,* August 10, 1988, 4. McFarland and Schuller are quoted in Mark Landsbaum, "Bishop, Schuller Join Voices Urging 'Temptation' Boycott," *Los Angeles Times,* August 10, 1988, sec. 2. Mother Theresa is quoted in John Dart, "Church Declares 'Last Temptation' Morally Offensive," *Los Angeles Times,* August 10, 1988, sec. 2.

59. Dart, "Church Declares."

60. "On the Verge of a Public Blasphemy," *New York Times,* August 12, sec. A.

61. On the Odeon, Aljean Harmetz, " 'The Last Temptation of Christ' Opens to Protests but Good Sales," *New York Times,* August 13, 1988, sec. C. and John Dart and Russell Chandler, "Full Theatres, Protests Greet 'Temptation,' " *Los Angeles Times,* August 13, 1988, sec. 1. On the Century Plaza, see Laura Sessions Stepp, "Long Lines for 'Last Temptation': Police, Tight Security Mark Film's Opening," *Washington Post,* August 13, 1988, sec. C.

62. On the Ziegfield and Avalon, Harmetz, " 'Last Temptation of Christ' Opens." On the Avalon announcement and Chicago, Dart and Chandler, "Full Theaters."

63. The press release and Pollack are quoted in Harmetz, " 'Last Temptation of Christ' Opens," and Beatty in Kim Masters, "Directors Back Scorcese: 'Cowardice' of Theatre Chain Decried," *Washington Post,* August 13, 1988, sec. C.

64. In *Hollywood vs. America,* Michael Medved argues that *Last Temptation* was less a box-office success than the press claimed (see Harmetz, " 'Last Temptation of Christ' Opens"; Aljean Harmetz, " 'Last Temptation' Sets Record as Pickets Decline," *New York Times,* August 15, 1988, sec. C; and Dart and Chandler, "Full Theatres"). Box-office figures, however, contradict this; the film averaged $44,579 per screen and had a first weekend gross of $401,211 nationwide, substantial considering the film's initially limited and subsequently problematic wider release (see Jeff Wilson, "First Showings Sell Out for Last Temptation," *Philadelphia Inquirer,* August 16, 1988, sec. D). According to *Variety,* the domestic box-office revenues for *Last Temptation,* meaning revenue prior to the film's video release, wound up at $8.37 million (see the cd-rom *Compact Variety* (Vol. 1: 1996). Considering that the film cost the studio approximately $6.5 million to produce and that Universal deliberately kept publicity costs low, it was at the very least profitable.

65. For more information about the protests and counterprotests in Boston, see Nickolas W. Pflugin and Gus Martins, "Protests, Counter Protests Greet 'Temptation,' " *Boston Globe,* September 6, 1988, 6. On the archbishop, Michael Vitez, "Religious Leaders React Mildly to 'Temptation of Christ,' " *Philadelphia Inquirer,* August 19, 1988, sec. C., and on the Ritz, Michael Vitez, " 'Temptation' Fails to Kick Up a Storm Here," *Philadelphia Inquirer,* August 20, 1988, sec. C.

66. On New Orleans, see Rebecca Theim and Chris Cooper, "St. Bernard, Kenner Officials: Don't be Tempted by Movie," *Times-Picayne,* August 18, 1988, 33, and on Santa Ana, Jess Braun, "Hundreds at Mall Protest Screening of 'Temptation,' " *Los Angeles Times,* August 20, 1988, sec. 2.

67. Hunt is quoted in "Stolen Print Is Latest Chapter in the 'Last Temptation' Saga," *Variety,* August 31, 1988, 25. On Pensacola, see "Judge Overturns Ban on Film," *New York Times,* September 10, 1988, sec. 1.

68. On Savannah, "Exhibs Digress on 'Temptation,' " *Variety,* August 24, 1988, 28, and on OSU, Jim Killackey and Michael McNutt, "Regents Block Controversial Film at OSU," *Oklahoman & Times,* September 23, 1988.

69. In Fort Worth, the chair of the Torrent County Republican Party resigned because the party's executive committee refused to join him in voting to condemn the film. See "The Last Temptation," United Press International, August 25, 1988. On the Atlanta protest, see "Stolen Print." On the Dallas protest, see "Peaceful Prayerful Protest Rally Opposes Opening of 'Last Temptation' in Dallas," *Southwest Newswire,* August 31, 1988.

70. On the Center, see "Stolen Print"; on the Showcase, see "Theatre Is Vandalized in 'Temptation' Protest," *New York Times,* September 6, 1988, sec. C. and Amy Daves, "'Tempt' Protests Continue; Vandals Damage H'wood House," *Variety,* September 7, 1988, 1.

71. Protests against the exhibition of *Last Temptation* in France were more violent than those in the United States. When the film opened in Paris on September 28, a riot followed in the foyer of the UGC Odeon. An arson attack on the Cinéma St. Michel left thirteen people hospitalized and the theatre gutted. The clubbing of moviegoers and the throwing of tear gas and stink bombs in theatres were recorded in Lyons, Nice, and Grenoble. These militant acts by ultraconservative religious groups such as Christian Solidarity led a representative of Universal International Pictures, which distributed *Last Temptation* in France, to say, "The opponents of the film have largely won. They have massacred the film's success, and they have scared the public" (Steven Greenhouse, "Police Suspect Arson in Fire at Paris Theater," *New York Times,* October 25, 1988, sec. C. See also James M. Markham, "Religious War Ignites Anew in France," *New York Times,* November 9, 1988, sec. A). Actions in other foreign cities were less violent, yet the film faced official censorship challenges in England, Australia, Greece, South Africa, Israel, Brazil, and Ireland. See "Last Temptation Touches Off Protests among European Groups," *Variety,* August 24, 1988, 5, 24.

72. *Last Temptation* suffered other censorships in the ensuing years. In 1989, Blockbuster Video, the nation's largest video chain, decided not to distribute the video version of *Last Temptation* in any of its stores. (see "Chain Won't Stock 'Last Temptation,' " *Fayetteville Observer and Times,* June 22, 1989, sec. A). In January 1991, the board of trustees of Seminole Community College in Orlando, responding to pressure from local religious groups, ordered the film moved from the 370-seat Fine Arts Concert Hall to a classroom that seated far fewer people. During the spring of 1992, the ACLU sued the college, holding that the film should be reshown in the larger theater (see Sara Isaac, "ACLU Poised to Go to Court over Screening," *Orlando Sentinel,* January 29, 1991, sec. 1).

CONCLUSION

1. "Hollywood Speech, Los Angeles, California, May 31, 1995," in "Bob Dole: A Vision for America: Collected Speeches, January–October 1995" (Washington, D.C.: Bob Dole for President, 1996), 34 (pamphlet).

2. W.E.B. DuBois, "Slanderous Film," *The Crisis* II (December 1915): 76.

3. Quayle's address to the Republican National Convention, August 20, 1992, is quoted in *Facts on File* (New York: Facts on File, 1992), 608.

4. "What's Happening to Disney" (advertisement), *New York Times,* April 10, 1995, sec. C. On Dole, see Frank Rich, "Dole's Moral Stand," *New York Times,* April 20, 1995, sec. A. For more on the controversy, see John Dart, "Miramax to Delay General Release of 'Priest' after Protest by Catholics," *Los Angeles Times,* March 25, 1995, sec. A; Bernard Weinraub, "Objection to 'Priest' Isn't Creating a Hit." *New York Times,* April 20, 1995, sec. C; and David Hunter, "Holy War," *L.A. Weekly,* April 14–20, 1995, 11. On *Priest's* prerelease censorship, see Wolf Schneider, "Forbidden Love," *Hollywood Reporter 65th Anniversary Issue,* November 20, 1995, 69.

5. As of September 30, only three NC-17 films had been released nationally in 1995, while in 1991 there had been a high of twenty-one. See Schneider, "Forbidden Love," 70.

6. Elaine Dutka, "Asian-Americans: Rising Furor over 'Rising Sun,' " *Los Angeles Times,* July 28, 1993, sec. F; see also David Ferrell and K. Connie Kang, " 'Rising Sun' Opens to Charges of Racism," *Los Angeles Times,* July 31, 1993, sec. 6.

7. Jennings is quoted in Karen Ocamb, "Human Tapestry," *Hollywood Reporter 65th Anniversary Issue,* November 20, 1995, 19–22, 106–107, which offers a detailed treatment of gays and lesbians in recent films.

8. See Andrew Hindes, "Activists Applaud Jackson Stand," *Daily Variety,* March 19, 1996, 5, 17; see also Pam Lambert et al., "What's Wrong with This Picture? Exclusion of Minorities Has Become a Way of Life in Hollywood," *People,* March 18, 1996, 42–52.

Index

Academy of Motion Picture Arts and Sciences, 26, 197–98n.15
Acid from Heaven, 33
Acid Rain: Requiem or Recovery?, 33
Acosta, John, 180
ACT UP, 123, 128, 130, 136
Addobbati, Aldo, 158
Advise and Consent, 22, 111
African Americans, anti-stereotyping campaigns by, 20, 82, 85, 185–86, 192
Agnos, Art, 127
AIDS, movie censorship and, 22–23, 123, 125–26, 190
AIDS Project Los Angeles, 124
Airplane, 79
Albee, Edward, 56
Allen, Nancy, 68
Allende, Salvador, 31
All the President's Men, 17, 31
American Civil Liberties Union (ACLU), 34, 39, 42–43, 50, 87
American Family Association, 160, 181, 195n.20
American Gigolo, 3, 22–23, 117, 120, 122
American Legion, 29
American Society for the Defense of Tradition, Family and Property (TFP), 174–75
Ancient Order of Hibernians, 153
Anti-Defamation League, 149
antitrust laws, movie studios and, 30
Artists and Writers Against Censorship, 179

Asian American Community Advisory Board, 105
Asian American Network, 104
Asian American Resource Workshop, 100
Asian Americans: anti-stereotyping protests of, 20–21, 54, 81–85, 88–93, 189–90, 207n.15; protest against *Year of the Dragon* by, 92–106, 189–90
Asian CineVision, 96–98
Asian Pacific American Media Watch, 99
Association of Asian/Pacific American Artists (AAPAA), 21, 89–91
Association of Motion Picture and Television Producers, 115–16
Association on American Indian Affairs (AAIA), 85
Atlanta Constitution, 165
Autin, Diana, 47

Baer, Ted, 195n.20
Bakker, Jim, 155–56, 181
Bakker, Tammy, 156
Bara, Theda, 55
Barnard College, 80
Barry, Kathleen, 61
Basic Instinct, 22–23, 107–8, 125–45, 205n.40
Bates, Pam, 135
Bay Area Reporter, 130–31
Beame, Abe (Mayor), 64
Beatty, Warren, 178
Beehler, Don, 161
behavioral theories, violence in movies and, 14–15, 60–61, 194n.19

Bell, Arthur, 115, 118, 120
Bennetts, Leslie, 122
Berns, Walter, 60
Beruit Agreement, film distribution
　and, 197n.15
Best Man, The, 111
Better Films Committees, 148
Bevilacqua, Anthony (Archbishop),
　179
Biberman, Herbert, 29
Birth of a Nation, The, 20, 82, 185,
　202n.10
Bisexual Public Action Committee,
　141
Black, Gregory, 17
Block, Mitchell, 36, 38, 43–46, 52
Blockade, 16
Block v. Meese lawsuit, 44, 50
Block v. Smith lawsuit, 42–44, 46,
　199n.29
B'Nai B'rith, 149
Bob Jones University, 156
Body Double, 79
Bogdanovich, Peter, 178
Bonnie and Clyde, 30
Bosco, Anthony, 169
Boston Globe, 100, 102, 142, 208n.32
Boulevard Nights, 14
Boy and His Dog, A, 66
Boys in the Band, The, 22, 115
Boys on the Side, 189, 190
Bram Stoker's Dracula, 195n.24
Braveheart, 191
Bray, Robert, 136
Brazil, religious film censorship in,
　217n.32
Brennan, William J. (Justice), 57–59
Bride, The, 102
Bright, Bill, 160, 162–63, 165–67
Britt, Harvey, 128, 130
Broeske, Pat A., 163
Broken Arrow, 190
Bronski, Michael, 126, 145
Brother Sun, Sister Moon, 155
Brown, Jennifer, 203n.26

Brown, Roscoe Lee, 207n.19
Brownmiller, Susan, 61
Buchanan, Pat, 168
Bullfrog Films v. USIA, 197–98n.15
Burger, Warren (Justice), 59
Burgess, Anthony, 156
Burke, Phyllis, 135
Burstyn, Joseph B., 8, 152, 154
Burstyn v. Wilson, 8
Bush, George, 9, 187
Busting, 115
Byron, Stuart, 114

Cage Aux Folles, La, 122
Caine, Michael, 68
Caldicott, Helen, 36, 40, 45
Caligula, 59, 202n.10
Callahans and the Murphys, The, 24,
　149
Campus Crusade for Christ, 160,
　161–63, 166–67
"Can Charlie Chan" campaign, 92
capitalism, censorship and, 5
Carnal Knowledge, 57, 59
Carolco Pictures, 126, 128–30, 133,
　143
Carpenter, John, 178–79
Carr, C., 124–25
Carrie, 72
Carroll, Kathleen, 73
Carten, Ellen, 136–37
Carter, Jimmy (President), 155–56
Casey, William P., 47
Castro, Antonio, 104
Catch 22, 30
"Catherine Did It!," 134–36, 140,
　212n.55
Catholic Action, 153
Catholic League, 187–88
Catholic Legion of Decency, 18, 151,
　154–55
Catholics: *Last Temptation of Christ*
　controversy and, 165, 169, 172–82;
　religious content of movies and,
　148–55, 157–59, 187–88, 217n.32

Catholic Theatre Guild, 149
Catholic War Veterans, 152–53
Cat on a Hot Tin Roof, 22, 111
censorship: defined, 4–5; evolution of, 4–12; history of, 3; in movie industry, 1–2; *vs.* protest, 1–2
Central Conference of American Rabbis, 148
"Certificates of International Character," 197n.15
Chalker, Ray, 107–8, 126–27
Chan, Jackie, 190
Charlie Chan and the Curse of the Dragon Queen, 3, 21, 54, 90–92, 207n.19
Charlie Chan character, Asian stereotyping and, 89–90
Charlie Varrick, 89
Cheat, The, 82–83
Chetwynd, Lionel, 195n.25
Chicago, movie censorship in, 13–14
Chicago Reader, 73
Children of Loneliness, 109
Children's Hour, The (1936), 109
Children's Hour, The (1962), 22, 111
Chile, U.S.-sanctioned coup in, 31–33
Chin, Frank, 92
Chinatown, 31
Chinese American Citizens, 99–100
Chinese Americans, movie protests by, 84-85, 90–91, 93–106
Chinese Consolidated Benevolent Association (CCBA), 93–94, 98, 103, 209n.35
Chinese for Affirmative Action (CAA), 90–91, 93
Christensen, Terry, 28–29
Christian Century, 216n.23
Christian Film and Television Commission, 195n.20
Church of the Way, 162
Cicognani, A. G. (Archbishop), 150
Cimino, Michael, 21, 93–94, 102, 105
Cineplex Odeon Cinemas, 160, 169, 175

Citadel Culture, 49
Citizens for a Universal Appeal, 174
civil rights movement, movie censorship and, 9, 11
Clark, Tom C. (Justice), 8, 154
Clarkson, Joseph F., 200n.39
Cleopatra (1917), 55
CNN News, 143
Coalition Against Violence Against Women, 204n.26
Coalition Against Year of the Dragon, 94–95, 98–99, 102–5
Coalition of Asians to Nix Charlie Chan, 92
Cochron, Clifford, 109
Cohn, Roy, 27, 40
college campuses, culture wars on, 193n.1
Color Purple, The, 122–23
Colors, 14–15
Coming Home, 31
Committee Against *Fort Apache* (CAFA), 20, 185
Concerned Women for America, 170
Conley, Hollie, 126, 130–31
conservative groups: defined, 9–10; *If You Love This Planet* controversy and, 34, 41–42, 45; movie censorship and, 1–3, 191–92; movie violence, campaigns against, 15–16; pornography opposition by, 18–19, 60–61. *See also* neoconservatives
Coolidge, Martha, 179
Corliss, Richard, 73, 154
Costa Gavras, 30–31
Council of Jewish Women, 148
counterculture filmmaking, 17–18, 29–30
Creative Artists Agency, 160
Crier, Catherine, 143
crime movies, censorship of, 13–16
Crowther, Bosley, 151
Cruising, 3, 22–23, 54, 69, 108, 117–22, 125, 127, 204n.26
Crying Game, The, 190

Cuba and Fidel, 197–98n.15
Cuban Americans, anti-stereotyping campaigns of, 20, 85–88, 93
cultural dominance, censorship and, 54–55
culture wars: AIDS epidemic and, 123; *Dressed to Kill* controversy and, 80; *Last Temptation of Christ* controversy and, 169–70; liberals and conservatives and, 10–12; movie censorship and, 3, 193n.1; political censorship and, 33, 50–52
Curley, 84
Curry, Richard O., 47

Dafoe, Willem, 178
Daily Variety, 72
Dallas Morning News, 102
Daly, Mary, 61
Daly, Robert, 92, 94
Davis, Nathaniel, 32
Death in Venice, 22, 115
Deathtrap, 122
DeCair, Thomas P., 41–42
Deep Throat, 59, 202n.10
Deer Hunter, The, 17, 31, 93, 207n.15
DeLaurentis, Dino, 92
Delta of Venus, 189
DeMille, Cecil B., 23, 82–83, 148–49
Demme, Jonathan, 124–25, 190
democracy, censorship and, 4–5
Denby, David, 72, 74
De Palma, Brian, 19, 68–76, 87–88, 93, 205n.41
Der, Henry, 93
Dershowitz, Alan, 205n.41
de Tocqueville, Alexis, 186
Devil's Advocate, 22, 111
Dewey, Thomas (Governor), 153
Dickinson, Angie, 68, 70
Diller, Barry, 159
Dinkins, David, 96
direct-action campaigns, *vs.* rating systems, 2
Director's Guild of America, 178

Dobson, James, 163, 181
Dodge-Aspen commercial, Asian stereotyping in, 89–90
Dole, Bob, 15, 184–85, 188
Donner, Clive, 90
Donnerstein, Edward, 205n.41
Dorfman, Dan, 51
Douglas, Michael, 128–29
Dr. Strangelove, 30
Dragon Lady, 84
Dressed to Kill, 3, 18–20, 53, 68–80, 143, 188–89; commercial success of, 70–71, 78–79; feminists' campaign against, 74–80, 204n.36
DuBois, W.E.B., 185
Dukakis, Michael, 9
Dupe, Leonard, 44
Dworkin, Andrea, 61, 80, 125, 143

Ebert, Roger, 167
Ecocide: A Strategy of War, 197–98n.15
"economic censorship," 197–98n.15, 200n.44
Edwards, James Jr., 169–70, 172–73
Emerson, Thomas I., 5
Emmanuelle, 59, 202n.10
Empire Strikes Back, The, 79
End of the Road, 149
Entertainment Tonight, 34–35, 38
environmental films, government censorship of, 18
Episcopal Church, 157
Episcopal Committee, 150–51
erotica, pornography and, 61
Eszterhas, Joe, 125, 128–29, 143
Eternal World Television Network, 169, 172
ethnic groups, anti-stereotyping campaigns of, 9, 82–86, 98, 206n.7. *See also* specific groups
Evangelical Sisterhood, 159
Evangelism, film censorship and. *See* Religious Right
Execution of Charles Harmon: An American Sacrifice, The, 31–32

Executive Order 12356, 47–48
Executive Order No. 9835, 17
extralegal censorship, defined, 5–6

Fail Safe, 30
Falling Down, 189
Falwell, Jerry, 24, 147, 156, 165, 170–71
Farewell to Manzanar, 207n.15
Fasteau, Brenda Feigen, 65
Fatal Attraction, 79
Federal Bureau of Customs, 36–37
Federal Council of Churches of
  Christ of America, 148
Federal Loyalty and Security Program, 17
Federal Motion Picture Council,
  214n.5
Federation of Chinese Organizations
  of America, 103
Feinstein, Diane (Mayor), 120–21
feminist groups: antipornography
  campaigns of, 18–19, 59–68, 79,
  188–89, 205n.40; *Basic Instinct* controversy and, 136, 138, 140–43,
  213n.59; *Dressed to Kill* campaign by,
  53, 68, 72–80, 204n.36; involvement
  in *Year of the Dragon* controversy, 98;
  movie censorship and, 29, 188–89
Feminists Against Censorship Taskforce (F.A.C.T.), 80
Ferguson, Eugene Jr., 47
Fiendish Plot of Fu Manchu, The, 21,
  90–92
Fifth Amendment, USIA film certification and, 197–98n.15, 200n.44
Filmways Pictures, 69–72, 75
First Amendment: *Basic Instinct* controversy and, 130; *Cruising* controversy and, 119; *If You Love This
Planet* controversy and, 44, 51;
  movie censorship and, 8, 29–30,
  32–33, 154, 185, 192; USIA film certification and, 197–98n.15
Fit to Win, 149
Flap, 86

Flower Drum Song, 84
Flynn, Raymond (Mayor), 100
Focus on the Family, 163, 181
Fong, Benson, 89
Foreign Agents Registration Act
  (FARA), 36–42, 44, 50–52
Fort Apache, the Bronx, 3, 20, 86–87,
  185–86
Fortune and Men's Eyes, 22, 114
Fowler, Chris, 136
France, *Last Temptation of Christ* controversy in, 180–81, 221n.71
Franklin, Gary, 167
Frasca, Jill, 141
freedom, public opinion and, 10
Freedom of Information Act (FOIA),
  Reagan Administration attacks on,
  47–48, 200n.39
Freedom Socialist Party, 98
free speech, government movie censorship and, 6–8, 27. *See also* First
  Amendment
Fried Green Tomatoes, 123
Friedkin, William, 117–19, 121–22
Friedlander, Miriam, 96
Friedman, Miriam, 105
From the Ashes . . . Nicaragua Today,
  197–98n.15
Front, The, 31
Fundamentalist Christians. *See* Religious Right

Gabrielson, Guy George, 110
Gallaway, Stephen, 195n.25
gang violence, movie violence linked
  to, 15
Gaudino, Annette, 134–35
Gay, Lisa, 139
Gay Activist Alliance (GAA), 115–16
Gay and Lesbian Alliance Against
  Defamation (GLAAD), 123–24,
  126–28, 130–33, 136–38, 141,
  143–44, 211n.33
Gay and Lesbian Resource Center,
  140

Gay Liberation Front (GLF), 113–15
gays and lesbians: anti-stereotyping
campaigns by, 22–23, 112–16,
204n.26, 205n.40, 211n.33; *Basic In-
stinct* controversy and, 107–8,
126–45; *Silence of the Lambs* contro-
versy and, 123–25
General Cinema Corporation, 121,
172–73
General Motors, 156–57
Gere, Richard, 122
Gever, Martha, 66
Gibbs, Joe, 177
Gielgud, John, 89
Godard, Jean-Luc, 24, 158–59
Godfather, The, 20, 86, 206n.9
Gods Must Be Crazy, The, 3
Godspell, 155, 216n.23
Gok, Forrest, 93
Gold, Ronald, 119
Gone with the Wind, 8, 24, 151
Good-Bye Billy: America Goes to War,
197–98n.15
Gossett, Lou, 207n.19
government censorship, 1–2; docu-
mentary films and, 30–31, 33; polit-
ical films and, 16–18, 26–52; Reli-
gious Right and, 147–48; threats of,
6–7
Great Society, alleged failure of, 9, 11
Griffin, Susan, 61
Griffith, D. W., 20, 82
Guardian Angels, 15
Gulf & Western Corp., 159
Guthmann, Edward, 121

Hail Mary, 24, 158–59, 217n.32
Haines, Randa, 179
Hall, Marg, 66
Hamby, Alonzo, 10–11
Hanks, Tom, 190
Harmon, Charles, 31–33
Haru, Sunri, 91
Harvey Milk Gay Democratic Club, 119
Hassanein, Salah, 159–60
Hatch, Orrin (Senator), 200n.39

Hau, Shubert, 91
Hauser, Thomas, 31–32
Hayakawa, Sessue, 82–83
Hayford, Jude (Rev.), 163
Hays, Will D., 83, 148
Hays Production Code, 2, 7–8; crime
movie censorship and, 13–14; ho-
mosexuality in movies and, 209n.4;
political censorship by, 28; religion
in movies and, 148–49, 215n.5
Hearst Corporation, 32
Heaven and Earth, 189–90
Hecht, Ben, 13
Hellman, Lillian, 109
Hergott, Alan, 133
Hill, Walter, 179
Hirsh, Richard, 173
Hitchcock, Alfred, 30, 71
Hoffman, Peter, 129
Hollywood Reporter, 72, 162, 166
Hollywood Supports, 145, 191
Home for the Holidays, 190
homosexuality in movies: AIDS epi-
demic and, 123; stereotypes of,
22–23, 107–17, 190–91, 209n.2. *See
also* gays and lesbians
"Houchi Kouchi" dance, 55
House Un-American Activities Com-
mittee (HUAC), 17, 37, 110
How to Make an American Quilt, 189
Hubbard, L. Ron, 155
Hueholt, Claire, 140, 144
Hughes, Howard, 13–14
Hughes, John, 55
Hull, Elizabeth, 51
Hunt, Guy, 180
Hutton, Lauren, 122
Hymers, R. L. Jr. (Rev.), 165–66,
171–72

I Am Curious—Yellow, 57
identity politics, liberalism and, 11
If You Love Free Speech, 199n.35
If You Love This Planet, 16–18; Justice
Department campaign against,
26–28, 33–52, 197–98n.15; "political

If You Love This Planet (cont.)
propaganda" label on, 33–34; print
advertisement for, 35
Incredibly True Adventure of Two Girls in Love, The, 190
independent filmmakers, political censorship and, 29–30, 51–52, 197n.15
In Our Own Backyards: Uranium Mining in the United States, 197–98n.15
Interchurch World Movement, 147–48
International Catholic Cinema Office, 159
International Convention of the Disciples of Christ, 214n.5
International Federation of Catholic Alumnae, 148–49
Inter-Racial Committee Against Fort Apache (CAFA), 86–88
Irish Americans, anti-stereotyping campaigns of, 206n.7
Italian American Civil Rights League (IACRL), 86
Italian Americans, anti-stereotyping campaigns by, 20, 85–86, 206n.9, 208n.32

Jackson, Jesse, 192
Jade, 189
Jansen, Sue Curry, 5
Japanese American Citizens League, 207n.19
Japanese Americans, anti-stereotyping campaigns of, 82–84, 190, 207n.15
Jennings, Richard, 124, 133, 191
Jesus Christ Superstar, 23, 155, 216n.23
Jesus of Nazareth, 24, 156–57
Jewish groups: anti-stereotyping protests of, 206n.7; religion in movies and, 148–49, 157–58, 165–66, 170–72, 218n.46
Jewison, Norman, 23
Johnston, Eric, 22, 110
Jones, Bob (III), 156
Joy Luck Club, The, 189
Julia, 31
Juliet of the Spirits, 56

Kael, Pauline, 71–72
Kappeler, Susanne, 61
Kaufman, Philip, 190
Kazantzákis, Nikos, 147
Kee, Virginia, 96–97
Keene, Barry, 43–44
Keene v. Smith lawsuit, 42–43, 199n.29
Kehr, Dave, 73
Kellner, Douglas, 29–30
Kelly, John (Father), 149
Kennedy, Edward, 36
Kids, 186
Killing Ground, The, 197–98n.15
King of Kings (1926), 23, 148–49
Kinsey, Alfred, 110
Kirsh, Steven, 203n.26
Kiss of the Spider Woman, 102, 122
Kite, Morris, 121
Klein, Alain, 134
Klondike Annie, 7
Knight, Morris, 115
Koch, Ed (Mayor), 117–19, 127
Kopkind, Andrew, 32–33
Koppes, Clayton, 16–17
Korean Americans, 189
Kraus, Bill, 119
Krimsky, John, 109
Kristol, Irving, 60
Kubrick, Stanley, 30
Kuhn, Annette, 54
Kunstler, William, 87

labeling of films, *If You Love This Planet* controversy and, 34–52
LaBelle, Beverly, 64
Labia, 107–8
Lady Chatterley's Lover, 57–58
Lai, Irvin, 99–100
Landau, Eli A., 56
Landsbaum, Scott Lewis, 51
Last Tango in Paris, 202n.10
Last Temptation of Christ, The, 23–25, 146–47, 159–82, 187, 220n.64, 221nn.71–72
Lawrence, D. H., 58

League of Black Cinema Artists, 207n.19
Lederer, Laura, 19, 62–64
Lederer, Susan, 61
Lee, Ang, 190
Lee, Margie, 81
Lee, Marilyn, 100
Lee, Paul, 101–2
Left. *See* liberalism
legal censorship: attacks on, 8, 191–92; defined, 4–5. *See also* government censorship
Legion of Decency, 28, 56
Leidholdt, Dorchen, 61, 77, 79, 204n.26, 205n.41
LeLorrain, Edward, 27
Lemmon, Jack, 31
Lewis, Anthony, 40–41
liberalism: defined, 9–10; *If You Love This Planet* controversy and, 34, 40–41; minorities and, 10–11; movie censorship and, 1–4, 185–86, 191–92
Live Nude Girls, 190–91
Lolita, 55
Lone, John, 100–102, 208n.32
Lord, Daniel (Father), 150
Los Angeles Times, 40, 100, 102, 133–35, 142, 144, 163, 166–67, 174, 208n.32
Lost Boundaries, 84
Lost Horizons, 89
Love in a Hammock, 55
Lovers, The, 57, 59
Low, Julian, 100
Lumet, Sidney, 8, 30
Lutheran Council, 157

MacKinnon, Catherine, 61, 80
Madame du Barry, 7
Mädchen in Uniform, 109, 209n.4
Madonna, 195n.24
Mafia, 86
Mahony, Roger M. (Archbishop), 165
Making Love, 122
Malle, Louis, 59
Man Called Horse, A, 86
Mann, Michael, 179

Man on America's Conscience, A, 84
Manzanar Committee, 207n.15
Mapplethorpe, Robert, 123, 186, 211n.34
Marais, Fernando, 217n.32
Marathon Man, 116–17
Marchett, Gina, 105
marketplace of ideas concept, censorship and, 5
Marnie, 30
Marshall, Alan, 128–29, 131
Martinez, Al, 142
Martinez, Guillermo, 88
Maslin, Janet, 142
MCA Corp., 160–61, 165, 170–71
McCaffrey, Edward T., 152
McCarran-Walter Act, 48
McCarthy era: homosexuality linked to communism in, 110; movie censorship during, 28–29
McFarland, Norman F. (Bishop), 173
McGoldrick, Thomas A. (Mrs.), 149
McGuinness, Richard, 114
McKenna, Joseph (Justice), 7
Media Focus, 160
Media Forum, 207n.19
Medved, Michael, 14, 167, 194n.19, 195n.20, 218n.48
Meese v. Keene lawsuit, 43–44, 51, 200n.36
Meet the Press, 188
Mexicans, anti-stereotyping protests of, 82–83, 85
Meyerhafer, William, 141
MGM Studios, 30, 114, 149–50
MGM/UA, 98–99, 102–5, 208n.32
Miami Herald, 88
Midnight Express, 20
Mill, John Stuart, 9–10
Miller, Janella, 205n.41
Miller v. California, 59
minority groups: anti-stereotyping campaigns by, 3, 9, 55, 82–83; liberalism and, 10–11
Miracle, The, 8, 24, 29, 151–55, 158, 197n.6

Miramax Films, 187
miscegenation, MPPDA ban on,
    82–83, 110–11
Missing, 31–33
Mitchell, George J., 36
Money Train, 14–15
Monty Python's Life of Brian, 3–4, 24,
    157–58
Moon Is Blue, The, 8, 55
Moral Majority, 24, 156, 159, 181
Morgan, Robin, 60–61
Mother Angelica, 169, 172
Mother Teresa, 174
Motion Picture Association of Amer-
    ica (MPAA): Appeals Board, 56–57;
    code revisions by, 110–11, 191; *Last
    Temptation of Christ* controversy and,
    167–68; movie rating system, 6–7,
    121; Ratings Board, 69
Motion Picture Herald, 152
Motion Picture Producers and Dis-
    tributors of America (MPPDA),
    194n.17; ethnic stereotypes in
    movies and, 83–84; homosexuality
    in movies and, 22, 108, 209n.2; po-
    litical censorship and, 29; ratings
    codes and, 7–8; religious content of
    movies and, 148–50, 151–52; vio-
    lence in movies and, 14
movie industry, censorship in, 1–2
*Mutual Film Corporation v. Industrial
    Commission of Ohio,* 7, 154
My Beautiful Laundrette, 122

Nash, Terri, 26, 34, 44–46
Nasty Habits, 155
National Asian American Telecom-
    munications Association (NAATA),
    93, 99, 105
National Association for the Advance-
    ment of Colored People (NAACP),
    15, 20, 82, 84, 185
National Association of Lesbian and
    Gay Filmmakers, 121
National Association of the Motion
    Picture Industry (NAMPI), 7

National Catholic Welfare Confer-
    ence, 148
National Clean Air Coalition, 36
National Coalition Against Television
    Violence, 195n.20
National Council of Churches, 157
National Endowment for the Arts, 3
National Film Board of Canada
    (NFB), 34
National Gay and Lesbian Task Force,
    116–19, 133, 136
National Organization of Women
    (NOW), 136, 138, 140–41, 143,
    203n.26, 205n.40, 213n.59
National Press Club, 36
Native Americans, anti-stereotyping
    protests of, 85–86
Natural Born Killers, 14–15, 195n.23
Navasky, Victor, 48–49
Nazi Love Camp, 66
Nazimova, Alla, 108
NBC Television, 207n.15
neoconservatives: anti-pornography
    issues of, 60–61; emergence of, 11
Network, 17, 31
Neuborne, Bert, 40
New Christian Right, movie censor-
    ship and, 3, 9, 11, 155
New Jack City, 14
Newsday, 73–74
Newsweek, 155
New York Board of Regents, 8,
    153–54
New York Daily News, 73, 134
New Yorker, 71–72
New York Holy Name Society, 153
New York magazine, 70–71
New York Post, 73
New York State Board of Censors, 58
New York Times, 40–42, 71, 110,
    114, 118, 122, 142, 166, 174–76,
    187–88
Nichols, Mike, 30, 57
Nightline, 27, 36, 38, 40, 172
Nixon, Richard, 11, 18, 59
Nosotros, 207n.19

nudity in film, censorship policies
and, 55–56
NYQ, 126, 145

obscenity laws: film censorship and,
55–59, 189–90; legal censorship
with, 29; PCA rule revisions on la-
beling and, 111–12
Office of War Information (OWI),
16–17, 84
Ogilvie, Lloyd John (Rev.), 162–63
Oliver Twist, 206n.7
Once Upon a Time in America, 205n.40
On Liberty, 9–10
Organization of Chinese Americans,
91
Orion Pictures, 124, 157
Outlaw, The, 55
Outweek, 124
Ovitz, Mike, 160
Oxenberg, Jan, 121
Oxford English Dictionary, 4–5

Pacino, Al, 121–22
Pally, Marcia, 205n.41
Parallax View, The, 31
Paramount Studios, 15, 30, 159–60
Paris Adult Theatre I v. Slaton, 59
Park, Mary Jamie, 120
Partners, 122
Pawnbroker, The, 8, 55–57
Payne Studies on social effects of
movies, 194n.19
Pedron, Eduardo, 88
Pee-Wee's Big Adventure, 102
Penetration, 66
Penland, Tim, 160, 163
Penn, Arthur, 30
Perez, Demetrio, 88
Perfect Couple, The, 22
Personal Best, 122
Petrie, Dan, 87
Philadelphia, 190
Philadelphia Inquirer, 168, 180
Pinky, 84
Pit of Loneliness, 22, 111

Poitier, Sidney, 207n.19
Poland, Larry, 162
political films, 3; government censorship of, 16–18, 28–32
Pollack, Sidney, 179
Pollock, Tom, 160
Poole, Cecil F. (Judge), 200n.44
pornography: *Dressed to Kill* controversy and, 72–80; feminist campaigns against, 60–68, 203n.23;
movie censorship and, 18–19,
57–60, 202n.10; PCA rule revisions
on labeling of, 111–12; violence
linked to, 60–61. *See also* obscenity
Powell, Jody, 41–42
Preminger, Otto, 8, 111
Priest, 186–88
prior restraint, censorship and, 5
Probst, John, 160
Proctor and Gamble, 157
Production Code Administration
(PCA): Catholic Legion of Decency and, 18, 150–51; homosexuality in movies and, 22; ratings
codes, 7–8, 110–11; violence in
movies and, 14
profanity, censorship policies and,
56–57
Professor Mamlock, 16
Program, The, 14–15
propaganda, films labeled as: *If You
Love This Planet* controversy and,
33–37, 42–52; PCA rule revisions
on, 111–12
Protestant organizations, religious
content of movies and, 148–49,
155–56, 181–82, 214n.5
protests, censorship and, 1–2, 6
Psycho, 71
Puerto Ricans, anti-stereotyping campaigns of, 20, 85–87, 185–86

Quayle, Dan, 187
Queer Nation, 107, 123, 126–28,
130–36, 141, 143–44
Quigley, Martin, 150, 152

Rabbinical Assembly of America, 149
Racket, The, 13
Radical Women, 98
radio stations, *Last Temptation of Christ* controversy and, 165–69
Rains, Claude, 89
Ramirez, Raul (Judge), 43
Randall, Richard, 14
rating systems, *vs.* direct-action campaigns, 2
Rawhide II (gay bar), 107, 126–27
Reagan, Ronald (President): attacks on FOIA by, 46–49, 200n.39; *If You Love This Planet* controversy under, 35–52, 199n.34; movie censorship under, 3, 16–18, 27–28, 33, 69, 147, 187; Religious Right and, 156
Reed, Rex, 73
religious movies, censorship of, 23–24, 146–82
Religious Right: *Last Temptation of Christ* controversy and, 146–47, 159–82; movie censorship and, 3, 9, 123, 192, 211n.34; political causes of, 11, 155–56; religion in movies and, 156–59
Return of the Living Dead, 102
Rice, Ann, 195n.24
Rice, Elmer, 111
Rich, Frank, 15–16, 188
Richey, Charles R. (Judge), 43
Rickey, Carrie, 102
Riese, Patt, 134
Right. *See* conservatism
Riley, John, 119
Rising Run, 190
Roberts, John, 35–36, 40
Roberts, Oral, 155
Robertson, Pat, 155
Rochester Women Against Violence Against Women, 68
Rones, Stephanie, 75, 78
Roosevelt, Franklin Delano, 10, 16
Rosaries for Peace, 174
Rose, Robert, 36
Rosenbaum, Ron, 124–25

Rossellini, Roberto, 8, 24, 151–52
Roth, Samuel, 57
Rothman, Frank, 103–4
Roth v. United States obscenity case, 57–58
Rourke, Mickey, 92, 100–101
Ruddy, Al, 86
Rumble in the Bronx, 190
Russell, Diane, 62
Russo, Vito, 108–9, 114, 117, 209n.4
Ruvolo, Rick, 130
Ryan, Michael, 29–30

Sagan, Leontine, 109
Sakamoto, Janice, 93, 99, 105–6
Salome, 108
Salt of the Earth, 29
San Francisco Chronicle, 134, 138
San Francisco Examiner, 131
Sarney, José (President), 217n.32
Sarris, Andrew, 73, 77
Save the Planet, 197–98n.15
Scalia, Antonin, 45–46, 200n.36
Scarface (1932), 13–14
Scarface (1982), 20, 87–88, 93
Schrader, Paul, 159, 161, 171
Schuller, Robert (Rev.), 173
Schumach, Murray, 191–92
Scorsese, Martin, 23, 146–47, 159–61, 167, 171–72, 178–79
Screen Actors Guild, 91
self-regulation, censorship as, 7
Selznick, David O., 7–8
Senate Bill 774, 47
Senate Bill 1730, 200n.39
Sense and Sensibility, 190
Serrano, Andres, 186
Sex, 195n.24
sexuality in movies: censorship of, 18–20, 59; *Dressed to Kill* controversy and, 55, 79–80; *vs.* obscenity, 58–59
Sheinfeld, Lois P., 205n.41
Sherlock, Jerry, 90
Showgirls, 189
Shurlock, Jeffrey, 56–57, 111–12
Sign of the Cross, 23

Signoreli, Michelangelo, 124–25, 145
Silence of the Lambs, 123–25, 134
Sims, Charles, 44–45, 50
Sisneros, Judy, 144
Smith, 50–51
Smolla, Rodney, 32–33, 50–51
Snitow, Ann, 205n.41
Snuff, 19, 25–26, 63–68, 203n.23
social effects of movies, movie violence and, 15–16, 194n.19
social groups, censorship and, 54–55
Soldier Girls, 197–98n.15
Some of My Best Friends Are . . ., 115
Southerner, The, 29
South Pacific, 84
Spacek, Sissy, 31
Spain in Flames, 16
Spanish-American League Against Discrimination, 88
special-interest pressure groups, censorship and, 1–2
Spellman, Cardinal, 152–53
Spitz, David, 12
Stalking Moon, The, 86
Steinem, Gloria, 61
Sterritt, David, 172
Stevens, John Paul (Justice), 44
Stone, Judy, 73
Stone, Oliver, 93, 189–90, 195n.23
Stone, Sharon, 125
Stonewall riots, 22, 113
Story of O, The, 68
Streetcar Named Desire, A, 55
Suddenly Last Summer, 22, 111
Suggs, Donald, 136
Supreme Court (U.S.): *If You Love This Planet* controversy and, 43–44, 200n.36; movie censorship decisions by, 7–8, 18–19, 154, 191–92; obscenity in movies, 57–59, 202n.10
Susskind, David, 86–87
Swaggart, Jimmy, 155, 181

Tajima, Renee, 95–96
Take Back the Night, 64
Tale of the Body Thief, 195n.24

Tan, Amy, 189
Tariff Act (1930), 36–37
Tashima, Wallace (Judge), 200n.44
Tate, Allen, 153–54
Taubin, Amy, 142–43
Taxi Driver, 31
television, homosexuality on, 115–17
Texas Chainsaw Massacre, The, 204n.26
Thelma and Louise, 189
These Three, 111
"Thirteen Points" concept, 7
Thomas, Kevin, 63–64
Three Days of the Condor, 31
Time, 73
Time-Life Films, 86–87
Titicut Follies, 30–31, 33
To Wong Foo, Thanks for Everything, Julie Newmar, 190
Transamerica Company, 120
Tribe, Lawrence H., 42
Tri-Star Pictures, 129, 137, 144
Truman, Harry, 17
Turner, Kathleen, 128
Turning Point, The, 117
Twentieth Century Fox, 30

Ufland, Harry, 159–60
United Artists, 15, 87, 120–21, 159–60, 172–73
Universal Studios, 146, 160–61, 163, 166–67, 169–71, 174–75, 182
U.S. Catholic Conference, 165, 173
U.S. Customs, 151–52
U.S. Information Agency (USIA), film certification practices, 52, 197n.15, 200n.44
U.S. Justice Department: film labeling policies, 36–52; Foreign Agents Registration Act (FARA) and, 37–52; movie censorship by, 26–52; Registration Unit of, 46, 199n.33
U.S. State Department, movie censorship and, 32–33
USA Cinemas, 15

Valenti, Jack, 57, 69, 167–68
van den Haag, Ernest, 60
Vanity Fair, 129
Variety, 78–79, 96, 102–3, 166
Verhoeven, Paul, 128–29
Victim, The, 112–13
Victor/Victoria, 122
Vidal, Gore, 111
Vietnam War, 11
Village Voice, 73, 77, 114, 118, 124–25,
    142–43, 211n.36
Vineberg, Steven, 3
violence in movies: campaigns against,
    63–66, 123–24; censorship and,
    12–16; decline of, 195n.25; *Dressed to
    Kill Controversy* and, 70–80; influences
    on behavior, 14–15, 60–61, 194n.19
Volunteers, 102

Waco Tribune-Herald, 168
Waiting to Exhale, 189
Waldman, Diane, 48, 50, 200n.39
Walker, Alexander, 56
Walker, Gerald, 121–22
Wall, James, 216n.23
Wall Street Journal, 170
Walsh, Francis, 150
Walsh, Moira, 216n.23
Walt Disney Studios, 30, 187
Wang, Wayne, 189
Warner, Albert, 148
Warner, H. B., 89
Warner, Jack, 56–57
Warner Brothers, 30, 56–57, 62, 157
Warriors, The, 14–15
Washington Post, 40–41, 127, 131,
    134–35, 166, 177
Wasserman, Lew, 165, 171–72, 179, 181
watchdog groups, movie violence
    and, 195n.20
Wedding Banquet, The, 190
Weintraub, Jerry, 117, 119
Werckmeister, O. K., 49
West, Mae, 55
West, Morris, 111
What's New, Pussycat, 56

White, Diane, 142
Who's Afraid of Virginia Woolf?, 55–57
Wilde, Oscar, 108
Wildmon, Donald (Rev.), 160–63,
    165, 169–70, 172, 181–82, 195n.20
Willis, Gordon, 120
Wilson, Rich, 134
Windows, 3, 22, 54, 117, 119–22, 125,
    204n.26
Winston, Archer, 73
Wiseman, Fred, 30
Women Against Pornography (WAP),
    19, 53, 61, 64, 74–76, 79, 203–4n.26
Women Against Violence Against
    Women (WAVAW), 19, 53, 64,
    75–78, 203–4n.26
Women Against Violence in Pornog-
    raphy and Media (WAVPM), 62–63,
    76–77, 203–4n.26
Women's Health Action and Mobi-
    lization, 141
Wong, Eugene, 84–85
Woo, John, 190
Woo, Michael, 103–4
Wood, Robin, 115
Workman, Philip, 157
World of Susie Wong, The, 84
Wu, Robert, 91
Wuntch, Philip, 102
Wyler, William, 111

Year of the Dragon: Asian-American
    protests against, 20–21, 81–82,
    92–106, 189, 208n.32; critical re-
    ception of, 102–3; defenders of,
    100–102, 208n.32; financial success
    of, 102–3
"Yellow Power" movement, 85
Young v. American Mini Theatres,
    202n.10

Z, 30
Zeffirelli, Franco, 24, 156–57, 170,
    218n.46
Ziener, Robert, 174
zoning ordinances, X-rated films and,
    202n.10